The Ethics of Cities

THE ETHICS OF CITIES

Shaping Policy for a Sustainable and Just Future

TIMOTHY BEATLEY

The University of North Carolina Press

Chapel Hill

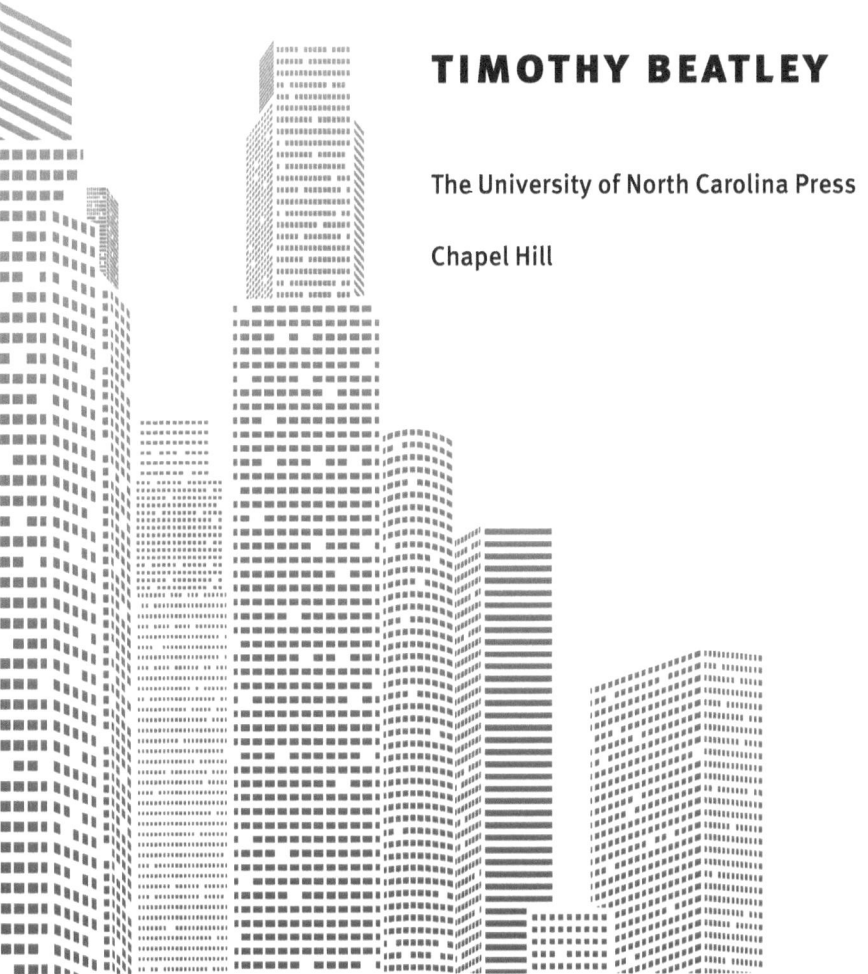

*This book was published with the assistance of the
William R. Kenan Jr. Fund of the University of North Carolina Press.*

© 2024 Timothy Beatley
All rights reserved
Designed by Richard Hendel
Set in Quadraat and Meta types by codeMantra
Manufactured in the United States of America

Cover art: buildings © iStock.com/R. M. Nunes; park © iStock.com/BIN WANG.
Image of city skyline used in interior © iStock.com/meen_na.

Complete Library of Congress Cataloging-in-Publication Data is available at
https://lccn.loc.gov/2024000331.
ISBN 978-1-4696-7862-7 (cloth: alk. paper)
ISBN 978-1-4696-7863-4 (paper: alk. paper)
ISBN 978-1-4696-7864-1 (epub)
ISBN 979-8-8908-8700-9 (pdf)

Contents

Preface. In Search of the Ethical City vii

Introduction. An Ethical View of Cities 1

1. The Core Values of an Ethical City 18
2. Virtue in the City: Virtuous Leaders and Citizens 31
3. Equality, Opportunity, Inclusiveness 44
4. Rights in and to the City 64
5. The Extent and Limits of Freedoms in the City 76
6. Ethical Policing and Use of Force 87
7. Panopticon City: Surveillance and Privacy in the Ethical City 101
8. A City's Obligations to the Future 109
9. The Ethics of Local Democracy and the Need for Fair and Shared Governance 122
10. The Ethics of Public Spaces and the Public Realm 135
11. The Ethics of a Healthy and Flourishing City 152
12. The Ethics of Biophilic Cities 168
13. What Is a City's Duty to the Larger World? 182
14. Working toward the Ethical City 198

Acknowledgments 209

Notes 211

Index 229

SIDEBARS

1-1. Descriptors of a Good or Ethical City 19
2-1. Some Important Urban Virtues 35
2-2. What Do We Expect of Citizens?
 What Are Some Examples of Expanded Citizenship? 38
4-1. Seven Principles of the Right to Housing 66
5-1. Tree Psychology: Some of the Factors Influencing
 Decisions to Remove Trees 81
6-1. Camden, New Jersey, Directive on the Use of Force 88
8-1. Krznaric's Six Ways to Think Long 112
10-1. What Are Some of the Values We Want to See
 Expressed in Public Spaces? 136
11-1. What Steps Could Cities Take to Address the
 Public Health Risks of Guns? 160
13-1. What Can Cities Do to Reduce Poverty and
 Raise Living Conditions beyond Their Borders? 183
13-2. Some of the Many Networks Cities Belong To 184
14-1. Alternative Metrics for an Ethical City 201

Preface In Search of the Ethical City

Ethical dilemmas and quandaries are pervasive in matters of urban governance and planning. Whether it's the fairness of police stop-and-search practices, the humaneness of a city's animal control service acts, or the extent to which citizens are engaged directly in the many municipal decisions made, an almost limitless set of ethical questions about cities emerges on a daily basis. This book looks at those questions, keeping in mind cities and their power. Cities today are vectors for political and economic change and have the resources and policy levers to take significant steps that can greatly affect human lives.

Though profoundly value laden, such decisions and policy choices are rarely framed as ethical choices. They may often be perceived as economic, legal, or political problems but are not often understood as ethical problems. That is the principal goal of this book, to reframe them as being imbued with ethical ambiguities, nuances, and judgments. Ethical choices and judgments, in cities as elsewhere, are not optional; failure to see a housing policy or local environmental decision as an ethical choice is itself a choice. Part ethics primer, part introduction to urban policy and planning, this book aims to frame and guide the many ethical dilemmas faced by mayors, city managers, planning commissioners, and citizens involved in decisions in and about cities.

This book builds upon my earlier book *Ethical Land Use: Principles of Policy and Planning*, which remains the only full-length book addressing the ethical and moral issues faced in land use planning and decision-making. Published more than twenty-five years ago, it has been declared by the American Planning Association one of the "100 Essential Books in Planning." This book expands on *Ethical Land Use*, addressing the ethical dimensions of a wider range of important urban policy issues, from public health and food to the need to connect urban residents to nature.

Though cities are faced with a host of problems, they have the ability to significantly improve the lot of their residents. They can work to, among others, reduce economic and racial inequality and overcome systemic racism and sexism; deliver safer living environments and adequate levels of affordable housing; ensure that the police force is used sparingly; and protect rights to minimum levels of clean air, water, and contact with nature. Cities can work to consider the broader constituencies and present and future members of our moral community, embracing a morally inclusive vision of what a city is and could be.

Cities also have the power and ability to significantly influence the pain and suffering and flourishing of humans, and of many other forms of life from birds to whales, and to take steps to stem the growing loss of species and biodiversity worldwide and the damaging progression of global climate change. Cities can play a meaningful role in shaping and guiding the use and consumption of natural resources and can take action to conserve nature even beyond their own borders or boundaries.

This book explores the ethical and value dimensions of a number of urban policy areas not usually viewed in this way. While I often dig deeply into the policy weeds, I work from the premise that every policy sector raises serious and difficult ethical issues and that we need to understand them as such. There is, of course, a long history of writing and thinking around ethics. From John Locke to John Rawls, there is a remarkable body of work. Much of this content is relevant to the subject of ethics in cities, but it is clearly not my intent with this book to make original contributions to the theory and literature of ethics more generally. Rather, this book is translational and synthesizing in nature; it is an attempt to introduce those interested in cities (and hopefully many who work in or with cities, or plan to) to the variety of ethical issues and quandaries faced there, as well as some of the key ethical ideas and concepts that are useful in sorting them out and in making ethical judgments about such urban content. It is not meant to be exhaustive. The book aims to survey the ethical landscape of cities and to provide to readers a sense of the scope and nature of the ethical issues and dilemmas faced there.

The chapters that follow also draw heavily from my own personal experiences, especially those from growing up in my home city of Alexandria, Virginia, where my father served as mayor for many years. Many of the ethical issues described in this book are ones that he and I discussed and ones that have been percolating for some years now. From time to time, I provide specific examples from Alexandria as well as from my current home in Charlottesville, Virginia, where I have lived and worked for the last thirty-plus years.

It is hard to overstate the importance of my years growing up in Alexandria and the impact they had in shaping my perception of what a city could be and what ethical leadership could look like. My father served as mayor for five terms (covering much of my elementary and high school years), and I had a front-row seat to his visionary leadership and his passion about what the city could be. His accomplishments continue to be evident even today, more than forty years later: Alexandria is now a much more walkable city, with public connections to its waterfront, a world-class historic district, an innovative arts center converted from a facility that made wartime torpedoes, and a city bus system (that at the time was known as the "Beatley Bus"). We had many conversations about what Alexandria might become, and his pride about this city was infectious. He also governed by listening to and respecting the many positions and points of view in a diverse city. He was known for long council meetings, partly a result of his belief that everyone who wanted to speak ought to be able to. In his inclusive and informal (some would say folksy) manner, and the fairness and decency with which he treated everyone, he was, and still is, a remarkable role model and example of an ethical leader.

The qualities of Alexandria, its urban and physical form, were an early education for me. I walked everywhere there, and I have especially fond memories of spending time in the forest behind our house, wading in a nearby stream, and exploring all over the west end of the city. It was not perfect, but it served to lay much of the mental groundwork for my understanding of what a good and ethical city might look and feel like.

The Ethics of Cities

Introduction An Ethical View of Cities

Could a city ever truly and legitimately declare itself to be an ethical city? That seems a bold and most unattainable claim. It reminds me of Rotterdam's famous goal of becoming a climate-proof city (by 2025, no less). It is an equally unrealistic and unattainable vision, but proponents will argue it is nevertheless a meaningful goal. In a similar way, that is what is meant here by the term *ethical city*—it is something that urban leaders and citizens alike can at least aspire to move toward. And it creates space in which to have an important discussion about the normative aspects of city life and city policymaking. That is the key intention of this book.

Open any newspaper, local or national, and you'll see a daunting range of pressing issues facing local governments. Cities face numerous difficult policy issues and deep ethical and value divides that underlie major controversies. From adapting to climate change and dealing with homelessness to tackling racial injustice and reparations for slavery, there are so many topics on the urban agenda that are deeply value laden. Few issues facing cities today would be considered trivial, simple, or truly solvable, at least in the short term.

Most of the decisions cities have to make are not unusual or extraordinary; rather, they are common and recurring: how to spend the local budget, what kinds of infrastructure investments are needed, whether teachers (or police officers or firefighters) deserve and are entitled to pay raises, or whether a zoning change is acceptable or desirable even though it will increase density and traffic in a mostly low-density neighborhood. But such policy and planning choices have substantial and lasting impacts on actual human lives: when and where we arrest and prosecute citizens, what standards guide the use of force and the vehicular pursuit of criminals, and how we mete out fair justice when those who break the law are prosecuted, recognizing the ethical need to forgive and to provide second chances.

Can a City Be Ethical?

It is the premise of this book that it is in fact possible and sensical to describe a city as ethical (or unethical). There are many objections to this position, I know. Some will say that a city is not, at least technically, a being with any form of agency or ability to act ethically (or not). To be sure, there are countless actors, countless people, who live and work in a city who do have the ability to act ethically and make decisions large and small. Mayors, city councillors, and other elected officials can and do act in principled ways and do indeed exercise personal judgments and make ethical choices. In their official capacities, they are making ethical judgments that represent the city.

Is an ethical city a place where most of the official policies and city decisions are deemed to be (on balance) ethical (or responsible or equitable or just)? Does a city treat its inhabitants, human and otherwise, with compassion and care? Does it seek to create conditions where every child begins a flourishing life and where the basics of health care, food, and housing are ensured? Does it forthrightly and honestly confront racial inequities and social inequality and work to rectify harm done in the past? Does a city take the long view, taking into account the needs and interests of future residents, many of whom may not even exist yet?

These are some of the questions we might use to determine whether a city can be described as ethical (or not). One problem, of course, is that there is not likely to be agreement on what constitutes "ethical" policy or actions. For example, San Francisco established a policy forbidding city employees to travel to or contract with companies based in states that restrict a woman's right to choose to have an abortion. I believe the right to choose is a human right and one that every city should acknowledge and protect. But someone with a right-to-life view will see this policy differently, of course, and may conclude that San Francisco is an unethical city. The city voted to repeal the policy in 2023, citing doubts about its effectiveness and worries that it was adding to the costs of contracts.[1]

A related problem is that a city makes thousands of decisions and policies, spread out over scores of years. Which city is the ethical city: the one that decided 100 years ago to erect a racist statue, or the city today that seeks to bring it down and works in small and large ways to compensate for and repay past injustices? And even in a single small span of time—say, the decisions of a city council over a two- or three-month period—there will be a mix of exemplary and not-so-exemplary decisions made. No city is perfect or devoid of politics and actors who exhibit more self-interest than interest in the larger public good.

In some clear legal ways, it does make sense to speak of the *agency* of a city. In this book, I define a city in terms of its status as a municipal government—an incorporated jurisdiction with boundaries, legal duties, and the ability to take legal and other steps. Does it make sense to describe a corporation as ethical? A university? These things make sense intuitively and legally today, so we can also answer in the affirmative for cities. A city can sue and be sued, enter into legal agreements, establish employee pensions, and, in short, function in ways quite like an individual, university, or corporation. Granted, individuals with specific roles are usually required to carry out such agency (e.g., a city council adopting an ordinance, a policewoman enforcing a traffic code, or a city manager establishing a line item in a budget to fund a local improvement of some kind). For me *ethical city* is shorthand for the totality of ethical actions, behaviors, and policies undertaken on behalf of a city government, in the government officials' capacity of representing, articulating, or implementing that city's positions.

What about the actions of nongovernmental actors: a homeowner who might erect on his lawn an anti-immigrant sign or a shop owner who refuses to serve customers because of the color of their skin? Is a city to be judged by the larger totality of actions of its residents? I am more agnostic on this point, but I will say that the connections between citizen opinions and city government actions are often clear and transparent; a racist and exclusionary zoning code does not simply appear from the ether but is usually a direct reflection of what a number of residents feel the city should do on their behalf.

Is one way, then, to define an ethical city by judging or taking stock of the many potentially ethical actions of its residents and citizens? How much money do they give to charitable organizations, for example, or what is the rate at which they volunteer for causes in the community?

Ways to Think about Ethical Cities

This book represents a broad examination of the ways in which it makes sense to say a city is ethical. In the end, I conclude there is no single or definitive way. But that does not vitiate or prevent our calling out or describing a city as ethical. What are the different ways a city might be thought of as ethical?

ETHICAL PEOPLE

A city, and its daily grind of people, represents the locus and venue for many different personal and collective choices about how to use resources, how to live our lives, how to treat other people and the larger environment, and what values to pursue. In this way, an ethical city is a city of ethical people. The cultivation of deep citizenship—and of a virtuous, generous, and compassionate citizenry—is a goal, or should be a goal, and I take up this topic in more detail in a later chapter.

There are, of course, many individual roles, some overlapping and many held simultaneously by actors in an ethical city. How ethically and conscientiously do professional police officers go about their jobs? What about firefighters or EMT operators or the many other less public roles, from city attorneys to social services workers?

Developers operating in a city have special influence in shaping the physical and built form and thus shaping impacts and patterns of opportunity. Later, we consider a variety of innovative and creative ideas for new housing projects and other forms of development. Often the most impactful and most progressive are driven by civic-minded developers who can see beyond the narrowness of profit motive. Recently, one developer in Bethlehem, Pennsylvania, agreed to protect and work around the chimney of an older manufacturing plant that served as a critical nesting site for hundreds of migrating chimney swifts.[2] It is not clear whether the chimney will be saved permanently, but if not, the developer has committed to replacing it with a bespoke swift tower that would serve the same purpose. Just being willing in this case to meet with local bird advocates, and to be open to considering a broader set of goals and purpose, is a hallmark of a more ethically minded developer.

ETHICAL POLICIES AND PROGRAMS

We might, on the other hand, judge a city's ethical bona fides by judging not the actions, judgments, and behaviors of individuals but rather the ethics and fairness of the policies, programs, and laws that a city adopts and implements. That is largely the way I define an ethical city in this book.

Does a city adopt policies that seek to treat all people fairly and consistently? Does it take steps and actions that are consistently in the larger public's interest, and does it adopt policies that seek to protect the health and well-being of its citizens and environment?

We can sharply disagree about what package or suite of policies a city might adopt and implement that would allow it to call itself ethical—that is an important open question in the book and one that I try to give some guidance about as we go along, but there are not going to be any hard and fast ethical litmus tests to apply to the policies, programs, and decisions made by a city and its official agencies and offices.

Is a city defined by the ethics of the behaviors and actions of its employees working in their official capacities? Most of us would not judge the morality of a city by the actions of a few individuals, I suspect. Say a policeman carelessly shoots his gun in the direction of a criminal but hits a nearby bystander: a bad decision. Does this one faulty choice made by an employee of a city implicate the city itself? Perhaps not, though if there is a pattern of disregard for the safety of citizens and bystanders, then perhaps yes. If in response to a spate of such incidents the city fails to adjust its policies and training, then it becomes more squarely implicated as unethical.

ETHICAL PLACES

A city's shape, form, and physical structure might also be assessed against the standards of ethics. A city's history of policies and actions, as well as the accumulated actions of others operating in the city—from developers to nonprofit organizations and neighborhood associations—manifests in the physical conditions of a city. In her book *Feminist City*, Leslie Kern describes what it is like to move through a city like London as a pregnant woman and mom.[3] Nothing is designed with her circumstances in mind; rather it's the able-bodied man that too often serves as the default model for the design of a city. She observes how antifeminist cities like London and Toronto can be, how hard it is to use public transit and navigate these cities with a stroller, and how these cities lack spaces for breastfeeding and bathrooms. Cities are a physical manifestation of maleness and can be rightly labeled sexist. A sexist city, as I discuss in more detail in a later chapter, is an unethical city; an ethical city must be a feminist city and more.

So the idea of the ethical city is messy, to put it mildly. But this book persists with the idea that it is a useful and meaningful moniker, if for no other reason than it sets forth an aspiration, the idea that we are looking at cities through an ethical lens, judging their decisions and agency, holding them up to the scrutiny of rightness and wrongness. We are starting a discussion about how cities can be understood to do the right thing, to address the wrongs and injustices that exist and that have existed, to be morally inclusive and compassionate, and to be able to take the position of the many people (and other species) that inhabit that city, seek to understand their life circumstances, and work to improve them.

What Kind of an Ethical Question Is a City?

A city is a difficult ethical question, or really many complex questions presented at the same time. Perhaps it is something like a puzzle but one where the sizes and shapes of the pieces are constantly changing. No pieces fit very well, and once you think you have found a fit, it may not last. As difficult and as challenging as the urban landscape is to make sense of morally and ethically, there are few places where so much good and goodwill can be amassed. Cities, again, are engines for improving life, enhancing opportunities, deepening and fostering human relationships, and connecting us with the larger natural world. Pushing for cities that acknowledge and earnestly work through ethics is well worth it and an essential task on the way to creating a better world.

A city, and the struggle to advance the vision of an ethical city, is an example of what Simon Sinek calls an "infinite game."[4] Rather than being a finite game—where the actors are fixed, the goalposts are clearly established, and the game ends at some point—cities involve many actors and entities changing over time, without agreement on a desired outcome or end point, and the game never ends; it continues potentially forever. A city is more than a destination and never a completed project; it is a journey, an endless striving for a more just world. The ethical quandaries and questions discussed in this book will never be "solved," and there is no end to the job of imagining (and reimagining) what cities ought to be or to the work of advancing the agenda of ethical cities.

The Moral Authority of the Righteous City

Can a city be said to have moral authority? Not always, but it does seem possible and plausible. Cities can often take risky and bold positions and in the process help set society down a different path. Cities can and often do make righteous decisions and take bold actions, often unpopular and sometimes even illegal ones.

Sometimes public officials will see an ethical pathway or a set of actions of an ethical stand that might put them in conflict with the law. One example emerged in the aftermath of the 2018 Parkland, Florida, shooting and the strong sense of the need to take action to prevent such tragedies from happening again. Mayors and council members have grappled with what they can do.

The City of Coral Gables voted unanimously to enact its own citywide ban on assault rifles, in the absence of similar federal or state actions. But in 2011, the Republican-controlled and very gun-friendly state legislature in Florida had passed a law prohibiting localities from adopting any form of gun control.

When Coral Gables voted for the assault rifle ban, it did so, remarkably, against the strong opposition of its city attorney, who advised that under the 2011 law municipal officers could be fined $5,000 and removed from their positions. The city attorney also informed government officials that she would not be permitted to defend them. "This is more important than us keeping our jobs," said Commissioner Frank Quesada. "Could we possibly be one cog or one domino in the process of improving the safety of kids throughout the state of Florida? I think the answer is yes," he said in the *Miami Herald*.[5]

Many cities have taken remarkable steps to address environmental degradation and, in the face of little action at the national or federal level (at least in the United States), have set ambitious targets for reducing their greenhouse gas emissions. Pittsburgh set a goal of achieving the targets of the Paris Climate Accords, even when the Trump administration declared its intent to pull out of this agreement.

Cities such as San Francisco have taken steps to significantly reduce the use of toxic pesticides and herbicides in the management of parks and landscapes. A graph of San Francisco's declining use over time of the herbicide glyphosate, a chemical we now know to be a likely human carcinogen, is impressive: it is now a fraction of what its use was in the past, and the city has instituted policies and best practices to ensure its use is a matter of last resort.[6] There can be little doubt that such steps are helping to reduce the damage to both humans and the natural environment. It may be many years before the benefits are completely clear, but the import and significance of the actions cities can take are simply undeniable.

There are a variety of policy levers at cities' disposal and numerous ways cities can work to protect the environment and the health and well-being of their citizens. Cities have considerable power to do good and to help their citizens flourish. This is one of the key messages of this book. An ethical city is not a city that passively stands by and waits to simply mediate or judge a debate or conflict; rather, it takes initiatives, makes decisions, and takes steps to effect positive change in both the near and distant futures. Cities can, and thus must, make a difference; there is no standing on the sidelines.

What Can Cities Do?

Cities have the ability to do things, via their funding and programmatic decisions, that can profoundly improve the well-being, health, and quality of life of their residents. Examples include Boston's decision to invest in universal pre-K for all its kids; San Francisco's decision to fund health care; or legacy cities' decisions to upgrade antiquated water systems to replace lead pipes. More than forty cities around the United States have raised the local minimum wage and have taken many steps to expand the supply of affordable housing. Cities can also take important moral stands and set ethical examples through their decisions, commitments, investments, and purchases.

Cities, especially larger cities, are increasingly engaged in global diplomacy in one form or another. Cities are members of global networks, which accelerates their progress in reaching global targets and aspirations (such as the United Nations' Sustainable Development Goals or the climate change targets of the Paris Accords). The richer cities of the Global North can take steps to help other cities, for instance by sharing technology or financial resources, to address pressing environmental and social problems. And even more proactively, I argue that cities must become more politically active on the global stage and can and must be leaders in support of global conservation and human rights.

As the chapters that follow argue, cities can and must also recognize their place in the larger world and can and must take steps to be good global actors. A modern city today exerts a large and negative ecological footprint on the world: consumption in cities results in distant ecological destruction and impacts workers and others in faraway parts of the world. But cities can be responsible, and take responsibility, using the actions and policy levers at their disposal to reduce consumption and its negative impacts. They can, for example, steer their procurement mechanisms to support products and companies that treat workers humanely and fairly and steer their municipal investments away from companies and enterprises that lead to global habitat destruction and exacerbate climate change.

Ethical Choices Are Complex and the Outcomes Uncertain

That is not to say that it is always clear what actions a city should take. In fact, the ethical choices and policy dilemmas a city faces will also vary over time and through the different steps or phases of a program or intervention. And for many of the decisions that cities must make, the long-term impacts and outcomes will be uncertain. What will be the long-term ecological and health effects, for example, of continuing to use herbicides and pesticides in managing a city's parks? A clear and definitive answer is unlikely, and whether to ban or restrict the use of such chemicals will necessarily be a decision made without full and complete information.

How to pay for improvements, then, raises a host of additional ethical concerns, as we know that some taxing tools, such as the use of sales tax, tend to be highly regressive, meaning they disproportionally burden those of low or middle incomes (the effective tax rate decreases with income). How to implement neighborhood amenities creates another set of issues: When should they be implemented, and in what order? Which neighborhoods should receive a makeover first, and what should be done when there are individuals who simply don't want their neighborhood to change? Thus, cities face various, though intersecting, sets of ethical questions:

- What kind of city do we want or need? What constitutes a fair and ethical set of living conditions for residents in the city?
- How do we fund, design, and implement the changes we envision in our city, or the necessary steps needed to bring about the city we want?
- Whom will we consult and whose voices will be heard in the design and planning of this desired future?
- Once the improvements have been made, what happens when there are outcomes, such as gentrification and displacement, that we may not have anticipated? And why didn't we anticipate them?

Cities Make Many Kinds of Ethical Choices

A city, even a small one, has many moving parts and, of course, many kinds of responsibilities and functions, each with a particular set of ethical issues, dilemmas, choices, and challenges. Cities have departments with quite different aims: there are police, fire, and emergency services; there are social services and those primarily focused on health; and there are quasi-independent organizations that are often supported by the city, such as the local Society for the Prevention of Cruelty to Animals or animal shelter. It is hard to generalize about ethical decision-making and reasoning with all the various functions inherent in what we call a city. But one conclusion is clear: cities engage in many, many kinds of ethical choices and decisions, with significant and lasting impacts.

In September 2021, the Texas legislature adopted legislation that essentially banned abortions, nullifying the constitutional protections under *Roe v. Wade*. The City of Portland, Oregon, sprang quickly into action, adopting an emergency resolution banning "future procurement of goods and services from, and City employee business travel to, the state of Texas."[7] Indeed, cities deliberate on and adopt budgets that represent choices about how to spend the city's resources. Deciding which constituencies, causes, or problems receive attention and funding is one of the most important ways a city can make a difference. Support for particular programs, causes, and organizations may come in the form of grants but might also take the form of technical assistance from the city or community. Cities do many things to influence growth patterns and land use, from creating direct regulation through zoning and subdivision ordinances to imposing impact fees that require developers (and, indirectly, homeowners) to help pay for parks and other services. They can regulate, but they can also directly purchase land and property; cities are usually land and property owners themselves, raising important ethical questions about how they manage these public assets.

How a city raises the funds to make allocations creates yet another set of ethical dilemmas and choices. No taxation or revenue-raising decision is morally neutral. Rather, there are implicit (and often explicit) biases and priorities embedded in different revenue tools and in the different ways groups in the city are treated. We would generally agree that approaches to taxation and revenue-raising should be progressive rather than regressive—an approach is progressive when those who have higher salaries and more wealth are asked to pay a higher proportion of their income or property value in taxes. Often this is not the case, of course, and as recent examples show, local property taxes, a main source of revenue for cities, is regressive—those with less wealth end up paying disproportionately more in taxes.[8] Deciding which revenue-raising tools and mechanisms to use is a significant category of ethical dilemma for a city.

In addition to managing its own property and treating its own staff and employees in particular ways, a city also can impose standards on businesses and other actors operating in the city. One way it can do this is by requiring companies to adopt certain health and safety protections for their employees and customers. One example is a city-imposed minimum wage requirement, which essentially establishes a floor for what a company must pay its employees. Another example is health care; cities such as San Francisco have imposed a requirement that companies must provide health care for their employees. Though the requirement covers only medium and large firms, it is a bold move for a city to mandate such coverage, creating a potentially huge benefit for workers in the city.

Cities and their agents have the power to kill and maim. Police officers can choose (or not) to draw and fire their weapons or engage in a dangerous high-speed chase through the streets of a city. But their decisions are also constrained by guidance and policy adopted by the city. Many cities are adopting new policies and protocols to ensure the safety of bystanders and the general public, for instance by prohibiting high-speed chases (unless the suspect poses a risk to the public) or prohibiting no-knock searches to issue low-level drug warrants, where the high risk to the public is unjustified, not to mention the unjust and excessive use of deadly force often used against people of color in such situations.

Ethical Cities Can Lead

From climate change to human rights, cities have the chance to take a stand, offer a positive example, and influence thinking and practice in the larger world. As important as it is to work on the ethics of one's own city, it is also important to understand how a city can itself act as an ethical leader. There are many examples of this in the chapters that follow: times when a city chooses a particular path, sets a positive example, or establishes an ethical benchmark against which other cities (and states and even national governments) measure themselves anew. When Donald Trump announced in 2017 that he was withdrawing the United States from the Paris Climate Accords, it was cities and city leaders who immediately responded. When Trump declared that he represented "the citizens of Pittsburgh, not Paris," Pittsburgh mayor Bill Peduto tweeted, "Pittsburgh stands with the world and will follow the Paris agreement."[9] More than sixty mayors soon thereafter expressed a similar level of commitment to the Paris goals, and even though Trump succeeded in pulling the United States out, cities have generally moved to fill the void in climate leadership left by their national government.

In the realm of human rights, many cities have led the way on LGBTQ+ protections, ahead of or in the absence of state and federal protections. Cities such as Philadelphia, Seattle, and Atlanta have adopted antidiscrimination laws that ensure nondiscrimination in cases of hiring, real estate sales and rentals, and business, and these cities have also established special services and programs for the LGBTQ+ community.[10]

In 2004, under the leadership of then mayor Gavin Newsom, San Francisco led the nation on gay marriage, issuing the first marriage licenses for same-sex partners at a time when this was quite controversial and many in the country were vehemently opposed to the idea. An emotional picture of Phyllis Lyon and Del Martin, the first recipients of such a marriage license in San Francisco, puts a touching human face on this form of inequality and discrimination. They were the first gay couple to be granted a marriage license, a milestone for San Francisco and for all LGBTQ+ citizens and an example for other cities. Recently the city has been working to protect and make visible historic sites of gay life, including making the Lyon-Martin House at 651 Duncan Street a historic landmark, with the ordinance signed by Mayor London Breed in May 2021.[11]

It is a bit of a cliché to say that cities (and city leaders and legislators) are closer to the people than state and federal governments are, and perhaps more attuned to the shifting views of right and wrong, but there is much truth to this, and there is little doubt that cities can be moral bellwethers, setting directions and staking out bold positions that might be difficult in other arenas.

Cities Structure How the Most Important Decisions Are Made

Perhaps even more important than the ethical content and boldness of the decisions a city makes are the many process and procedural decisions (and values) it puts into place. How easy or hard is it to express your opinion about your city's priorities, and how actively inclusive and diverse are the points of view that are considered and taken into account in making the city's decisions? How evenly is political power distributed in your city, and are there particular voices (e.g., corporate entities or members of the business community) that are outsize in their impact?

There are of course many factors that influence the fairness of the processes by which decisions are made. Are decisions made by elected (or unelected) officials in ways that are not transparent, with little effort to understand how they might impact the public and little effort to solicit input from those who would be impacted? Are the people making decisions unduly influenced by special interests who have made significant campaign contributions? (They often are.) So-called pay-to-play is a common feature of American politics at the local level, where donations and conflicts of interest are the norm, but as some new restrictions in some cities suggest, it doesn't have to be this way.

Whose voices are included, who is consulted, and how much direct control citizens and neighborhoods have in making decisions are major questions that determine the ways that cities can structure the fairness of decision processes. As discussed in later chapters, there are many ways to make a city's political system fairer and more inclusive, from banning pay-to-play and other excessive campaign contributions to making it easier for rank-and-file citizenry to vote in elections.

Causal Uncertainty and Policy Complexity

Most of the ethical quandaries we face in cities are especially difficult because they involve many different actors and institutions and lots of uncertainty about the likely outcomes of the policy and planning proposals on the table. The actual impact of an ordinance or a program, however well intentioned, may be unclear and even contrary to intentions. Causal uncertainty is a given in most matters of local governance, and an ethical city is one that understands the importance of assessing, evaluating, and taking the appropriate steps to correct, adjust, or even completely change direction if necessary.

It is certainly true, as well, that many of the issues faced by cities, in part because of their complexity, involve balancing competing interests and perspectives. There are many different perspectives, stakeholders, and interests at play in a city, and often they are at serious odds. Ethical judgments will often be difficult, and policy and political outcomes will need to take account of this diversity of opinions.

Time Frames Short and Long: City Decisions Profoundly Impact the Future

Many of the decisions faced by elected and nonelected officials alike involve working through alternative temporal dimensions. Local politics is frequently driven by short-term demands and crises. In the face of hearing a room full of unhappy constituents, it is not surprising that city councillors favor those more immediate voices and concerns. Longer-term considerations, especially ones that might be more than a few years into the future, often receive less weight in this decision-making climate. The present almost always trumps longer-term thinking and considerations.

However, in cities a raft of potential ethical duties emerges regarding the future. Indeed, the very nature of urban planning is about taking steps today, and making investments in the near term, to achieve a desired quality of life in the future. Without sufficient advance thinking, the future qualities of place, the livability we seek, may be difficult to achieve.

And the temporal issues are often even more complex. It is often a question of which time frame is privileged among the many different competing time frames and is often more complex than simply "present versus future."

The Special Ethics of Geography and Space

The physical form and design of a city raise important ethical issues and help shape and reinforce particular values. The so-called contact hypothesis suggests that the more we interact with those who are different from us, the less they will seem to us as "other." In these ways the spatial form and configuration of cities are important factors and ingredients in moral circumstances. The moral and ethical dilemmas and judgments cities face are not simply to be worked out in a dark room, in front of a computer screen; rather, they arise from and are intimately influenced by the physical conditions of cities. This makes them distinct and different from many other policy dilemmas.

And just as moral circumstances are physical and place based, so are many of the important responses of an ethical city. Indeed, the design and planning of the physical setting can, we increasingly recognize, have a significant impact in shaping the moral attitudes and perspectives of its residents. Cities can provide ample space for public meetings and assemblies, for celebrations, and generally for opportunities to bring people together in actual physical space. The contact hypothesis, though far from settled, argues that we become more tolerant, more accepting of diversity, and perhaps more empathetic when we are exposed to people who are different from ourselves. In contrast, in the past much physical planning and design has tended to emphasize designed separation and isolation and, in many American cities, racial segregation. These are physical and spatial patterns that do just the opposite and that work to reinforce a sense of difference, intolerance, and perceived superiority on the part of some classes and races.

Our work around greening and naturalizing cities suggests, as another important example, that the greater the exposure to nature, the more likely we are to be generous and cooperative and that nature-rich cities will help bring out the better angels in all of us. We certainly know as well that the health of people, places, and the planet will increasingly depend on physical planning and design.

The physical environment of cities conveys many ideas and signals about what we believe to be important and what or who matters in the world. The recent discussion in many American cities around statues and the naming of schools and streets illustrates this well. Whom and what do we celebrate with statues in public parks? In many cities, including my own, this turns out to be people and monuments to a racist past—which has led many cities to take down such statues. And it leads to a broader discussion about whose stories, histories, life journeys, and perspectives are being presented in public spaces and whose are being left out.

A City Is a Physical Embodiment of Past Decisions (and Past Injustices)

It is undeniable that the current life circumstances of people of color in US cities are a result of a long-standing pattern of discriminatory decisions made in the short- and longer-term past: decisions to dislocate thriving Black neighborhoods and to annihilate and destroy them through the building of interstate highways, redlining, and extensive use of racial covenants to curtail opportunities. These are all determinants to a considerable degree of the current economic and health conditions of the residents of these cities today.

What we must or should do about these current circumstances remains an open question, taken up in the subsequent chapters of this book. Do these long-standing patterns of racial injustice and systemic racism, leading to dramatic gaps in wealth and life expectancy, require actions today to correct or compensate for them? And if so, what kind and degree of compensation is ethically required? A number of American cities have already taken steps, though still early and limited, to provide some form of reparations for slavery and discrimination and for the direct and harmful actions cities have taken in the past (destruction of Black neighborhoods through urban renewal, for example).[12]

Can a city have a moral debt? Just as a company or an individual can be said to have a debt—say financial or personal—can a city have something that needs repaying? There are certainly many things a city can do to correct past harms. Many cities are looking to reconfigure and redesign destructive highways, in some cases capping them or even taking them out completely. So-called freeway lids can help stitch communities and neighborhoods back together and can provide parks and green spaces and other often-lacking amenities. As one San Diego activist said in a recent *Los Angeles Times* article about the potential of freeway lids, "By creating a place where people can meet, walk their dogs, providing passive recreational areas, then you're going to be able to mend . . . the gash in the community. It creates the threads to pull networks back together."[13] Mending past damage is required and can happen in many different ways.

It can also be said that cities have ecological debt.[14] Ecological debt is of particular interest and importance in an era of climate change, and it is unquestionably true that the damages and dangers faced today by low-lying nations such as Bangladesh or the Maldives are a result of consumption and industrial production and the resulting greenhouse gas emissions of cities of the Global North. More locally, there are many examples of cities, from Boston and San Francisco to Washington, DC, that owe their creation and existence to extensive ecological disruption and damage. To whom is the debt owed in such cases? Perhaps to the neighborhoods and individuals directly harmed (often the poor and people of color) but also to nature itself. The Anacostia River in Washington, DC, has been heavily polluted and its sediment is contaminated with toxins, a result of industrial pollution beginning in the 1800s.[15] The District of Columbia is currently implementing a sediment remediation project to contain and clean the sediment, repair this ecological damage, and eventually bring the river back to a "fishable and swimmable" condition.[16] River pollution was the price of income, jobs, and economic prosperity in the short term; those living in the city then and today have benefited from these ecological harms.

Washington, DC, then, can be said to carry an ecological debt on its books (whether written down or not) and has a strong moral and ethical duty to repay it. An ethical city would want to repair harms done and repay debts accrued. Every city sits floating in a river of time, impacted by its past decisions, and faced with the need to correct and adjust for those past deeds, while working to create a just and ethical future.

What or Who Counts in the City? The Expanding Moral Community

"A city that is good for a hummingbird is also good for humans," *Last Child in the Woods* author Richard Louv recently told me. That makes a lot of sense from a human self-interested perspective. We want and need to live in environments where there are plenty of flora and fauna; the kinds of conditions in which hummingbirds thrive are also the conditions we need to thrive.

So does that mean the hummingbird matters? Or the tree that this special bird depends on for its habitat? What, in short, is the moral status of nonhuman life, and what is a city duty bound to do if we believe that other forms of life do have inherent worth and moral status? Cities are full of many kinds of life: birds and wild animals but also domestic pets. Which biological constituencies do we, or should we, represent? Giving voice to other forms of life and standing up for them when they are in trouble is a significant and important ethical duty, and while there are many things that we can do as individuals, there are so many more that a city can do.

As blasé as we often are about the loss of species, there are ethical excuses for cities not to take action today. As I discuss later, we have duties to the many life-forms that inhabit cities alongside us, from the sturgeons in the Potomac River to the monk parakeets of Brooklyn. We also have duties to act in ways that conserve and protect more distant life beyond our borders.

Conclusions

Cities themselves, as legal and political entities, make many kinds of direct decisions—they regulate, buy land and property, and procure goods and services. They can be judged by the fairness, equity, and ethics of these decisions and actions. There are many different kinds of actions and decisions that cities can take, and too often we view them and deliberate about them in an overly narrow way, failing to uncover and discuss the full ethical dimensions often involved. Cities also structure the processes, political and governmental, by which decisions are made and the extent to which they are fully reflective of the many voices and perspectives in the city and are fully democratic. This introduction also began to describe some of the unique and special ethical challenges cities face that reflect a long history of past actions. Cities face complex, overlapping issues and make decisions that impact a broad and moral community, including future residents and generations and many different nonhuman lives.

There is a strong case to be made that cities can and should take strong ethical and moral positions and can serve as leaders, setting ambitious goals and staking out often controversial, but ethically correct, positions.

Discussion Questions

Does it make sense to describe a city as ethical or unethical? Why or why not?

What factors or considerations should go into determining whether a city can consider itself to be an ethical city or not?

Are there particular functions or kinds of decisions that cities typically make that are especially ethically charged or ethically difficult?

The Core Values of an Ethical City

In beginning to answer the question "How can a city be ethical?" one initial task is to identify any key principles or core values that would seem to define or clarify this kind of city. What follows is not exhaustive but meant as an initial parsing of some of the ethical and moral ideas and concepts that underpin a city that seeks to be ethical.

It is a good question to ask ourselves and one another: What do we expect from a good and virtuous city, a place where we want to live? What are the values we want and need our city to acknowledge and put into practice? Below is a quick summary of what I argue are some of the main ethical values we want to see in cities (see also sidebar 1-1). In most cases, even the most exemplary city falls short. But we can and should be aspirational. And we should have a public discussion about the values and principles that we expect public officials and citizens alike to at least work toward.

Public Good over Narrow Self-Interest

What constitutes a good or ethical decision? For many who enter public service, it is precisely the word *public* that matters the most. An ethical policy or decision is one in which the interests of the larger public are decisive. In contrast, there are many local policy decisions that seem more about satisfying individual egos or narrow self-interest or advancing the well-being of a few at the expense of the many.

Here we enter into the realm of moral philosophy and the different ethical positions and theories that might guide our decisions in cities. There is an important classical distinction between teleological ethical theory and deontological theory. The former judges the rightness of an action or

Sidebar 1-1 Descriptors of a Good or Ethical City

Caring and kind	Open, diverse
Compassionate	Generous and sharing
Gentle	Inclusive (of humans and nonhumans)
Fair/equal/equitable	In pursuit of the common good
Democratic, participatory	Restorative/healing
Tolerant	Future-looking, future-caring
Forgiving	Creating public value/public benefit
Respectful	

decision by its consequences, specifically by the amount of good or benefit brought into existence as a result. The best-known version of this is utilitarianism, typically associated with historical thinkers such as Jeremy Bentham, Henry Sidgwick, and John Stuart Mill, among others. In contrast to the historic importance and priority given to the aristocracy or the clergy, utilitarianism is a profound ethical advancement: we count the benefits and harms, pleasure and pain, and good and evil experienced not just by the few but by the many (more about this below).

Many of the policy directions that help define a good and ethical city are strongly supported by utilitarian logic. Efforts to restrict guns in schools, public buildings, and public spaces are often met with vehement opposition by gun owners and gun organizations, despite the evidence that a majority of Americans do not support guns in public places. A 2017 survey of nearly 4,000 Americans, for example, found strong support for limiting where guns could be freely carried: "Most Americans, including most gun owners, support restricting public places [where] legal gun owners can carry firearms."[1] In this survey, less than 20 percent of the respondents thought gun owners should be able to carry guns into schools, bars, or sports stadiums—that is, more than 80 percent thought it inappropriate and wrong.

How do we make sense of issues like guns, and what is the right and ethical pathway for a city in terms of regulating and controlling guns? Guns and gun violence, as I argue at several points in this book, are serious public health problems, and cities should address them as such, but can we apply a utilitarian frame in deciding what to do? Perhaps. Do the many perceived benefits of unfettered gun use (safety, security, recreation) outweigh the perceived benefits to those who would rather see more restrictions placed on guns? Which policy choice or pathway, or combination of policies, maximizes social benefits?

For cities, the polestar that should guide them to take actions and policies will, other things being equal, benefit the largest number of people. Cities should strive to do what is best for the broader public. Philosophers sometimes use thought experiments to illuminate ethical intuition. Thought experiments are one way to confirm some intuitions about the rightness of city policies and programs. One frequently cited example is the so-called trolley dilemma.[2] It goes like this: An out-of-control trolley is hurtling down the tracks about to hit and kill five people. You are standing nearby and could easily pull a lever that would send the trolley car onto another track, where only a single person would be hit and killed. Would you, and ethically should you, take this action?

Most people say they would. The logic is that taking the action would, on balance, save lives, perhaps many lives. There is intuitive support for the consequentialist utilitarian result in this scenario. Change the specifics of the dilemma, though, and people's instincts about rightness or wrongness change also. What if there is a large man standing next to you on a bridge? By pushing the man over the bridge, the trolley can be knocked off the tracks, again saving the five lives. This is an action most people say they would not take. It seems the action is seen as more like murder and seems to many to violate human rights in a way the first scenario does not. So while there is strong support for cities that take actions and undertake programs that benefit the many, there are other more deontological values and principles that are also important and that place constraints on what cities can do. Deontological ethics (from the Greek *deont*, meaning "duty") holds that an action is deemed right or wrong not by adding up the quantity of good it brings about but by invoking some other (nonutilitarian) moral concept or duty (for instance, acknowledging a human right or protecting the environment for future generations).

Perhaps needless to say, the self-dealing actions of politicians and other city leaders epitomize the ethical inverse of the principle of the public interest. Yet the story of many cities is full of actions of often corrupt individuals primarily seeking private gain at the expense of larger public goals.

How we define or determine the "public good" remains an open and difficult question. The goal of maximizing "utility" is, for economists, determined best by the transactions of a free market, and when we attempt to determine (through tools such as benefit-cost analysis) the benefits over the costs, we usually seek to approximate the outcome we believe the free market would have reached if not for imperfections or market failures.

One important open ethical question here is how we define or think of a good life, which cities seek to maximize or make available to their residents.

Aristotle famously presented the distinction between a life of pleasure (hedonic) with a meaningful life (eudaemonic). Recently, psychologists have sought to identify a third kind of good life—a life of psychological richness. This kind of life is perhaps characterized less by pleasure or comfort and more by challenges, stimulating experiences, and even hardships. We can and must debate, in a city that thinks about ethics, the question of what we are trying to generate in the aggregate, the character and quality of the pool of public good we are seeking to create. Books such as Charles Montgomery's *Happy City* may reinforce the notion that it is some aggregate measure of happiness that should guide us, but my own instincts lead me in the direction of a broader, more inclusive notion that acknowledges also the importance of deeper meaning and purpose in life, certainly as newer ideas of psychologically rich lives arise in cities.[3]

It may be as communitarian Amitai Etzioni believes, that happiness is an especially inadequate measure of the good life. He rightly points out that many of the decisions or actions we take in life are other-regarding and respond to a sense of caring and commitment. Many of these important acts, such as caring for a spouse with Alzheimer's, donating an organ, or stepping in to rescue a swimmer in trouble at the beach, are not pleasurable in the usual sense—they are hard things and often include a significant amount of pain and sacrifice. The motivations to act in these cases, Etzioni believes, involve satisfying one's "moral commitment."[4] *Flourishing* is better at capturing this moral component of the good life but is not fully adequate.

Utilitarian Ethics

Utilitarianism is arguably the dominant ethical framework used in city decision-making, sometimes informally when an elected official weighs in his or her mind which option will produce the largest gain or positive impact for constituents. A common practice is responding to the number of citizens who attend a public meeting on some controversial subject by counting the number for and against as a crude guide for how to decide. More formally, the practice of benefit-cost analysis is commonly used as a decision method in planning and public policy and is often codified or enshrined as a necessary step in the decision-making process.

When the moral philosophy of utilitarianism first emerged through the writings of theorists such as Bentham, Sidgwick, and Mill, among others, it was an improvement in the way public decision was derived. The interests and welfare of everyone counted—not just of the wealthy and the powerful. In this way, utilitarian thinking was and is highly egalitarian. "The greatest good for the greatest number" is the classic shorthand for this moral rule.

Bentham's so-called greatest happiness principle gives expression to and comports well with the intuitions of many of us—that we should and must act, choose, and legislate in ways that benefit the greatest number of us.

Bentham's classic moral direction to maximize social utility, and to seek to bring about the greatest good for the greatest number, has considerable intuitive appeal. Cities have the chance to do many things that elevate and benefit their citizens and inhabitants, and a utilitarian goal underpins much of the history behind efforts to protect health and safety, advancements in sanitation, creation of parks and green spaces, and many other things that cities do. Cities are and ought to largely be about programs, policies, and actions that make life better for the vast majority of their citizenry.

How to define *good*, of course, has always been open to discussion. Typically, we hold that because the "good" is (and ought to be, we believe) a personally or individually defined thing, it is best to defer to the choices and expressions of individual choice in how we cast our "dollar votes." In this way, it is argued, the free-functioning, unfettered market system is the best way to reach the utilitarian result we seek. We calculate the benefits by imagining what would have resulted from free-market transactions if not for certain and serious market failures (such as the presence of negative externalities, incomplete information, or high transaction costs).[5] To many, utilitarianism seems a reasonable and defensible moral position. Elected officials, for example, would want to work on behalf of a larger public interest, where laws and policies benefit not just a few people but many, perhaps the majority, of one's constituents.

Many of our toughest urban policy dilemmas raise precisely these kinds of questions about how widely disseminated the benefits of a policy are. Indeed, it can be argued that many of the positions we have taken, for instance around guns, heavily favor the positions and opinions of a minority of the public. It should be about benefiting the many and not the few. Larger public interests necessarily trump personal gains as well.

Equality, Equity, and Inclusiveness

Are there some values that trump the greatest happiness principle?

While there is much to recommend a city (or city officials) that takes a utilitarian approach, we must also acknowledge the weight and significance of other values that serve to constrain or place parameters on the utilitarian result. Here we invoke the deontological theories of ethics. Derived from *deont*, Greek for "duty," the idea is that there are many other nonconsequentialist values and considerations that might support a decision contrary to or different from that which maximizes social utility.

There are a broad range of values that have to do with fairness and fair treatment, equality and equity, and what individuals are entitled to in terms of living conditions and life circumstances. It is ethically intolerable, for example, for some citizens of a city to live in abject poverty and experience deeply unhealthy living conditions. Individuals are owed dignity and autonomy and, as discussed later, rights that are basic and inviolate. These include rights to things such as minimum levels of housing, safe and healthy environments, connections to nature, and procedural and political rights, such as the right to participate in making a decision that affects you and the right to have your voice heard on matters of local import.

Residents of cities experience a host of unfair and unjust inequalities that must be addressed. We are motivated to make a person or community whole, not because of economic efficiency or the logic of utilitarian maximizing, but rather out of a deep sense of fairness and equity—the understanding that there is a fundamental duty to compensate for past harms, to make right the wrongs of the past, and to seek and achieve social justice.

Kindness and Care

It's a common perception that kindness is in short supply in modern cities. Yet there is an important value here that makes any human community where people live close together tolerable: kindness is what we hope others show toward us and what certainly buffers us against the many other stresses in urban settings. While there are a variety of definitions of kindness, it is defined by the *Cambridge Dictionary* as "the quality of being generous, helpful, and caring about other people or an act showing this quality."[6] Synonyms for *kind* include words like *respectful*, *gentle*, *tender*, and *good*. And there are obviously a host of similar overlapping philosophical and inspirational concepts, including love, in the way it is discussed in this book's introduction, and compassion (more about this concept below). There is something very intuitive about the need for kindness—and for cities especially to avoid the inverse, cruelty. Just as we avoid and shun people who are cruel, no one wants to work or live in a city whose policies and practices are cruel.

Kindness can also be seen in the official positions and policies of a city government; it isn't just something shown by one individual to another. It may come in the form of time off for employees to care for family. It may be seen in the way a city treats animals, for instance by taking steps to make glass more visible to migratory songbirds. These are some ways—and there are many—that a city can be kind. When it comes to nonhuman animals, cruelty seems more the norm than the exception.

A connected notion, then, is altruism, the ability of a person, and a city, to act in selfless ways—to do things for others with their interests in mind primarily, rather than one's own benefits or good (e.g., doing something solely to get positive publicity and acclaim for one's actions or a city garnering publicity that adds to its reputation, tax base, or desirability).

Gentle is another synonym for *kind*, and it's a word I like a great deal. Growing up in the Washington, DC, area, I was always pleasantly surprised by the signs you would see as you crossed into Maryland: MARYLAND WELCOMES YOU. PLEASE DRIVE GENTLY.[7] I very much liked the idea that official road signage would invoke such a rarely used word, but more important, I thought it was spot-on as a message. Driving is inherently dangerous and often leads to violent outcomes; "Drive gently" was a handy way of saying "Be careful; be considerate of the lives of others; slow down; don't drive or behave aggressively." Gentleness is a value we want to see in cities and in the ways cities operate and implement programs and policies. *Humane* is yet another possible moral descriptor of a city and its landscapes. It's frequently used to describe the caring treatment of animals, for example, and it may be understood as another version of kindness.

Some might object to an ethical city founded primarily on the value of kindness; it seems to some to be an optional virtue, something we should exhibit but maybe don't always have to. You might say, "I don't expect you to treat me that way out of kindness but rather because I have the right to be treated this way." More later on deontological and rights-based ethics, but here we view kindness and its associated constellation of values as foundational for a good and ethical city.

Interestingly, there is abundant research that demonstrates that the more kindness exists in the world and in the city, the more happiness we see. Acting with kindness delivers personal benefits as well, and in some studies just watching and paying attention to the acts of kindness taking place around us has been shown to deliver happiness.[8] But much of what happens in cities, many policies and decisions, might to the contrary be described as cruel, not kind.

It also makes sense to talk about toxic masculinity in relation to cities and city governments. So many aspects of society reflect this tendency, but it seems an apt description of much of the policing philosophy of cities, for instance. We see this in the way city police brook no talking back or resistance when someone is stopped or questioned on the street. But we also see these tendencies in the highly aggressive ways we manage landscapes: here we don't brook weeds that are out of place and viewed as undesirable, and we nuke them with herbicides and pesticides. Our gun culture and hubris about guns reflects toxic masculinity, as does our tendency to favor, invest in, and build large infrastructures that knock down forests, alter rivers, and destroy coastal ecosystems.

What we need more of is the inverse of hubris, the inverse of a hypermasculine approach: we need approaches to landscape, policing, and infrastructure that eschew the mindless and destructive results of brute force in favor of humbleness, gentleness, and sensitive and appropriate design that emphasizes intelligent, smaller-scale interventions that fit within and respect nature. Tolerance and kindness should carry the day in our ethical city.

Dignity and Autonomy

Dignity and autonomy are related concepts and foundational for a city that seeks to be ethical. Most would agree that we want to work to protect the dignity of every resident of a city. Yet often we don't. "Dignity violations," or moments in which we inflict humiliation, disrespect, and feelings of inferiority and powerlessness, happen constantly through municipal power. Think of the recent sweeps of homeless camps, the ways many are treated in the criminal justice system, or the daily harms and harassments endured by residents of color who experience systemic racism.

During the pandemic, federal and state governments have stepped in to prevent evictions. Few things are likely more humiliating than experiencing firsthand an eviction, with one's possessions thrown into the street.

Katrin Grossman and Elena Trubina identify three conceptual elements that make up dignity: self-respect ("to be able to meet one's own self-image"), self-determination ("to decide about one's goals and means"), and public recognition ("to be respected as a fundamentally equal member of society"). Autonomy is an essential companion cornerstone, similar to self-determination. Autonomy can be defined as "the capacity to be one's person, to live one's life according to reasons and motives that are taken as one's own and not the product of manipulative or distorting external forces, to be in this way independent."[9]

Tolerance is also an important, related value. A good and ethical city is one that understands and appreciates that residents will have a variety of valid life plans and lifestyle preferences. Cities can tolerate and celebrate this diversity.

Moral Imagination and Reflective Equilibrium

Moral imagination is at the heart of the project of understanding city life and city policymaking as an ethical activity. It is a skill, a perspective, perhaps likened to a muscle—a moral muscle that needs exercising.

We want citizens, consumers, and elected officials with the deep ability to engage in moral imagination: the ability to put yourself in someone else's place, to see and understand their point of view. "A critical feature of the moral imagination," says philosopher David Bromwich, "... is that justice to a stranger comes to seem a more profound work of conscience than justice to a friend, neighbor, or member of our own community."[10] To be able to see the merits of another's view or outlook is a key feature of an ethical life and, as I argue throughout this book, something that cities can support and cultivate. Moral imagination helps us to make better, more ethical judgments when it comes to city policy.

Intuition is important, certainly, but so is ethical reasoning. How many times have we reacted to something we've experienced or a story we've heard that has an outcome that strikes us as simply unfair or unjust, something that feels wrong, something that our gut is telling us is a morally wrong result? We each have an ethical compass—call it our gut instinct—and we make many of our daily decisions unconsciously through the guidance of intuition.

Philosopher John Rawls offers a very useful way to think about this process of making ethical judgments in what he calls "reflective equilibrium"—the idea that we move back and forth between what our intuition is telling us and what our value commitments to ethical rules seem to require, reaching a point where we are happy (or equally unhappy) with the outcome or result. That's not to say we shouldn't value our intuition. It is a good starting point for what we feel is right or wrong. But it must be balanced against the ethical or legal principles we have embraced and adopted as a society or as a city, so moral judgments will always be more complex than simply what our gut tells us.

Empathy and Compassion

Empathy and compassion are universal human values that govern and guide much of daily life as well as policy and planning decisions. But can a city be compassionate? Indeed it can, and compassion is really at the heart of an ethical city. There are now a number of cities that have embraced compassion as a guiding principle and are taking tangible steps to put this value into practice.

One city that sought to define itself by compassion is Louisville, Kentucky. Several years ago, I interviewed then mayor Greg Fischer about how he made compassion a goal for his city. As a new mayor coming from a business background, Fischer believed in the importance of putting values front and center, and for him, compassion fit well with his vision. Fischer's definition of compassion is "respect for each of our citizens so that their full human potential is flourishing." Empathy is not enough, he argues; *compassion* is a more active word, one Fischer says implies putting values into practice.

As part of its commitment, the city signed the Compassion Charter, a succinct but powerful four paragraphs. The charter calls on us "always to treat all others as we wish to be treated ourselves" and "impels us to work tirelessly to alleviate the suffering of our fellow creatures." We must refrain from "inflicting pain" and "transcend selfishness." More than 2 million individuals have "affirmed" the charter, as have over seventy cities, including Rotterdam, Cape Town, Tucson, and Denver.

When Fischer spoke of this frame and aspiration for his city, it seemed to be clearly about equity and interdependence, with a deep sense of fairness and an acknowledgment of how everyone's lives, especially in a city, are intertwined. "It is much more difficult for everyone in the city to see the interdependence they have on each other. They may not look the same, they may live in different parts of town, [have] different economic situations, but we're all interconnected in terms of our common fate."

There are also practical implications and many ways to give expression to this value. In Louisville, one way has been through the city's annual Give a Day, a week in April when citizens are challenged to volunteer and help out in a variety of different ways. There are community trash cleanups, tree plantings, and food collections. In 2018 some 205,000 volunteers—about one-quarter of the city's population—participated, breaking a record.

The vision of a compassionate city, in turn, serves to elevate the importance of and guide a variety of city policy areas, from affordable housing and homelessness to health care and gun violence. I was especially interested to hear how Louisville's agenda of compassion might connect to the agendas of environment and sustainability. Fischer pointed to several key areas. Compassion for animals is one, and it guides the city's animal services, he told me. Fischer is proud of the city's shift to no-kill animal shelters: kindness toward animals is part of a compassionate city.

While Louisville has striven to become known as a compassionate city, 2020 challenged those credentials when a twenty-six-year-old Black woman, Breonna Taylor, was killed during a late-night police raid, an attempt to serve a no-knock warrant at her apartment that ended in gunfire. The tragic events of that evening, and the public protests that followed, shocked the city to its core and raised questions about Fischer's leadership and transparency in handling the crisis, leading the city council to pass a "no confidence" vote. The pain and anger in the community remain, though some positive steps have resulted. The practice of no-knock warrants has been banned, for example, and Fischer issued an executive order declaring racism a public health crisis and laying out a comprehensive set of goals and actions for addressing racial equity in that city moving forward.[11]

Stories like this show how fraught and complex the moral quandaries facing cities often are. There are various actors and interests to consider, competing values to balance, and a need to hear and consider many different voices and perspectives. Finding an ethical path for a city may not be immediate or linear.

A City Is a Bundle of Living Things That Deserve Respect

One of the most important questions about how we define the moral community has to do with what ethical consideration is given and due to the many other nonhuman lives a city's decisions touch or impact. Within the bounds of a city there are thousands, indeed millions (or more!), of other living creatures. Many of these are sentient, meaning they are capable of feeling pain. How we operate as a city, how responsible we are in protecting and stewarding the trees, land, and nature within that city, has serious impacts on these other life-forms. Go to any city's Wikipedia page and you will readily and prominently find its population—the number of *human* residents, that is. That is one way we tend to understand cities and how we tend to judge and classify them. You would be hard-pressed, however, to find out much about nonhuman species.

A city usually has extensive biodiversity—many flora, fauna, and fungi exist within its boundaries—and is, in addition to many other things, a "habitat" for wildlife and wild nature. We tend to pay most attention to the larger animals we see, especially the critters—birds, squirrels, other larger mammals—we think are attractive. As a bird lover I advocate for the need to make cities bird friendly and bird safe, and this includes the need for buildings to be fitted with bird-safe windows. Birds are an important part of my own definition of moral community, and I believe we have a strong ethical obligation to do what we can to reduce their pain, suffering, and human-caused mortality; it is estimated that upward of a billion birds die each year from window and building strikes in the United States alone. We are less enamored with snakes and spiders, but cities are home to many such forms of life, and how we care for and treat them is a significant ethical question.

The moral status of plants is an open question, but cities contain (and want to contain) extensive trees and vegetation. New research suggests that trees engage in communication and help each other, cooperate, and form communities of life not unlike those in the human world.[12] Botanists and plant lovers are quick to charge society with "plant blindness," suggesting that we pay more attention and attach greater importance to animals than plants, but this is changing. There is evidence that our historic view of plants as inert, passive, and lacking in agency may be profoundly wrong, which brings with it some serious ethical implications.

How important to us, then, is this incredible stock of life we co-occupy cities with? Are they a meaningful part of our moral community? And if so, what do we owe them and how do we treat them?

Impacts Near and Distant: The Future Must Be an Ethical Priority

There is an important temporal dimension to how we think of a city and its moral community. Are we duty bound to consider only the current occupants of a city (human or otherwise) in many decisions? Or should we think longer-term, taking into account the impacts of decisions of future residents, perhaps those who may not live in the city for another twenty, fifty, or even 100 years?

Given the number and diversity of the kinds of moral judgments and ethical decisions a city is faced with, the extent of future impacts will certainly vary. Some decisions will have clearly immediate or near-term effects, such as decisions about roadway design or pedestrian safety, but many decisions play out in a much longer temporal stage.

Many decisions will potentially have serious and longer-lasting impacts and affect the quality of life or ecology of a city for many years (or even generations) into the future. And it may often be hard to tell what long-term effects will result from numerous and frequent short-term decisions. If we allow the felling of a tree here or there, do we set a precedent that then shapes the conservation (or lack thereof) of urban forests that would otherwise keep us cool and delight us with their beauty years into the future? A real and true ethical commitment to the future, moreover, requires cities to take many actions, and make many kinds of investments, with the quality of future life in mind.

Duties beyond Borders

There is a clear spatial or geographical aspect to our moral sensibilities. It is often observed that we are more likely to care about people, things, and communities that are physically closer. Yet we know that cities cause serious impacts hundreds or thousands of miles beyond their legal boundaries. Do cities have duties beyond their borders?

This book argues for a definitive yes. We know that large cities create impacts—air and water pollution, for example—that extend well beyond their legal boundaries; many impacts of local actions, whether traffic congestion, excessive light pollution, or combined sewer overload, affect residents of adjacent cities and may impact people and places farther away. Large cities sustain themselves on a large and elaborate flow of goods and materials—food, energy, water, building materials—coming into the city. The implications of such large ecological footprints and extensive urban metabolism are evident in faraway places—fisheries become depleted, mines pollute waterways, and forests and natural habitats are diminished to provide these local needs.

How to adjust or modify this destructive urban metabolism is one of the most important ethical challenges of cities today. Importantly, a core value of an ethical city is to acknowledge its moral responsibility for these external and beyond-border impacts and to take steps to minimize or eliminate them.

Cities also have the power and ability to positively influence things happening on the global scene, and this core value is not only about minimizing impacts but about taking affirmative steps and exhibiting impactful leadership to address problems at regional and global levels. Cities, especially in the Global North, also have the resources and wealth to play an important role in addressing global problems and challenges from hunger to climate change to biodiversity loss.

Conclusions

A city is ethical to the extent that it follows certain established core values and ethical principles. These include compassion and kindness, the notion of making decisions informed by a robust moral imagination, and the ability to effectively put oneself in the circumstances and place of others. There are valid and useful philosophical frames that an ethical city should attempt to follow, including (other things being equal) taking actions that benefit many rather than the few and that extend and expand the common good. An ethical city favors the collective good over individual interests.

While there is much merit to consequentialist theories such as utilitarianism, there are also many values more duty based or deontological that cities must acknowledge and defend as well, including notions of equality and individual rights of various kinds. A pluralistic set of these core ethical values can guide cities and city leaders in making policy decisions. It is important to acknowledge that while many of the ideas presented so far may seem overly analytical, there are other moral concepts that pursue ethical and moral ends that may be more about employing the heart as much as the head. Compassion, for example, is a key element of an ethical city.

Discussion Questions

What do you believe are the key values that should underpin the vision of an ethical city?

Are some values more important than others?

Do these core values sometimes conflict? And if so, how do we decide which are most important?

Virtue in the City
Virtuous Leaders and Citizens

Chelsea Johnson remembers well when she got word that the home builders association in Tampa was trying to push through changes to the city's iconic tree protection ordinance. These changes would have made it much easier for developers and home builders to cut and clear trees that stood in the way of new construction. Put another way, it apparently would allow "clear-cutting" on residential lots. The proposal seemingly came out of nowhere.

Johnson was the president of the South Tampa Neighborhood Association and, as she explained to me in a recent phone call, was not especially knowledgeable about trees or the city's tree protection ordinance when she heard about the eleventh-hour proposal.[1] But she did know that trees were an essential part of the quality of life in Tampa and an especially important part of the beauty of her own neighborhood. She understood that the value of trees and other urban ecosystems extends far beyond aesthetics. So she sprang into action, becoming, as she says, an unexpected tree activist. Convening warring groups around her dining room table, she helped hammer out a unique compromise between the tree-hugging residents and the developers and builders.

What motivates individuals to step forward to organize in such cases, to advocate, to often give hours of their time, in this case to ensure both tree protection and the ability of the city to grow? Surely there is often some element of personal benefit and reward, but often it is hard to explain; they are virtuous individuals acting beyond a concern about immediate self-interest. An ethical city is powered by the countless actions of virtuous individuals and organizations.

Virtuous Leaders and Citizens

It is often the case in history that change occurs through the actions of a few individuals selflessly and courageously standing up for what they believe in, taking direct action to redress an injustice or solve a community problem. People such as Jane Addams, founder of Hull House in Chicago, and Jane Jacobs, critic of the mainstream planning and development of cities, come to mind as such heroes, but there are many others. And there are thousands of less recognized people who have made similar contributions to the improvement of urban life and the protection of nature and environment.

What motivates these heroes, these leaders—some elected or with official positions, many without—to do things for their neighborhoods and communities and the larger public? This leads us to a different approach to the question of what makes a city ethical and what it takes to move a city in that direction.

The controversy surrounding dangerous drinking water in Flint, Michigan, is a telling example of the power of virtuous actors. The particulars of the story are now commonly known but worth repeating: To save money, the city shifted its water supply source from Detroit to the Flint River in 2014. A failure to apply anticorrosion chemicals to the water, as had always been done, meant that water with excessive and highly dangerous levels of lead was being delivered to homes in Flint, going unnoticed for months.

The actions of multiple individuals led (finally) to a recognition of what had happened and to a demand for action. It began with a concerned mom who wanted to know why her kids were sick and why their hair was mysteriously falling out. She set the ball in motion but quickly gained support from an Environmental Protection Agency official who investigated the issue and in turn reached out to an academic water scientist, who did additional testing. A physician at a local hospital also became involved, looking closely at the medical data and noticing a significant rise in children with elevated levels of lead. She stepped forward and became an important voice in the medical community calling for immediate action to address this serious health threat.[2]

We see similar virtuous acts and heroic actors every day in every city. Each person is motivated by a complex mix of values, and in many cases they derive personal benefit and gratification from selfless acts, but there is more at work here than self-interest. Consider firefighters, who charge into a burning structure to save a family, something for which they have trained and a risk they have voluntarily accepted; yet that act still requires sacrifice and courage. Or consider police officers, who similarly place themselves in danger and must make snap judgments, sometimes about when to draw their gun, in order to protect the public and enforce a city's laws; they may also often feel like a target of criminals and others who wish them ill. And doing these jobs is increasingly demanding and complex. We now expect police officers to do their job courageously but in strict accordance with their city's specific use-of-force policies and standards, making their on-the-spot judgments in the face of unforeseen danger even more difficult. Or consider bus drivers, who are often the frontline face of the city, forced to confront many unexpected events and crises, from health emergencies to traffic accidents, and to make many snap judgments as well (and, we hope, to do their job with care and compassion). From forgiving a fare for a homeless rider to giving life-saving assistance to a rider in need, care and compassion are, we hope, the guiding virtues in these exchanges.

Here we consider an important alternative (or perhaps additional) ethical frame for cities, which sees the many ethical outcomes and decisions and the good work of cities as a result of the character and virtues of its citizens and individual leaders. The heavy ethical lifting in this framing is not done by judiciously balancing and weighing options or by laying out specific ethical principles and applying them to specific circumstances; rather, the task is to cultivate and nurture ethical individuals whose character and virtues will lead them to make consistently good decisions that ideally consider the greater common good, equality and fairness for others, and the interests of future generations.

Like in the Flint and Tampa examples, the stories of virtuous individuals can be found every day in the pages of newspapers. There is the savvy and committed Australian who dressed up as a black cockatoo and confronted his premier in public about why his administration was allowing the destruction of an ancient banksia woodland. Or the individual in Maine who single-handedly saved the lives of thousands of horseshoe crabs by searching the beaches every day for those that had been overturned by the surf (and thus were not likely to survive). Or the individuals along the Texas coast who sprang into action during Texas's recent freeze to save many sea turtles by loading them into the backs of their cars and taking them to warming stations. Individuals will take remarkable actions and make sacrifices on behalf of animals, nature, and humans in need to help achieve a larger public good.

It Takes a Virtuous Village

A 2016 *Mother Jones* story about the Flint saga, with the headline "Meet 5 Everyday Heroes of Flint's Water Crisis," is worth drawing attention to.[3] It is often not a single person but a network of virtuous citizens and leaders who together solve a problem or raise an alarm bell. It takes a virtuous village, one might say. One person can certainly make a difference, but that difference can be multiplied and amplified when activating and reinforcing a larger community of virtuous citizens.

This is the realm of virtue ethics. It is another important approach to ethics, quite different from the teleological or deontological perspectives we have discussed so far. It holds that, following Aristotle and Plato, the important task is the cultivation of personal ethics and integrity. It is less about the equity or justness of a decision or outcome and more a question of the goodness of people. Virtue ethics shifts the emphasis from decisions or rules that might bring about an ethical result to the character of the actors making those decisions. It shifts from the question "Is that a fair, just, or ethical outcome?" to "What kind of person should I be?" or "What kind of life should I lead?"

This is one important way to understand an ethical city: it is a city that at once is animated, guided, and lived in by virtuous individuals who take stands and undertake heroic actions on the part of others and the larger public interest. When we think of a good and ethical city, we imagine a place where many individuals think beyond their narrow personal self-interest and work on behalf of some larger good. It is a city where average citizens understand the importance of stepping up. But it is also a city where countless elected and unelected officials perform their appointed duties with care, integrity, and solemnity.

There is an active philosophical discussion about, and an extensive literature around, virtue ethics—how cultivating virtues helps enhance meaning in life, what precise set of virtues society believes are valuable or beneficial, and importantly, how to cultivate virtuous citizens and leaders. It is believed that this creates the most successful, most effective way to ensure that ethical decisions are made. Thousands or millions of decisions—made by those on a planning commission or a city council, for instance—will be guided not so much by ethical principles as by ethical and virtuous individuals who have inculcated, absorbed, and internalized an ethical sensibility.

Sidebar 2-1 lists a few of the more important virtues we might like to see displayed or expressed in cities. Philosopher Ronald Sandler identifies a number of these as important environmental virtues in his book *Character and Environment*.[4] This is by no means an exhaustive list. I would add courage: we want those forging a life in cities to be willing to take chances, experiment, and lead the way, for instance by connecting to nature by riding a bicycle (ditching the car), installing rooftop solar panels, and taking many other actions that may seem odd or different but that will ultimately be important to creating a healthier, more sustainable city.

Sidebar 2-1 Some Important Urban Virtues

Love	Loyalty	Humility
Cooperativeness	Honesty	Gratitude
Care	Optimism	Frugality
Compassion	Creativity	Farsightedness
Justice	Wonder	Ecological sensitivity

Environmental virtues drawn from Ronald L. Sandler, *Character and Environment: A Virtue-Oriented Approach to Environmental Ethics* (New York: Columbia University Press, 2008).

How we defend or argue for specific virtues is an active philosophical debate. Traditionally virtues are understood to have both self-regarding benefits and larger benefits for the common good (other-regarding value). As an individual works to become a good and virtuous person, many individual benefits accrue, of course. Virtuous behavior and a virtuous life can help create the conditions for personal happiness, but more commonly philosophers argue for virtue based on its value in creating conditions for meaningful and flourishing lives. Purpose and meaning are elements of a satisfying life, a life of making connections with, caring for, and working on behalf of others.

Some philosophers have emphasized the larger social benefit and value of cultivating virtue. In her book *Uneasy Virtue*, for instance, Julia Driver offers a consequentialist defense of virtue ethics: it is not just about achieving individual excellence or flourishing but about the larger benefits to society. "On my theory," she says, "the value of all these traits resides in their tendency to produce good consequences."[5]

What Motivates Those Who Are Virtuous?

Why do they do it? And how can cities cultivate and reinforce such qualities and character? More broadly, from an ethical perspective, how do we go about defending or arguing a virtues-based approach to urban ethics?

As mentioned earlier, Amitai Etizioni, a leading voice for communitarianism, believes that we often fail to grasp the importance of moral commitments as motivators. Instead of a framework that seeks to maximize pleasure, and in which people are seen to be primarily motivated by self-interest, he sees a different path, one that believes much of our motivation stems from a desire to "affirm" our moral commitments. These actions and behaviors are often decidedly not pleasurable but often painful and difficult.

He disagrees with those who attempt to explain much of this behavior in terms of the pleasure or benefits gained by the actor. "In sharp contrast to the thesis that acts motivated by attempts to live up to moral commitments are but another source of satisfaction, one ought to note that practically all affirming behavior is in effect painful or deprives one of pleasure. Fasting, donating an organ, attending to the sick, speaking truth to power, and so on are all cases in point."[6]

Where those moral commitments come from is an open question, but Etzioni and other communitarians would argue they derive from the larger communities of which we are a part and are a result of the shared values we hold. One task then becomes to inculcate or reinforce these social values, or the need each person has to act in ways that are not just self-serving but also protect and advance the larger common good. Discussing specific society-strengthening virtues that cities can bolster is a good start.

Toward a Deep(er) Citizenship

An ethical city depends heavily upon its citizens, and it counts on them to do many more things than we have typically or commonly expected. It is a cliché, but an accurate one, that we ask very little of citizens and that our concept of citizenship is limited in scope. A good citizen, conventionally anyway, is understood as someone who obeys the law, pays her taxes, perhaps does the minimal things that society (and a city) asks of her, including occasionally voting and serving on a jury. Citizenship is a sporadic, limited thing, not something most Americans spend much time thinking about.

David Orr, professor and former head of the environmental studies program at Oberlin College, has written extensively about the potential of asking and expecting more from citizens. Orr asks us to consider our citizenship in a larger biotic, or biological, community, echoing the ideas of Aldo Leopold. "The ecological emergency," Orr says, "is about the failure to comprehend our citizenship in the biotic community." We ought to acknowledge our status as "plain members" of this community of life, as Leopold so eloquently expresses in his book *A Sand County Almanac*.

How must our notions and expectations about citizenship change given our current global predicaments? For one, the scope of citizenship must be enlarged. Being a good citizen is no longer just about voting, paying taxes, and obeying the law (though we still have a hard enough time with these). Orr contrasts this traditional limited scope of citizenship, what he calls "cheap citizenship," with the kind of expanded citizenship needed today, or "deep citizenship." Citizenship entails more today: what and how (and how much) we consume is now a legitimate question of citizenship. For instance, we know that individuals can effect significant change in the world by how they choose to direct their purchases.

We especially need words and a political language, Orr says, that acknowledge the importance of the natural world and the severity of our current ecological crisis. Patriotism, for instance, is usually understood in a very narrow way. "However, it must come to include the use one makes of land, forests, air, water, and wildlife. To abuse natural resources, to erode soils, to destroy natural diversity, to waste, to take more than one's fair share, to fail to replenish what has been used must someday come to be regarded as unpatriotic and wrong."[7]

Orr has also written compellingly of the importance of "ecological literacy"—the essential knowledge about ecology and sustainable place-making that all citizens should be expected to be conversant in. For the most part, our collective level of ecological literacy is rather small, but that could be different. As the environmental challenges we face accelerate and become ever more complex, there is an ethical duty that individuals have to learn and a societal obligation to teach or convey this basic knowledge. What is the stock of knowledge, the subject areas, that citizens of cities today are duty bound to learn? It is an open question, but it should include intimate knowledge of the ecologies of one's city—its natural systems, flora, and fauna (and fungi) but its human ecologies as well, including the deeper histories of the city. There are all kinds of knowledge needed to participate in the political and social life of a city and to make meaningful contributions to its growth and development over time. And such knowledge is essential for acting in ways that are ethical.

How Do We Cultivate Virtue in the City?

An important question is how we go about cultivating virtuous leaders and citizens. How do we especially go about creating the next generation of hyperengaged, ethically aware citizenry that we so desperately need today? There are renewed calls for civics education in high school, for example, and this would be a welcome new emphasis, though we likely need to begin the education process even earlier.

Citizenship must also be increasingly understood and defined in terms of geography and place, and more of us should be challenged to invest emotionally in the communities and neighborhoods in which we live and to, when needed, stand up (and speak up) on behalf of the many inhabitants of our "home," human and nonhuman.

Sidebar 2-2 lists some of the possible behaviors and actions we might expect from good citizens. Many entail active steps that reflect care and

> **Sidebar 2-2 What Do We Expect of Citizens?**
> **What Are Some Examples of Expanded Citizenship?**
> Helping a neighbor who is housebound
> Checking in on an elderly neighbor during a heat wave
> Cleaning off snow from the sidewalks in front of our homes
> Attending a public hearing and voicing concerns about the homeless
> Standing up for endangered flora and fauna
> Placing feather-friendly dots on windows to prevent bird collisions
> Volunteering to give nature walks in the neighborhood
> Growing a garden and donating the food to a food bank
> Picking up garbage on your morning walk
> Coming to the aid of someone who has fallen off a bike
> Turning down the thermostat to reduce energy consumption
> Attending a climate change rally
> Lobbying your city council for stronger energy standards
> Installing a rooftop photovoltaic panel system
> Knowing your neighbors' names
> Participating in community events such as parades, cleanups, and celebratory gatherings

compassion for others, such as giving aid and help when others are in need. In an ethical city, being a good citizen means being a good neighbor: perhaps looking in on the elderly, watching kids playing in or near the street, or offering to give someone a ride or to run an errand. These are old-fashioned virtues of neighborliness that ought to be rediscovered.

This mode of more active citizenship also challenges the idea that all social functions are farmed out to specialized agencies and staff of a city government: we need not pick up trash from the street, because that is something we pay city trash collection and street maintenance personnel to do. In this mindset, safety becomes something we assume and expect police to take care of.

Making a city safer for women, some believe, will require more of us to directly take actions to make a positive difference. As Paul van Soomeren of the International Crime Prevention through Environmental Design Association notes, "One of the big errors is thinking that safety is something only for the police. . . . You live in your dwelling, but you also have a responsibility for your neighbors and people in the street." "Convincing people to act as custodians of their immediate environment is essential," says Anne

Quito, as she surveys opinions and ideas about how to respond to the tragic Sarah Everard case that unfolded in 2021. Everard was a thirty-three-year old resident of London who, while walking home one evening, was abducted, raped, and killed by an off-duty police officer who used his badge to force her into his car. The case triggered a national outcry and a series of Reclaim These Streets vigils.[8] For many, it showed how much greater the dangers in cities are for women (even when women take all the precautions they're supposed to) and how, in some cases at least, the police themselves are to be feared.

In imagining a virtuous city, we might understandably hope that people look out for and care about their fellow citizens and extend helping hands when they are able. An ethic of active care and assistance might be cultivated in cities in many different ways but might especially suggest the need for more specialized workshops and training programs that give citizens the tangible skills to effectively offer assistance. The problem of street harassment that women face is a case in point and suggests how difficult it may be to activate citizens. Some 90 percent of women who report being harassed also report that they received no help from the people around them, suggesting the critical importance of bystander training programs such as Right to Be's Stand Up against Street Harassment campaign.

One important point is that we should want to cultivate an urban citizenry of common virtues, perhaps as contrasted with heroic virtues. Yes, we need and want individuals to spring into action when fellow citizens are in need of help, for instance by giving life-saving assistance or medical care. But we also want to live in a city where people simply treat each other with respect and kindness, reflected in the many small actions and behaviors we undertake—holding open a door, smiling and offering a friendly greeting, giving directions. I have a personal memory from a short time living in Sydney with small children: it was a remarkably common experience when riding the public buses there that almost without fail someone would offer to help lift our heavy stroller when boarding. A virtuous city, it should be remembered, is largely defined by the many smaller, daily expressions of kindness and compassion.

Being a good citizen is clearly also about being a good neighbor. So many of the urban challenges we face—growing social isolation, rising rates of depression, the challenges of an aging population—call for some form of renewed neighborliness, such as the willingness to watch out for other people's children playing in the street or to check on elderly neighbors or ask if they need a ride or something from the grocery store. In the ethical city, we need to relearn many of the virtues of being good neighbors.

Cultivating compassion—for people and other forms of life—is a special challenge in an ethical city. Seeing and experiencing problems such as homelessness through the faces, voices, and stories of actual people serves to deeply educate us and humanize this problem. The *Los Angeles Times* reported recently on a unique "immersion course": three days of walks and discussions aimed at exposing police and prosecutors to what the life of a homeless person might be like, in this case in the Tenderloin district in San Francisco. The course includes early morning and evening walking tours of the neighborhood, led in one case by a former homeless person and drug addict, and one day serving food to the homeless in a church basement. Another day they stand in line for food themselves.

There are also positive techniques for strengthening compassion toward the many other living creatures that we co-occupy cities with, including efforts to engage in a kind of exercise: What if I were a bird or snake or other animal? How would I live, and what challenges would I face? I watched a group of elementary school kids engage in precisely this kind of exercise in a canyon in San Diego, one of the hundreds of largely forgotten canyons in that city. This canyon, like many, held an incredible amount of biodiversity but was to the surrounding communities considered a dangerous place, a place for children to avoid. On this day, I watched a program called Kids in the Canyon in action. Organized by the local chapter of the Sierra Club, it introduces kids to these magical canyons and the life they hold. I listened as one by one, children explained the animal they had chosen and what it might be like to be that animal.

Giving something a name, individualizing another person or form of life, is another way to foster compassion. It is a way to overcome the abstraction that in so many ways and in so many cases allow us to ignore pain and suffering: we don't know who that homeless person is, so we have no direct responsibility to them. Ignorance is bliss and forgiving. We are often told that giving a bird or even a tree a name is anthropomorphizing, or attaching a human trait or quality to something nonhuman. Yet this is a way of declaring value, highlighting the presence of something living, and signaling the need to consider the well-being of that living creature.

Virtues such as compassion are formed early in life, so schools are an essential tool for cultivating virtues. The nation of Denmark has long valued the development of empathy, teaching it in schools and nurturing it as an important educational goal there. "Empathy is very important for democracy," said Mette Løvbjerg. She is the headmaster of the Møllevang school in the Danish city of Faxe, not far from Copenhagen, and believes strongly in the need to teach and model values like compassion. "You can't have a democracy that is functioning if nobody puts themselves in another one's shoes," she told the *Christian Science Monitor*. "If we don't teach our children that, then we don't have a democracy in 50 years. It's under pressure already." "Many parents consider their children's kindness in the classroom just as crucial as their math or science skills," the article's author added.[9] There is an important role for parents in emphasizing these virtues at home but also in supporting school initiatives to give them priority alongside more typical educational goals.

What else can cities do, especially to enhance and deepen the commitment of citizenship? It is now quite common for local governments to offer some sort of training program for citizens, especially as a way to prepare them to participate in the political life of the city. These are often called citizen academies, usually taught by city staff to expose citizens to the various departments and functions of local government.[10] My hometown of Alexandria, Virginia, offers one of the more comprehensive such academies, offered in two-hour evening blocks over a nine-week period. Perhaps there could be more explicit discussion of ethics and philosophy here, but it does seem designed to bring citizens up to a minimum level of knowledge about the workings of city government. And facilitating community activism should be a goal in every city as well.

We want not only citizens who will be willing to serve on planning boards and help out with other city functions but citizens willing to invest their time, energy, and commitment in the future of the city. In short, we need citizens who are embedded and who care deeply and personally about the places in which they live.

We especially expect our elected officials—mayors, city councillors, city commissioners—to exhibit virtuous behavior, though we are often disappointed. We want them to be honest, be inclusive when making decisions, consider all points of view, and have the interests of the larger public be foremost in their minds. Of course, the reality is often different, muddled by a desire for influence and power, support for pet projects or special interests, and in the case of a not insignificant number of local elected leaders, graft and conflict of interest. The political system in place in most cities serves to discourage virtue—rather, shortsighted action (what gets rewarded at the ballot box), pay-to-play (where access depends on campaign contributions), and self-dealing carry the day. Many decisions are made behind closed doors, with little sense of transparency or accountability, and with self-interest or special interests in mind. Too many elected officials can be described this way.

There are many reforms that would help foster greater virtue in our elected officials. Limits on campaign contributions, for example, and greater limits on pay-for-play (or indeed outlawing the practice) would help, as would more stringent conflict-of-interest provisions. Efforts at expanding local voting, avenues for participation, and co-design throughout a city's governance structure would undoubtedly help as well.

Creating vehicles and mechanisms for greater public scrutiny would in turn serve to reinforce more virtuous elected officials. A robust local press is one important element, though it is in decline in many cities. "Local journalism has been in dramatic decline over the past 15 years," writes journalism professor Penelope Muse Abernathy, "as news organizations and journalists have disappeared."[11]

In many places, newspapers and radio and television stations are diminishing in number, and their ability to cover local news is increasingly limited. These are often the most trusted local sources of news, and without them a community is more susceptible to misinformation and fake news.

The City of New York recently took a unique approach to financially subsidizing local news outlets. In May 2019, then mayor Bill de Blasio issued an executive order directing all city agencies and departments to spend at least 50 percent of their advertising budgets on "community and ethnic" media outlets. According to the CUNY Center for Community Media, this resulted, in the first year alone, in the expenditure of $10 million (by fifty-one city departments) in media purchases from 220 local media outlets.[12] Part of the goal is to support news outlets that are able to reach the city's diverse population, which speaks more than 200 languages.[13]

Conclusions

There is much intuitive support for the notion that a just and ethical city will depend on the presence of an active citizenry that cares about doing ethically correct things and who, in countless ways, will work on behalf of a larger common good. There are many specific, albeit intersecting and overlapping, virtues that are necessary to create an ethical city: compassion, courage, and long-term thinking, among others. How we ensure that citizens in an ethical city hold these many important virtues remains an open question; how do we encourage, cultivate, strengthen, and support them? What can cities do to create the conditions that support or strengthen "the better angels of our nature," to invoke Abraham Lincoln's powerful words?[14]

There is, it seems, a special need to cultivate the next generation of caring and compassionate citizens and, especially, elected and appointed public officials. We want to have confidence that our leaders will be honest and temper their political aspirations in favor of the welfare and interests of their constituents. This is a difficult request in an era of politics where money plays such an outsize role and where self-promotion and political advancement often seem more important.

Discussion Questions

What do you believe is the promise or potential of taking a virtues-based approach to ethics in cities?

Is it a better approach to focus on cultivating and nurturing virtuous citizens and leaders than on developing and applying ethical standards and principles to guide decisions? If we could count on the good character and virtuous leanings of those who serve on boards, commissions, and city councils, perhaps that is enough?

Which specific virtues do you believe are the most essential to strengthen or cultivate and why?

How might a city go about educating its citizens about ethics, and how can it effectively teach and inculcate the virtues we need and want to see (as well as discourage the vices we don't want to see)?

3

Equality, Opportunity, Inclusiveness

Inequality is one of the most difficult challenges cities face today. There are many different kinds of inequality: economic, racial, gender, and sexual orientation, among others. Some forms of inequality are growing—economic, for instance—while others, such as racial and gender inequality, are long-standing and systemic. An ethical city works to identify inequalities and their negative effects and to take tangible and meaningful steps to reduce or mitigate them.

Americans count equality as a prized value, enshrined even in the Declaration of Independence. But paradoxically, the United States is a nation whose beginnings are steeped in slavery and a legal and economic embrace of the harshest forms of inequality, which continues to affect the unequal life trajectories of Black and brown Americans. Slavery, later Jim Crow, and still later urban renewal and redlining were woven into the very fabric of our cities and land-use patterns and manifest in the modern realities of discriminatory traffic stops, police brutality, and disproportionate rates of poverty, among many other results of long-standing and systemic racism.

It is important to acknowledge that there are multiple versions or flavors of equality, and all come into play in cities. There is a vaunted American ideal of equality of opportunity—the notion that all Americans should at least have an equal starting point from which to begin and an equal chance to cultivate the skills to succeed in life. Philosopher John Rawls, in his important book A Theory of Justice, argues for the notion of *fair* equality of opportunity, understanding that simply ensuring that individuals have equal access to or a chance to be considered for a job or a life opportunity is not enough—societies (and cities) must also invest in educational and other resources to ensure that someone is able to fairly compete for those life opportunities.[1]

Cities indeed are often understood as one of the most powerful mechanisms for providing such conditions for excelling, succeeding, and getting ahead in life. And we believe as a matter of fairness that cities should invest in the institutions, programs, and infrastructures to ensure an equal and fair starting point for all.

Equal treatment is another variation: the idea that similarly situated individuals should be treated similarly. Fairness and equity require equal treatment, for instance in the renting of an apartment or the assessing of a fine. This ideal is enshrined in the equal protection clause of the Fourteenth Amendment of the US Constitution.

We know that historically in many cities, minority residents have not received the same level of treatment, for instance by police or law enforcement. For many years, the pervasive use of restrictive covenants in cities around the United States prevented the sale of homes to Blacks and Jews, and later the practice of redlining made it difficult for Blacks to secure a mortgage to buy a home.[2] The results are unjust and explain the vastly lower levels of income and wealth enjoyed by African Americans. Inequalities are often compounding and immensely unfair.

Pursuit of these different, yet important, notions of equality might together characterize an egalitarian city, an aspiration many of us would like to see cities embrace. An egalitarian city reflects the spirit that all residents are equally worthy of respect and are owed a life of decency and autonomy. We also want to acknowledge the uniqueness of each person, his or her particular preferences and life plans, and the need for a city that makes it possible to pursue many different life experiences. Equality of outcome should not mean sameness of lives. An egalitarian city does not require all residents to have the same kinds of homes and other material objects, the same lives, or the same patterns of life. Diversity is good, and the ability to freely choose one's lifestyle and one's life plan is, as I discuss in a later chapter, another mark of an ethical city. A diverse and inclusive city is one that recognizes, respects, and tolerates the many ways in which individuals are different, including many personal attributes and qualities, for instance sexual orientation or the color of one's skin.

Some philosophers (and economists) argue that some degree of inequality is good in the sense that it creates incentives to succeed and excel in life, or that we will naturally work harder in an economic system where we are rewarded for our work and the cultivation of our skills. John Rawls develops, as we have seen, a comprehensive moral theory leading to a set of just principles to govern society. One of Rawls's key arguments is that we would accept and prefer inequality only when it works for the benefit of the least-advantaged members of society. Some degree of inequality would likely help lift everyone's boat and improve everyone's lot—so the argument goes. We can tolerate some inequality, Rawls believes, as long as we choose societal options that maximize benefits for those on the lowest economic rung—what he referred to as the "difference principle." He also believed there would be support for an extensive social net that would ensure no one lived in conditions of severe poverty.

There are many other kinds of inequality that manifest in cities. The physical design of cities favors those who are able-bodied, for example, and many of the spaces and aspects of city life favor men over women. American cities in their dependence on car mobility are ageist, making mobility, and life more generally, difficult for both the young and the old. Those who are too young for a driver's license or too old to safely drive a vehicle are relegated to second-class-citizen status, though in many cities this has been changing. An ethical city is one that recognizes the existence of these profound and impactful inequalities and works hard to overcome them.

The Problem of Inequality

Inequalities in cities represent a challenge to the ethical city in several ways. The lived conditions of many people in cities violate our basic values of dignity, sense of fairness, and what we feel every person has a right to expect. Cities have always been places of social and economic opportunity, engines for uplifting the lives and lots of their inhabitants, but they have often also been places of extreme and brutal inequality. Images of Latin American cities, such as Rio de Janeiro or São Paulo, Brazil, are extreme examples, where favelas literally bump up against luxury towers. Where cities can do something to reduce these conditions, there is a moral duty to try.

Income and wealth inequality have also been increasing in the United States, especially in the last four decades, and the implications are significant. In 2020, the Pew Research Center reported that there has been a significant rise in income at the top, especially among those in the top 5 percent of the richest Americans, while the middle class has seen a decline in its share of income (as a proportion of aggregate income).[3] Interestingly, the Pew study found that a majority of respondents—some 61 percent—expressed the view that there is too much economic inequality, suggesting solid support for steps to address it.

Rising economic inequality strikes many of us as unfair, but there is also strong evidence that it is harmful to society in many ways. Richard Wilkinson and Kate Pickett, in their 2019 book *The Inner Level*, argue that there are many negative effects of inequality and, inversely, positive outcomes for societies with greater equality of income and wealth.[4] In unequal societies there is greater emphasis on "status consumption" and a greater willingness to work longer hours and assume higher levels of debt. It is harder to address sustainability in such circumstances, and there are clear implications for both health and civic life.

People in more equal societies, Wilkinson and Pickett tell us, "are more inclined to help others—the elderly, those with disabilities, or anyone else."[5] More equality leads to greater community life and, in turn, higher levels of social trust and social cohesion. Conversely there is a real price to pay for inequality: increased levels of heart disease, higher infant mortality, and more mental illness, for example. Less economic and social inequality in cities will in turn lead to more livable, pleasurable, enriching cities—in short, *better* cities, which will better fulfill the needs and aspirations of their citizens. And as Wilkinson and Pickett's analysis suggests, more equality will help strengthen other values, such as trust, willingness to share, and generosity.

Obviously, many bad things happen in life, such as being involved in a debilitating auto accident, being born with a birth defect, or contracting cancer or another life-shortening illness. There is an important role for cities to play in creating safety nets and helping social institutions that work to reduce the burdens associated with these unexpected life circumstances.

Here the commonsense notion of luck applies: the idea that so much of our position and lot in life is determined by factors beyond our control. From an ethical perspective, societies (and cities) are more likely to help an individual in tough times when circumstances seem like a result not of human agency or choice but of random events or circumstances—*bad luck*. It is bad luck to be born with spina bifida, to grow up in a poor and violent neighborhood, or to have abusive parents. It is precisely these kinds of unfair inequalities of life that call for and justify an ethical city's response.

In the end, an egalitarian vision of cities reflects a recognition that so much in life, so much of the success or failure we experience, happens for reasons largely or mostly beyond our control. We have no control over the kind of neighborhood or family circumstance we are born into, the kinds of parents we have (loving and nurturing, if we are lucky), or many of the specific causes of our good or ill fortune.

Your gender and the color of your skin are both beyond your control, and it is an element of bad luck to be born Black or brown in a society where racism and white supremacy are prevalent or to be born a woman where women are paid less, have fewer freedoms, and are subject to high levels of domestic violence. The causes of racism and misogyny are many, and you are unlucky if, as a person of color, woman, or both, you endure threats and violence, systemic discrimination, insecurity, and so on. Discrimination in seeking housing or applying for a job is debilitating and painful—one of life's sharpest and most lasting cuts for those who experience it.

A key idea Rawls posited is that we will make more ethical judgments if we are divorced from specific information about our own life circumstances (social position, level of wealth, ethnicity, and so on). He calls this the "veil of ignorance" and speculates about the principles of justice we would adopt to guide society if we were able to cloak ourselves with this kind of impartiality.[6] At an intuitive level this idea is very appealing and a sensible step we should all attempt to take (even beyond Rawls's thought experiment). If we did not know, for instance, whether we were disabled and unable to move through the city without the aid of a wheelchair, would we ever support the design of a city that did not accommodate wheelchair accessibility? It would be too great a risk. Similarly, if we didn't know our race, we would be more likely to support a society and societal principles of justice that are race-neutral. Adopting the "veil of ignorance" is a helpful way of identifying the many ways that our actual life circumstances bias our ethical choices, and hopefully this awareness helps to neutralize them and leads to fairer, more just outcomes.

So many of the sources of inequality are the result of factors that are morally arbitrary and counter to the view that one's income, status, and material well-being are functions of merit or hard work. We can debate how much inequality in cities is acceptable, though discrimination and unequal treatment because of race, gender, or sexual orientation are never permissible.

Let's explore in more detail some of the different forms of inequality we see in cities.

Addressing Unfair and Unequal Burdens

A long history of racial violence and systemic racism is baked into American cities and has resulted in dramatically unequal living conditions. The murder of George Floyd in 2020 (and many other Black and brown citizens before and since) and the rise of national protests organized by Black Lives Matter and others have raised awareness about the real extent of the violent and unequal treatment of people of color.

How cities can and should address this long history of violence and injustice is an important and unresolved question. In many cities there are now active discussions about reparations, and some have begun to take tangible steps to correct for the past and rectify current racial inequalities.

Minority neighborhoods have long endured disproportionate dangers and harms as the preferred locations for waste transfer stations, port facilities, and other noisy and dangerous urban uses. Neighborhoods of color consistently and historically experience higher levels of environmental pollution than white neighborhoods do, as the result of unfair distribution and discriminatory siting of things such as hazardous waste facilities, municipal trash dumps, and various kinds of polluting industries. A growing recognition of these unfair patterns in the 1970s and '80s led to the emergence of the environmental justice movement and a growing political activism to try to stop or reverse them. *Environmental racism*, a companion term, describes the racial animus that underpins these siting and land use practices. One of the early examples of organized protest and opposition to such practices came in 1982, when the State of North Carolina planned to transport PCB-contaminated soil to the predominantly African American Warren County and dispose of it there. Extensive protests did not stop the disposal plans but signaled the beginning of a period of activism and a framing of these issues as an extension of the civil rights movement. Too often, minority communities have little political and economic power and little direct involvement in decisions that deeply impact their health and well-being. And the many cumulative effects of these decisions over time have led to disproportionately lower life expectancies and greater health impacts.

Robert Bullard, considered by some to be the father of the environmental justice movement, was one of the first to systematically document these cases of unfair facility siting and the opposition and activism emerging around them, most notably in his influential book *Dumping in Dixie*, originally published in 1990. It presents a compelling picture of the extent to which environmental racism exists in the US South and the ways in which it is evident in the patterns of siting decisions for polluting industries, hazardous waste facilities, and municipal waste dumps. Bullard's book begins with his own early research in the late 1970s on the unequal siting of municipal waste dumps in Houston. "Growing empirical evidence shows," he writes, "that toxic-waste dumps, municipal landfills, garbage incinerators, and similar noxious facilities are not randomly scattered across the American landscape." Rather, "the siting process has resulted in minority neighborhoods (regardless of class) carrying a greater burden of localized costs than either affluent or poor white neighborhoods."[7]

Concerns about environmental justice are present in every city, and serious examples abound. Latinx neighborhoods in Houston experience dangerous emissions from nearby chemical plants. Rates of leukemia and other cancers are dramatically higher in the areas near the plants; one local activist refers to these neighborhoods as "sacrifice zones." In Los Angeles, efforts are underway in the Watts neighborhood to curtail the noise and toxic dusk of the Atlas Iron and Metal Company, located immediately adjacent to Jordan High School there. The company has operated for many years with impunity in this African American neighborhood, something that would be unthinkable, it is believed, if the neighborhood were white. To the north, residents of mostly Black West Oakland endure high levels of particulate pollutants from the many diesel engines that run the Port of Oakland. Opposition is mounting there to a proposed expansion of "turning basins," which would allow for a significant increase in the number and size of the container ships the port can service, in turn worsening the air quality in West Oakland. The Oakland port example illustrates the reality in many cities: the burdens of the services and facilities that benefit the larger city and society (e.g., transport of commercial goods) are not evenly or fairly shared but are "piled on" in the places and neighborhoods least able to endure or oppose them. Also true is the reality that serious ecological harm (e.g., serious toxic pollutants) should be seen as unacceptable anywhere and unethical when imposed on anyone (or anything). A tolerance for environmental injustice facilitates and normalizes such ecological damage.

While the practice of unequal siting of hazardous facilities continues, and many neighborhoods of color continue to experience disproportionately high levels of health hazards, there has been some positive progress to note. In April 2023, the Biden administration issued an executive order (building on a 1994 executive order issued by the Clinton administration) requiring federal agencies to "identify, analyze, and address disproportionate and adverse effects (including risks) and hazards." Each agency must now prepare an "environmental justice strategic plan" and evaluate its progress in advancing environmental justice over time.

There is also progress at the city level. One example can be seen in Chicago, a city that illustrates well the past history and impact of environmental injustice but also a growing commitment to address it. In this city there is a sharp spatial division between the largely white neighborhoods in the north and the mostly Black and Latinx neighborhoods in the south. A long history of siting polluting industries and allowing other noxious projects in the southern neighborhoods has led to a serious gap in life expectancy (it is a disturbing ten years lower for residents in the neighborhoods of color in the south part of the city). Partly in response to the activism of community-based organizations, the city is taking action to address these historic disproportionate risks. In 2023, outgoing mayor Lori Lightfoot signed a sweeping executive order mandating, among other things, the preparation of a citywide "cumulative impact assessment" and the mapping and designation of "environmental justice neighborhoods," which will receive funding priority; the designation will be used to guide future land use, transportation, and other city decisions. The order also created the new position of justice project manager and laid out new process requirements for notifying impacted neighborhoods, providing opportunities for public participation, and establishing new procedures for registering complaints. Whether future decisions in Chicago will in fact be guided by this new framework and set of commitments is unclear, but there are already positive signs, including significant new levels of funding ($188 million in fiscal year 2022) for projects in underserved neighborhoods.

The environmental justice movement has achieved much, though planning professor Julian Agyeman argues for a language and framing for these equity issues that might overcome the activist view of environmental justice. Is it possible to imagine a time when equity and justice are baked into a city's policies? Agyeman calls for "just sustainability," a recognition of the need to place justice and fairness at the center of our efforts in urban and environmental planning.[8] Cities are moving in this direction but are still far from a time when vigilance and activism become unnecessary.

It is important to recognize that the burdens of inequality manifest in many pervasive and overlapping ways. Nature in cities, for instance, is not evenly or fairly distributed but rather reflects the larger historical patterns of segregation and discrimination. In American cities, the greenness of your neighborhood, the extent to which you enjoy trees, and the size and extent of the tree canopy will all vary depending on income and race. Neighborhoods of color tend to have fewer trees and a lower canopy, reflecting long-standing policies and practices such as redlining.

"Tree equity" is increasingly recognized as an important goal in cities and by tree conservation organizations such as American Forests. With more trees and more canopy come lower heat levels and, in turn, better health and more livable, enjoyable neighborhoods. And with few to no trees, there are few birds and little birdsong. The health disparities are considerable, but so are the disparities in wonder and delight attached to places that have less nature.

Many cities are now working to address disparities in trees (and heat). The City of Pittsburgh's Shade Tree Commission unveiled its Equitable Street Tree Investment Strategy to begin to combat these disparities. The city will initially focus on ten neighborhoods (described as "low-income and low-canopy") and will aim to increase tree plantings, maintenance, and education there.[9] Severe disparities also often exist when it comes to parks and other kinds of neighborhood green spaces. The parks that exist in neighborhoods of color, if they exist at all, are often smaller (half the size, on average, of those in white neighborhoods), and they may or may not be very accessible or welcoming or feel very safe.

What can cities do to correct these kinds of inequalities in access to nature? Many things are being tried, and cities are developing and adopting equity targets to guide them. In Richmond, Virginia, African American mayor Levar Stoney has sought to expand the amount of green space in the city's underserved neighborhoods, especially where the dangers of urban heat are high, and in 2020, he unveiled five new parks in the city, created from land the city already owns.

Cities can also change the model by which they plan and design new parks and make them profoundly more inclusive and participatory, giving residents real power and real say in their design. One example is Cully Park in Portland, Oregon, where a minority and underserved neighborhood was given the chance to shape and design a new park. Through innovative community engagement policies (from provision of day care to payment of stipends for those in the community who were able to devote time to the project), and managed by local nonprofit Verde, a wonderful park and neighborhood amenity was created. A former twenty-five-acre landfill, it is now a park that is "community-designed and community-built."[10] The direct hand of the community is seen throughout its design: impressively, the raised-bed community garden was designed by children in the neighborhood, and the park's inclusive elements include a Native Gathering Garden. The transformation here is impressive: "Where it once served as a repository for refuse, this park now provides opportunities for people in the community to grow and thrive."[11]

Equal access to parks and green spaces is not enough, though, says Kim Moore Bailey, who runs the nonprofit organization Justice Outside. Long-standing racism and discrimination cannot be overcome so easily. A park may be physically nearby, but if residents of color do not feel safe or welcome there, that physical proximity may, as a practical matter, be meaningless. More needs to be done, says Bailey, including taking steps to foster deeper feelings of ownership (and to overcome a sense of exclusion). Changing policing patterns and actively engaging neighborhoods and residents would help immensely.

One innovative initiative is Oakland Goes Outside, an effort of the Oakland Unified School District in California. With the assistance of a three-year $1 million grant from the San Francisco Foundation, the school district engages in teacher training and will eventually organize overnight camping for all 7,200 of its middle school students.[12] The experiences in and enjoyment of nature that camping allows is something few children from less affluent neighborhoods usually enjoy but which can be life-changing.

It is important to understand how life chances and trajectories are affected by the major institutions of a local government. We know that individuals of color are more likely to have a tangle with the law, are more likely to end up incarcerated, and are more likely to be on parole, for example. Such long-standing inequality and systemic racism have further served to deepen wealth and income disparity today. A recent report by the Brookings Institution concludes that there are "staggering racial disparities" between the wealth of Black and white Americans. It notes that white Americans have a net worth some ten times that of Black Americans: "Gaps in wealth between Black and white households reveal the effects of accumulated inequality and discrimination, as well as differences in power and opportunity that can be traced back to this nation's inception."[13] This wealth gap continues in part through inheritance, which allows white households to pass their wealth along (an estimated $765 billion in 2020), which the Brookings authors note is only "lightly taxed."

What else must cities do to overcome and address long-standing racial inequality? Making equity and equality key goals in city development and in city decision-making would go a long way. A number of cities have now created new positions—chief equity officer, for instance—and new processes and structures to better understand how decisions lessen or exacerbate inequalities. Washington, DC, for example, has created the Council Office on Racial Equity and adopted legislation that now requires the preparation of a racial equity impact assessment for new laws under consideration by the city council.[14]

Ageist and Ableist Cities? In What Ways Do Cities Discriminate by Age and Physical Ability?

Urban planner Steve Wright, an advocate for the disabled and someone who himself uses a wheelchair, writes compellingly in a recent issue of *Planning Magazine* about the need for cities to embrace universal design. The Americans with Disabilities Act—which mandates that (among other things) the design of public facilities and buildings include wheelchair ramps, elevators, and other elements that make them accessible to the disabled—while a good start, is not sufficient.

The difficulties of navigating the public transit system in any major city for disabled people are immense and debilitating in terms of being mobile and living a reasonably normal, functional life. A recent study of New York City's Metropolitan Transportation Authority underground metro stations found that many were lacking in functional elevators, for example. The study concluded that only 124 of the 493 subway stations were wheelchair accessible, though it determined that most could be retrofitted with elevators. That is a huge number of stations, and the cost of retrofitting is high, and consequently the city will likely only make a gradual dent in this number (funds to retrofit sixty-six stations at a cost of $5.2 billion were included in the Metropolitan Transportation Authority's most recent five-year Capital Program).[15]

Wright notes that much of the new discussion around the "fifteen-minute city" makes ableist assumptions that everyone can move around the city by foot or bicycle. "But the in-vogue concept is undermined," Wright says, "by dozens of cities with inaccessible subways and elevated trains, sidewalks too narrow for wheelchairs, and recreation space in need of retrofitting to provide basic access. Without eliminating these kinds of barriers, the 15-Minute City and other concepts like it will simply perpetuate our existing failings in accessible design."[16]

Anna Zivarts, a self-described "low-vision mom," agrees and, writing in *Bloomberg CityLab*, argues that what is especially needed is extensive, reliable fixed-route transit and a disability-accessible pedestrian infrastructure that connects to transit. "Able-bodied folks might be able to dash across a highway or edge along a muddy shoulder, but to many disabled people, the lack of sidewalk or curb ramps to get to a transit stop, or the absence or an accessible pedestrian signal makes the transit stop inaccessible."[17]

Similar concerns about accessibility and safety exist for particular age groups—the young and old—living in cities today. Again, the design standard seems to be by default for the healthy (white) adult male, age eighteen to sixty. As one gets older, and less capable of safely driving a car, the typical car-dependent sea of suburbia that looked good to child-rearing families stops looking so good. Without the ability to drive a car, the chances of social isolation rise markedly, and the ability to socialize and to enjoy the company of others goes down. Any difficulty in walking, or walking more than a few hundred feet, make that park a half mile or quarter mile away difficult or impossible to reach.

There is much attention paid, as there should be, to thinking about age-friendly cities, how they should be designed, and what experiences, services, and opportunities they should include. Aging in place is a desire for many entering what geriatrician Louise Aronson calls "elderhood," and I do believe cities have a responsibility to do what they can to facilitate this choice; universal design will help here as well, but so will investing in services that will allow residents to live independently as long as possible.[18]

Cities need to do a better job helping citizens think about the full potential of their lives and the many new opportunities for reimaging their later years. As life expectancy globally continues to rise (though we have seen a dip in the United States), we must completely rethink the stages of life, shifting from a conventional three-stage notion (your youth and education years, your working years, and your retirement years) to something much more creative and ultimately empowering. Lynda Gratton and Andrew Scott argue for a need to plan for the "100-Year Life," seeing the potential for many different phases, including training for a new profession later in life, starting a nonprofit perhaps, or entering public service.[19] A city can invest in conditions and experiences that allow residents to stay healthy into elderhood, such as building walkable and bikeable neighborhoods, providing extensive chances for socialization and friendship formation, investing in holistic geriatric care, and establishing the necessary opportunities for retraining and re-employing older folks.

Many older residents of cities are not healthy, of course, and many have limited incomes, facing serious problems of lack of housing, health care, and access to nutritious food. On the other end of the age continuum, we rarely ever think about how a city should be designed for children and kids. Many of the things that would make a city child friendly, such as abundant parks and walkable neighborhoods, would also help make them more family friendly. The organization 8–80 Cities makes precisely this point: that we must design our cities for both an eight-year-old and an eighty-year-old.

Planning cities for teenagers or young adults is especially challenging but necessary. They need and deserve the ability to get around, visit friends, and safely travel by foot or bike to their schools. Independence is a precious commodity that cities can foster and facilitate. I saw this firsthand when living in the Netherlands with my family in the late 1990s on a sabbatical year.[20] The relationships we saw there between younger kids and their parents were remarkable for the lack of conflict and angst. The physical freedoms kids enjoy there, especially the freedom to safely ride bicycles, seemed to us to lead to healthier, less stressful relationships with their parents. This is not a secret, certainly, and part of the reason some have declared Dutch kids to be "the happiest in the world."[21]

Gender and Sexual Orientation

It is commonly and correctly observed that cities and the built environments that we live in are for the most part designed by men and that, not surprisingly, the perspectives and interests of women have been secondary. In the United States, while about half the students graduating from architecture schools are women, they are severely underrepresented in the field. In a 2018 essay in the *New York Times*, Allison Arieff asks, "Where are all the female architects?"[22] It is a complex answer, certainly, but discrimination in the workplace and the failure to pay women and men equally and to value the work and voices of women are important reasons for the disparity. Having female role models and mentors is also important. Arieff asks as an aside, "Apart from Zaha Hadid, how many female architects can you name?" "Not many" is the clear answer, and that must change. An important part of the solution to this inequality is ensuring that more clients are women, too. There has been a rise in the number of female mayors of cities around the world and this is a positive trend, but female representation in local city councils is still low, nationally only about 30 percent but often higher, which is positive news.[23] Without nearly equal representation of women on local governing bodies (city councils, yes, but also planning commissions and a city's many other advisory boards and committees), it is likely the needs and priorities of women in cites will be ignored or undervalued.

Women face extra burdens when it comes to participating in local political systems and running for public office. What to do with children, for example, is a major concern, one that many male candidates do not worry about. Cost and availability of childcare are major limitations to participation in politics or any form of political engagement, whether serving on a planning commission or simply attending a public hearing as a citizen. Recently the Federal Election Commission ruled that congressional candidates can spend campaign funds to pay for childcare, a positive step, but much more is needed.[24]

Women face incredible dangers in their normal, daily navigation of cities that men don't face. The abduction and murder of thirty-three-year-old Sarah Everard in London by a police officer was a shocking case in point. The official governmental response was to invest millions of pounds in more streetlights and cameras—and of course, more policing. This, many women especially have observed, is shortsighted and profoundly inadequate.

Creating safer streets and public spaces, where there are more people and more "eyes on the street" (a famous recommendation of American urbanist Jane Jacobs), would certainly help. Tackling in a serious way the verbal and physical threats and sexual harassment women experience each day in cities would also be elements of a minimum response. Statistics show that street harassment is pervasive and a daily experience for many women. In one study of three Spanish cities (Madrid, Seville, and Barcelona), nearly 80 percent of women reported experiencing street harassment. A recent survey in Washington, DC, found that approximately 70 percent of respondents had been harassed in the last year.

Some have argued that street harassment should be made illegal in cities and the men doing it arrested and prosecuted. Yet laws that criminalize street harassment seem not to be very effective, causing some cities to search for alternatives that emphasize education and culture change. Washington, DC, took this approach in 2018 by adopting the Street Harassment Prevention Act with a focus on education and training.

What else can cities do? A recent BBC video, "What Would Cities Look Like If They Were Designed by Women?," offers some hope for the future and reports on progress in Barcelona to better address women's needs. There are efforts to design community play spaces that better balance the play needs of boys and girls (rather than simply giving all the space to soccer-playing boys) and antimachismo stands at major public events to aid and assist women. There is an effort to map sites in the city where sexual assaults have happened and to take steps to prevent them from occurring again. And there are perennial efforts to rethink mobility in the city (women are more likely to walk or to use public transit than men) as well as redesign bathrooms to more fairly account for women.

Leslie Kern, author of the book *Feminist City*, offers many recommendations for change in cities, again invoking Everard's abduction and murder:

> Anti-harassment public awareness campaigns are one option. Cities like Stockholm have *banned sexist advertising* from public spaces. Symbolic gestures such as *naming streets and squares for women* and including more monuments to women may also, slowly, shift the mindset that public space belongs to men. Cities can adopt gender equity standards to ensure that *a gender perspective* is brought to all planning decisions. Working to improve women's representation in city government and services as well as training and retraining public sector workers on issues related to gender equity are important interventions.
>
> Crucially, we must rethink who we assign to the role of overseeing safety. Everard's murder is far from the only case where police officers have been charged with violent crimes against women, an issue that particularly impacts Black and Indigenous women. Women will not feel safe while those entrusted with this role continue to abuse their power.

The bathroom issue—what is sometimes referred to as "potty parity"— has been particularly vexing. The profound inequity in bathroom facilities between men and women is especially evident at sporting or other public events where women must wait in long lines while men get to quickly zip in and out of a usually lineless bathroom. Part of the answer is for cities to modify their plumbing standards and codes, and some cities have done this. Texas law now requires twice the number of women's toilets as men's in newly constructed sports or entertainment venues. This kind of code change is a good first step, but there are deeper problems with what law professor Mary Anne Case refers to as laws that establish "urinary segregation."[25]

Much fairer would be the approach taken on commercial airliners, where passengers of both sexes have access to and queue up for the same bathrooms. This approach also helps address several other "anxious dilemmas," as when trans or nonbinary individuals are forced to choose between the men's or women's bathroom or when men need to accompany their young daughters to the restroom (and are not happy about having to take them into the men's room or sending them unaccompanied to the women's).

Another kind of sexist design can be seen in the way we set the temperature of indoor offices and environments. Building heating and cooling standards, it turns out, have historically been based on an assumption of the resting metabolism of a forty-year-old man, resulting in spaces that are often too cold for women. A 2015 study in *Nature Climate Change* concludes that this metabolic assumption "may overestimate female metabolic rate by up to 35%."[26]

Safe mobility through a city is another perennial need for women and another especially critical issue to address. Urban public transit systems often don't serve women very well. They are designed primarily as radial spoke-and-hub systems to accommodate the typical home-to-work journeys of men, and only recently have they started implementing the more lateral routes that better reflect journeys made by women. Transit remains a dangerous space for women and also does not match well their daily needs and the way they live their lives.

Far fewer women than men can take advantage of bicycles and other forms of micromobility. They feel (and are) less safe on bicycles and tend to commute by bicycle at far lower rates than men. A very disturbing study conducted by researchers at the University of Minnesota found that when motorists passed female bicyclists, they tended to come much closer than when overtaking male riders.[27] Many cities around the world have taken steps to address the safety of public transit for women. In Indian cities, for instance, there are women-only train and transit cars, and in many cities there are women-only taxicabs.

Caroline Criado Perez, in her important book *Invisible Women*, provides a comprehensive catalog of the many ways that we design and plan with male physiology as the default assumption, often with deadly results for women.[28] From crash dummies and car seat designs that reflect male anatomy to the design of personal protective equipment that fails to fit or protect average women, the design process seems to begin with a male user in mind.

Members of the LGBTQ+ community also continue to experience significant discrimination, and even violence, despite the progress made over the last several decades. And they continue to face significant health challenges. An ethical city is one that works to address the inequalities and inequities connected with sexual orientation. Many cities have now adopted antidiscrimination or nondiscrimination ordinances that seek to prevent sexual orientation and gender identity discrimination in hiring, real estate, and the provision of city services.

Atlanta has even established the nation's first director of LGBTQ+ affairs position, reporting to the mayor, as well as a Mayor's LGBTQ+ Advisory Board.[29] Seattle has created an LGBTQ+ Commission to advise its mayor and city council.[30] The Human Rights Campaign Foundation produces an annual report that scores and evaluates cities on how well they are doing on LGBTQ+ issues. In 2020, the number of cities with the highest possible score (100 points) rose to 94 (out of 506).[31] Those cities have designated an LGBTQ+ liaison, enforced contractor nondiscrimination, and banned conversion therapy.

Addressing the Many Aspects of Urban Inequality

There are many potential leverage points cities can use to correct or work to address urban inequality. Much of the inequality, especially racial inequality, is systemic and finds its roots in the slavery baked into the genesis of our nation and will defy easy solutions.

One important point is to encourage all cities to look closely at the ways current policies may serve to reinforce inequalities. Many systemic biases are rarely thought about or discussed. Take, for instance, the ways cities go about raising the revenues they need to support the services and infrastructures they provide. Some of these revenue-raising devices are regressive, meaning that they fall harder on those who are least able to afford them. We should seek to raise public funds in cities through mechanisms that are progressive, or that ask those with the greatest income or wealth to pay a greater share.

Some of our most common revenue-raising methods at the city level have serious biases built into them. A recent study concludes that local ad valorem property taxes systemically and unfairly overtax lower-income and Black homeowners. Because property tax assessments are largely unable to take into account interior spaces and improvements, they tend to over-assess, or overvalue, property in lower-income, minority neighborhoods and underassess property in more affluent neighborhoods. And, not surprisingly, people in more affluent neighborhoods are able to successfully challenge these assessments (and get them lowered by a city assessor) to a disproportionate degree.

Ethical cities should choose revenue-raising measures and mechanisms that reduce inequalities or at least don't exacerbate them. Debate has raged in Seattle about the need to tax very wealthy people and wealthy corporations there, notably Amazon, to pay for proposed affordable housing projects. A guaranteed, or basic, income proposed there could also be funded, some believe, in this way.[32]

In the context especially of long-standing systemic racism, there are now conversations underway in many cities about the need for some form of reparations, and some cities such as Evanston, Illinois, and Asheville, North Carolina, have already taken tangible steps to do so. Evanston has made a commitment of $10 million to fund reparations over ten years, with one of the first specific programs being a housing grant for those who lived in the city between 1919and 1969 (the year the city began implementing a fair housing policy). By providing reparations we acknowledge the need to treat individuals unequally as a matter of fairness and equity in order to compensate for unfair treatment in the past.

The Evanston proposal has not been without controversy and has been criticized as a small and piecemeal approach (the housing grants are only $25,000) that may undermine the push for larger reparations, more likely through direct cash payments (and which many believe will require the federal government to intervene). Those defending the city's efforts acknowledge that more must be done but argue that a housing grant is a sensible aspect of reparations and helps address the fact that lack of access to housing historically has deprived Black people of significant wealth accumulation. Evanston is taking other actions as well, for instance funding a minority business incubator program and a pilot basic income program.[33]

Robin Rue Simmons, the Evanston alderman largely behind the reparations program, acknowledges that much more must be done. "It's a start," she says, noting that the hope is that revenue from recreational cannabis sales and private donations (including from local churches, which she optimistically observes have been supportive) will grow the reparation fund.[34]

In whatever form cities provide reparations, they must also include steps to rectify the physical and spatial inequalities that continue to exist and that isolate and determine the distribution of opportunities. Positive steps include taking away neighborhood and housing barriers, such as by introducing major reforms and rewriting zoning provisions, as has been done in cities from Portland and Minneapolis to Vancouver. This can include making "housing of the middle"—duplex, triplex, and multifamily units—as well as accessory dwelling units by-right uses and essentially banning the exclusive single-family zoning category that has been such an effective tool for excluding people of color and depressing the availability of affordable housing.

In a number of American cities there are efforts to take down highways, tear them up, or cap them; highways have historically also been instruments of exclusion and racism (and out-and-out destruction of Black neighborhoods). Already there are positive examples of this, such as in Rochester, New York. As Caitlin Dewey notes in a recent *Planning Magazine* article, "Since removing the so-called Inner Loop [in Rochester], the city has rebuilt the street grid and parceled out new spaces for affordable housing, retail stores, and a local museum expansion."[35] But there are also worries that such projects could lead to displacement and gentrification.

Many cities are experimenting with basic, or guaranteed, income, which provides residents with a set monthly allocation, no strings attached. Compton, California, a city of around 100,000, was one of the first cities to experiment with this, under the leadership of mayor Michael Tubbs; 125 residents, randomly chosen, received $500 a month for two years under a pilot initiative. A larger program began in 2021, providing some 800 residents with $1,800 every three months. Called Compton Pledge, it claims to be "the largest city-based guaranteed income pilot in the U.S."[36]

There are also many things a city can do to try to ensure that all residents are able to experience a fair and equitable start in life. Equality of opportunity (or *fair* equality of opportunity, to use Rawls's terminology) is an important goal in cities, justifying many kinds of early leveling investments, including more equal and equitable school systems and education. Boston is notable for its investment in universal pre-K education, something that can have a profound long-term positive effect and help create a more equitable beginning for kids in cities. Boston mayor Michelle Wu recently announced new funding that will allow an expansion of this program.

New forms of local economic development, and new forms of economy, that provide higher wages and more vesting of ownership would seem ethically justified. There are extensive debates about the need to raise minimum wages, which some forty US cities have done recently. Cities can do many other things as well, such as provide more support for worker-owned businesses, where accumulation of wealth, not just an hourly wage, is possible.

Support for a profoundly different kind of economic model, one that puts equity and ecological regeneration at the center, is also needed. Cities around the world are beginning to question the very assumptions of a traditional capitalist paradigm of unlimited growth and a definition of success tied almost entirely to supply and demand, prices, and a rising GDP.

There has been a strong consensus for decades about the need for a model of economic growth that would put the welfare of people and the planet at its center. British economist Kate Raworth has been especially effective in stimulating new discussion and, importantly, action on the part of cities. Her vision of a different economic system is captured through the picture of a doughnut—and a model she calls Doughnut Economics. Much of the growing popularity of Raworth's idea is due to the power and simplicity of this picture: we need an economic system that ensures, on the one hand, that everyone's needs are taken care of and no one falls below certain social and health thresholds (no one falls into the hole in the doughnut) but also, on the other hand, that the economy does not exceed the planetary ecological boundaries.

Amsterdam is one of the first cities to attempt to put this doughnut economic vision into practice and officially adopted it as its guiding framework. This laid the foundation for Amsterdam's commitment to becoming a "circular city" (a fully circular economy) by 2050, where resources and materials are fully and completely reused and recycled, over and over again.

Addressing inequality in cities will require new approaches to making decisions and new metrics for judging success and progress. The City of Pittsburgh, for instance, published the Pittsburgh Equity Indicators, a comprehensive set of measures meant to provide a baseline sense of how the city is doing. Data was collected and analyzed for eighty indicators grouped into four "domains," utilizing a methodology developed by the CUNY Institute for State and Local Governance.[37]

While the indicators show very serious inequalities between white and Black residents on some measures—especially homicides (per 100,000), homelessness, incarceration, and asthma hospitalization rates—on other measures the news is better. For example, both Black and white residents in Pittsburgh have very good access to green space (scores of 93.5 and 91 out of 100, respectively). Cities can do a lot to address inequality, but having an accurate and detailed sense of where inequality exists, and developing a comprehensive set of indicators that are collected and updated yearly, must be a key part of a city's overall strategy. It may also be the only way to hold elected officials and others accountable for progress made (or not).

All city comprehensive plans—the main planning instruments intended to guide a city's future development and growth—must address equality and equity. Some local comprehensive plans now include explicit references to equity and social justice. Portland, Oregon, for example, has developed a

"Framework for Equity," which is a chapter of the Portland Plan. The framework has a strong statement acknowledging the city's duty to ensure all residents have access to "a high-quality education, living wage jobs, safe neighborhoods, basic services, a healthy natural environment, efficient public transit, parks and greenspaces, decent housing and healthy food."[38]

Conclusions

Many different kinds of inequality exist in cities, and there is a strong ethical and moral obligation to work to reduce or eliminate them. Doing nothing or very little is not an option in a city that seeks to be ethical. Cities hold the potential, because of both their often-progressive politics and their economic and other opportunities, to make meaningful progress in reducing or overcoming profound inequalities. Furthermore, cities have many tools and policy levers at their disposal to address inequality, from housing and land use decisions that expand opportunities to use of the tax code and choices about how to fund and implement a wide variety of local programs.

We need to be as inclusive as possible in the decisions we make, and we need to explore many new ways of planning to make sure that we move in the direction of reducing, rather than extending or even expanding, the inequalities that have existed in the past. Reckoning with racial inequality and systemic racism in American cities is an especially pressing need.

Discussion Questions

What are the most serious or ethically troubling inequalities that we see in cities?

There is no question that systemic racism is baked into American cities. How can cities begin to effectively address these inequalities? And what tangible steps can an ethical city take to repair, correct, and compensate for these past and current injustices?

How much inequality in cities is acceptable?

What can cities do to ensure that they are fairer and more inclusive for women, older and younger residents, members of the LGBTQ+ community, and those with disabilities?

Rights in and to the City

The concept of rights is an old one and enshrined in many societal documents and legal frameworks, from the US Constitution to the UN Declaration of Human Rights. Some legal rights emerge from common law, such as the public trust doctrine, which establishes a public right to access shorelines and navigable waters, and other moral or political rights emerge from statements and documents. There are many different rights that cities can recognize; that is, many urban challenges turn on an acknowledgment or a claim of a right.

We also find rights referenced in the ways we speak about cities and their governance. I may declare that "I have a right to be in the room" when a certain decision is made or that a neighborhood "has a right to be consulted" before the final decision about a road alignment or other city outcome is reached. A right is something that everyone deserves and is entitled to, and the list of rights related directly to cities is potentially quite long: some believe there are rights to personal safety, housing and food, minimum levels of clean air and clean water, and access to and connection with the natural world, to name a few.

Most of us argue for rights as a form of deontological ethics—a duty or claim based not on the extent of the benefit or utility brought about but on something other than an outcome or consequence. These are things that bring ethical fulfillment or satisfaction even when they might not result in the larger public interest. However one arrives at a condition of poverty, hunger, or homelessness, the notion of a right establishes an entitlement—usually by virtue of one's humanity—and a corresponding duty to satisfy that right. There are many different kinds of rights and claims to rights that arise in the context of cities.

Is There a Right to Housing?

Few issues have become more difficult to solve at the local level than the interconnected issues of gentrification, housing affordability, and homelessness. The problem of homelessness is complex and complicated, and the reasons people are homeless vary (there is often some element of mental illness). However, the high price of housing is a major driving force behind homelessness, as residents begin to camp or live out of their cars because they have been evicted or can't find adequate affordable living spaces. California cities have been on the front lines of this issue. Cities such as San Francisco and Los Angeles have some of the highest costs of housing in the nation and some of the highest rates of homelessness. Nearly a quarter of the nation's homeless (some 134,000 people) are in California.

From an ethical point of view, what are people entitled to? Do cities have a duty to ensure that housing is available and affordable for all? And is there a duty to address—to solve or minimize—the related problem of homelessness? Should adequate housing be considered a kind of human right that every person is entitled to qua being human? There is a robust and extensive history of defense of human rights, and we can point to a number of documents that carry legal and ethical weight establishing such rights, including for instance, the UN Declaration of Human Rights, which dates to 1948.[1]

The National Economic and Social Rights Initiative is one organization that takes a strong position in support of such rights. It states its position in support of a human right to housing in this way: "Everyone has a fundamental human right to housing, which ensures access to a safe, secure, habitable, and affordable home with freedom from forced eviction. It is the government's obligation to guarantee that everyone can exercise this right to live in security, peace, and dignity. This right must be provided to all persons irrespective of income or access to economic resources."[2]

More specifically, the initiative identifies seven attributes, or "principles," of the right to housing: security of tenure; availability of services, materials, facilities, and infrastructure; affordability; habitability/decent and safe home; accessibility; location; and cultural adequacy. A brief definition of each of these principles is provided in sidebar 4-1.

This list of more specific attributes provides the sense of a full right to housing, not a right that is modest or "light." And it opens up the strong possibility of disagreement about what the right to housing in practice implies or requires. Some might argue that we are owed a safe structure at an affordable price but not necessarily one where there is access to all of the activities and services listed.

Sidebar 4-1 Seven Principles of the Right to Housing

Security of tenure: Residents should possess a degree of security of tenure that guarantees protection against forced evictions, harassment, and other threats, including predatory redevelopment and displacement.

Availability of services, materials, facilities, and infrastructure: Housing must provide certain facilities essential for health, security, comfort, and nutrition. For instance, residents must have access to safe drinking water, heating and lighting, washing facilities, means of food storage, and sanitation.

Affordability: Housing costs should be at such a level that the attainment and satisfaction of other basic needs are not threatened or compromised. For instance, one should not have to choose between paying rent and buying food.

Habitability/decent and safe home: Housing must provide residents adequate space that protects them from cold, damp, heat, rain, wind, or other threats to health; structural hazards; and disease.

Accessibility: Housing must be accessible to all, and disadvantaged and vulnerable groups must be accorded full access to housing resources.

Location: Housing should not be built on polluted sites, or in immediate proximity to pollution sources that threaten the right to health of residents. The physical safety of residents must be guaranteed, as well. Additionally, housing must be in a location which allows access to employment options, health-care services, schools, childcare centers, and other social facilities.

Cultural adequacy: Housing and housing policies must guarantee the expression of cultural identity and diversity, including the preservation of cultural landmarks and institutions. Redevelopment or modernization programs must ensure that the cultural significance of housing and communities is not sacrificed.

Source: The National Economic and Social Rights Initiative

Skeptics might point out that even those with the financial means to compete for market housing must make trade-offs between these different desired qualities. It may simply not be possible or realistic for a society (or a city) to commit to all of these qualities or characteristics (though the principles are still useful as an aspirational list).

Planning a city for all ages and age groups represents yet another dimension of urban equity and another way in which urban rights can and should manifest. Growing numbers of older people are developing Alzheimer's or experiencing some form of dementia. At once we know that the burden of caring for these individuals will continue to grow and is often overwhelming for those closest to them. What rights do dementia patients hold in the city, and do we have an ethical obligation to support their care and a minimum level of quality of life for them?

As with an accident or birth defect that might render a person disabled, there is a serious element of luck here: one's condition in life is random and undeserved. The determinants or predictors of Alzheimer's or other forms of dementia are still largely unclear and in any event are not *deserved* conditions in any sense but morally random. Laws like the Americans with Disabilities Act express that we are duty bound to provide access regardless of one's disabilities. The ability to move in a city and to physically access the spaces and opportunities it has to offer are ethical underpinnings of the act.

Rights to Mobility

Fair and equitable mobility in a city is a major point of discussion and debate in an ethical city. In the era of modern cities, we have heavily subsidized and prioritized private automobiles, though that is changing. Many cities have invested heavily in public transit, and transit is often framed as a public service that every resident is entitled to have access to.

Recently the country of Luxembourg made news by announcing plans to make all public transit free in that small nation. Some cities are also moving in that direction; in December 2019, Kansas City, Missouri, became the first major American city to announce its intentions to make all public transit free, which the *Kansas City Star* described as a "transformative advantage for low-income residents who need a ride to work or school."[3] City council member Eric Bunch, cosponsor of the measure, explicitly frames the decision as an ethical matter: "I believe that people have a right to move about this city," he says in a *Bloomberg CityLab* article about the decision.[4]

The bold move in Kansas City built on the successful experience with its streetcar line, which has provided free downtown service from the beginning. Streetcar ridership has been growing (it topped 6 million in its first three years of service), and there are plans to extend the line.[5] There is a cost, of course, to providing free fares: in Kansas City's case, an estimated $8 million from lost fare box revenues. But city officials seem unfazed by this and believe there are sources available to replace this revenue stream.

A right to mobility in the city could legitimately extend to many other modes of personal transport, such as access to safe and connected pedestrian paths and trails and bicycle lanes, paths, and routes. Adequate and fair accessibility to various forms of micromobility that are now being provided in cities is another aspect of this question. Companies that offer electric scooters, for example, have been found to serve more affluent neighborhoods of cities and avoid poor neighborhoods. One article about how this played out in Minneapolis describes it as a form of redlining and a violation of the city-issued license (which stipulates that at least 30 percent of the scooters must be placed in "areas of concentrated poverty").[6]

Rights to the Street

Planner and urban design professor Bruce Appleyard has been exploring the ways that ethics and rights apply to the pedestrian realm. We know that people walking around a city, especially if that is their primary form of mobility, often feel at a disadvantage or like second-class citizens, as it were, compared to those traveling by car. The potential proliferation of driverless cars might further increase conflicts.

Is a right to the street due to the pedestrian? As Appleyard and William Riggs lay out in an article in the *Journal of Transport and Land Use*, there have been a variety of different expressions of these rights.[7] At that core is an expression of the equal moral worth of those walking and those traveling by car, who have been given usual and historical priority. It is partly a response to the excessive commitment of space given over to the automobile, especially in American cities, and the general subjugation of the safety and legal rights of pedestrians.

There is a long line of planning heroes who have expressed similar versions of street rights. Jane Jacobs championed a pedestrian charter in Toronto. University of California, Berkeley scholar Donald Appleyard includes a "Statement of Street Dwellers Rights" in his important book *Livable Streets*. He speaks of the need to think of the street as a "safe sanctuary" and a "community."

What is the pedestrian entitled to? What specifically are the rights she or he holds when moving through the city, on its streets and sidewalks? One right might include the need to clearly shift liability from pedestrians to cars and car drivers, who are largely responsible for dangerous conditions. Appleyard and Riggs rightly identify a variety of "functional area ethics," for instance the ethical duties of various professionals who have a hand in designing streets (e.g., engineers and designers), those who are street actors (e.g., car drivers), and those who are involved in enforcing streets rules and laws (e.g., police). This typology is a partial answer to who is duty bound to implement or give meaning to pedestrian rights.

Right(s) to the City

A city is a set of physical places, to be sure, but it is also a bundle of assets, opportunities, and potential positive experiences delivered by these spaces and the people and activities they support. At its best, a city is a place that delivers culture, income, and health, but it can also deliver the reverse, and there is much in the distributive nature of contemporary cities that is unjust and unequal.

French philosopher Henri Lefebvre's 1968 book *The Right to the City* is a beginning point for many to describe the extent to which a city must be inclusive, shared space where residents are entitled to enjoy its many benefits. David Harvey explains the notion this way: "The right to the city is far more than the individual liberty to access urban resources: it is a right to change ourselves by changing the city . . . the freedom to make and remake our cities."[8]

Rights to the city are various in nature. For instance, there is the right to access and enjoy the special qualities of a city, including its spaces and uplifting physical attributes. There is a right to be in these spaces, to enjoy them equally with others, and to use them, for instance for protest or celebration. A city is a place that welcomes everyone and to which all residents feel they belong. And there is an expectation that each person, regardless of income, ethnicity, or social status, has a voice, has a say, and can participate in the political life of the city.

Some of these urban qualities are intrinsically difficult to exclude residents (or visitors) from: the beauty of the architecture of buildings and plazas, for example. The freedom of movement in a city is something mostly enjoyed by all, and the right to access public spaces is understood as a basic right. Yet as a practical matter, one's limited financial resources—whether to rent or buy a home, pay for a hotel room, or even to ride a bus or streetcar necessary to travel to many public spaces in a city—may profoundly limit this right of enjoyment or access.

As Harvey seems to suggest, the deeper and broader notion of the right to the city involves the right to be engaged in and participate in the life and governance of the city. Are the decisions by which the city is shaped, designed, and changed over time open to everyone, or do these decisions get made in exclusive places and ways? "Is the city *my* city? Do I belong?" These are central questions, Harvey believes. My own notion of the ethical city is of a city that is open and inclusive. This is your city; it is a city that is not simply for the elite or the wealthy but open to and works on behalf of everyone. And everyone is entitled to enjoy it.

Urban decisions and policies can affect all of these dimensions, all of these different forms of rights to the city. What are the specific rights we can acknowledge and seek to recognize in cities today? That is the primary subject of this chapter. It is important to begin by recognizing that while some of these rights might be seen as legal or constitutional (established through an ordinance or law or enshrined in a state or federal constitution), many may fall into the category of "social rights," that is, things to which we feel people are entitled, perhaps by virtue of their citizenship or humanity.

Health Care and Other Essential Services

Most would agree that health care is a human right, something that serves as an essential foundation for other rights and for human flourishing overall. Cities can acknowledge and work toward this right in many ways, for instance by funding public health-care clinics or stipulating that employers provide basic coverage. While few other cities do it, San Francisco mandates that employers over a certain size provide a minimum level of health benefits to their workers. Under the Health Care Security Ordinance, adopted in 2021, employers can satisfy the law by providing "payment for health insurance premiums or a contribution to a health care savings or reimbursement account."[9]

What we believe are deserved rights must also reflect important changes in society, and a good example can be seen in the essential importance today of internet access. When I was growing up, in a pre-internet world, a typewriter, and especially an electric typewriter, was a fascinating and at times important tool. But today, access to digital technologies provides more than access to entertainment; technology is essential to education, income and jobs, and arguably access to the larger benefits and pleasures of culture.

In Detroit, it is estimated that 70 percent of school-age kids lack internet access at home. There is a strong case to be made that along with equality of opportunity and a right to a minimum level of housing, internet access is equally essential. Some have called it "digital redlining," and efforts such as the Equitable Internet Initiative work to bring this essential service to all neighborhoods in Detroit, in this case through a "neighborhood-governed community wireless network."[10] These services are facilitated by volunteers called "digital stewards," who help homeowners get connected and work with them to ensure their internet is functioning well. Part of the idea is to "demystify technology."

The ability to secure health care and other essential services is, of course, related to a person's overall income and level of wealth. Is there also a right to a minimum level of income? In the previous chapter I discussed the idea of a universal basic income, an idea being piloted in a number of cities. The key idea is that a person is entitled to a minimum level of income, which they can control and choose to spend as they see fit. Such systems indeed provide a basic income—perhaps $500–$1,000 per month. It's not a generous income, but it's sufficient to forestall many of the most difficult circumstances, where choices must be made about how to distribute what you have to pay for food, shelter, heating and cooling, and medications. Evidence suggests that under such programs, participants mostly spend their monthly allocations on such essentials.

A Right to a Clean and Healthy Environment
In the early 1970s a number of US states began to include language in their state constitutions declaring a public right to a clean and healthy environment.[11] Some states went quite far with this language, especially Pennsylvania, which in 1971 placed a provision commonly known as the Environmental Rights Amendment in the state's Declaration (or Bill) of Rights. This strongly worded constitutional provision was adopted with overwhelming political and public support: both houses of the Pennsylvania legislature voted unanimously in favor of adoption, followed by ratification by a resounding popular vote with an almost four-to-one margin in favor. It was an auspicious beginning, but it has taken half a century for the state's courts to give the provisions the full weight of law. The Pennsylvania provision stands as a powerful ethical statement about what individuals can expect when it comes to a safe and clean environment. The key section is worth quoting here: "The people have a right to clean air, pure water, and to the preservation of the natural, scenic, historic and esthetic values of the environment. Pennsylvania's public natural resources are the common property of all the people, including generations to come. As a trustee of these resources, the Commonwealth shall conserve and maintain them for the benefit of all the people."[12]

The concept of environmental rights is certainly not new and can be seen in such common law principles as the public trust doctrine, which establishes the public's right to navigable waterways, beaches, and coastlines. And there have been many other tangible expressions of the basic individual rights that all humans hold, regardless of ethnicity, income, or status, as expressed for instance in the UN Declaration of Human Rights.

Such a statement of rights in a city places constraints on our collective tendencies to privilege what is profitable, expedient, or the utilitarian or majority-desired outcome. The Pennsylvania courts understood that individual rights to a clean and healthy environment are "inviolate" and the result of the "social contract between government and the people." It is an essential kind of assurance that, whatever your life circumstances, however lucky or unlucky you have been, whatever city or neighborhood you end up in, society declares that you have the right to a clean and healthy environment. In this way, Pennsylvania's Environmental Rights Amendment helps buttress the ethical and legal underpinnings of environmental planning: the environment is not understood as a luxury but must be protected in the same ways we protect freedom of speech or freedom of religion.[13]

There is a growing sentiment in many cities that nature is not optional but essential to human flourishing and should be understood as a birthright, not just something available to those in leafy, richer neighborhoods. The sense that contact with nature is a right to be enjoyed by all can be seen in initiatives such as New York City Nature Goals 2050, which pushes that city to do more to protect, conserve, and restore urban nature, in part through a "Declaration of Rights to New York City Nature."[14]

One frequent criticism is that such amendments are often worded so broadly as to seem meaningless. But this is no different than for any other of our fundamental rights, says Delaware riverkeeper Maya van Rossum, such as freedom of speech or freedom of religion. These all require further policy and legal deliberations to define more precisely their extent and practical meaning, but this does not mean the right is any less important or profound.

Like all rights, the right to a clean environment is not absolute but must be balanced against other rights. Just as there are constraints on one's free speech rights (such as in the classic example that yelling fire in a crowded movie theater is not protected speech), there will be times when environmental rights will need to be moderated or superseded by some other public interest. There will be times, van Rossum believes, when environmental rights will be overruled by a "compelling state interest." It will be up to the courts to judge these limits, as they do with other, more classic rights.

Contact with Nature as a Right

An especially interesting question is whether the Pennsylvania environmental amendment could be interpreted to require an affirmative duty to ensure that all residents have at least daily contact with nature. Sometimes contact with nature is considered a human birthright, though in practice we have difficulty achieving this vision. Numerous studies show significant differences in access to parks, trees, and nature depending on race and income. Greener, more nature-rich neighborhoods deliver many positive benefits, and evidence has shown that mental and physical health is better in such neighborhoods. Could a constitutional right to the environment serve as a legal basis for rectifying these often dramatically different (and unjust) environmental and health conditions? It seems a strong possibility.

A promising direction is the possibility of establishing an affirmative right to contact with nature and to nature-rich cities and urban neighborhoods. As van Rossum notes, Pennsylvania's Environmental Rights Amendment has a strong antidegradation focus—it aims to prevent harm to the environment. Yet at the same time, she also believes there is a duty to restore natural environments that have been degraded. "Everybody has the same right to a healthy environment," she says, "so if that right has already been taken, and if that right has already been infringed upon, there is a duty to restore. We believe that this is a part of the green amendment."

As a practical matter, what level of environmental restoration should an environmental rights amendment like Pennsylvania's mandate? One option might be restoration to a level of nature that represents the practicable best that might be achieved anywhere in a city—for instance, a dense tree canopy (60 percent canopy or more, as seen in some of the leafiest places in cities), easy access to parks and trails (e.g., a green space within a five-to-ten-minute walk of every resident), or a biodiverse neighborhood (e.g., one with all or most native species of birds).

Perhaps a more strident view would judge restoration based on the natural conditions and functioning of an urban neighborhood or site before it was developed. A functional equivalence might be invoked: it may not be realistic to assume a dense office building or an urban neighborhood would look like a Douglas fir forest, but it might be required to function like one (for instance, with respect to retention of stormwater, filtration and recycling of wastewater, or provision of shade and cooling, a set of natural performance standards met by new structures such as the Bullitt Center in Seattle or other buildings that satisfy the certification standards of the Living Building Challenge).

Some will object to the anthropocentric language employed in Pennsylvania's Environmental Rights Amendment ("the *people* have a right"). But they are *human* rights that are ratified here after all, with little acknowledgment of the inherent moral worth of the natural world. Yet environmental rights may be a necessary bridge to a more biocentric ethical shift.

The Pennsylvania amendment also establishes the constitutional rights of future generations. Ethicists sometimes argue that giving a right to something that does not yet exist is illogical and indefensible. But there are interesting possibilities here for establishing an even stronger basis for environmental law and planning: policies that do not allow the extinction of species, the exhaustion of woodlands, or the irreversible destruction of natural features of beauty and wonder, if they are viewed as important elements of a healthy environment, as I believe they should be, could all gain a legal (and political and ethical) ally.

The Limits of a Rights-Based Approach to Ethics in Cities

There are limits, of course, to a rights-based approach to urban ethics, and many would criticize this as a heavily individualistic, perhaps even self-centered approach to imagining a virtuous city. It conjures up pandemic-era images of screaming attendees at city council meetings, arguing at the top of their lungs about the right to visit restaurants or send their kids to public school without masks and without being vaccinated. To communitarians, it fails to sufficiently emphasize duties and commitments to others and the importance of working on behalf of a larger public good. They rightly note that we are quick to declare our rights—for instance to a trial by jury—but then we do everything we can to avoid jury duty. Perhaps we should equally emphasize the many obligations we have to help others and to work to address collective problems and needs—whether that is cleaning up trash in one's neighborhood, reducing the amount of driving we do, or turning down our thermostats to help address climate change. To some extent, this is the challenge of cultivating useful urban virtues and a virtuous citizenry (the subject of the next chapter), and too much of a hyper-rights-based vision of cities may distract us from this.

As Amitai Etzioni, one of the most eloquent proponents of this view, says, "The thesis that every citizen has not only rights but also responsibilities is a communitarian cornerstone."[15] Individual rights, and certainly the efforts to see one's rights acknowledged and respected, seem often unduly motivated by self-interest. Many good outcomes can result from tapping into the motivation of self-interest, but will it truly lead to the good and ethical city we want to see? Undoubtedly, affirming many legal or moral rights—such as those that ensure equal access to parks and nature—will help make a city more equitable and just. And that moves us in the direction of the larger common good.

Establishing legal or moral rights in cities will also raise difficult questions about when and how to balance rights when they conflict. A proponent of gun safety will think city regulations that require safe storage of guns are the very slightest of necessary constraints on the Second Amendment, while a card-carrying NRA member will see it as overreaching. Here we may often need to reference and be guided by a larger set of concerns about the public interest, and refer to and apply many of the other values and ethics described in these chapters.

Conclusions

The concept of rights in and to the city has been gaining traction in recent years, and the scope and content of such rights have been expanding. A rights-based approach to thinking about the ethics of cities is a valuable constraint on tendencies to maximize benefits of welfare; they hold that individuals are entitled to certain basic rights—to a clean and healthy environment, to contact with nature, and to minimum levels of housing, among others—that we are duty bound to satisfy and respect regardless of what maximizes benefits for all. The moral authority or source of such rights, and the precise extent of these rights, remain open to discussion. Many of these rights have their origin in federal and state constitutions, while others find expression in local or city documents or declarations (such as the Declaration of Rights to New York City Nature found in the New York City Nature Goals 2050).

A rights-based approach to thinking about ethics in cities has its limitations as well. Some people are critical that too much emphasis is placed on individual rights, to the neglect of more collective or public values. Especially in American society, we are quick to assert our individual constitutional or legal rights (e.g., to a trial by a jury of our peers) but less willing to acknowledge the corresponding duties that go along with these rights (e.g., actually serving on a jury).

Discussion Questions

What are the specific rights urban citizens are entitled to?
What do you feel are the most important rights that citizens of cities are entitled to?
Are these rights fixed and universal, or can they vary from city to city depending on what a city feels is ethically required?

5

The Extent and Limits of Freedoms in the City

Many of the most charged and controversial policy questions that arise in a city today involve conflicts between individuals' desires and the need to protect the health and safety of the larger public, who may be negatively impacted by the exercise of these freedoms. The exercise of personal freedom—the ability to do what one wants to do, when one wants to do it—is an important underpinning of an interesting and meaningful life. Yet in cities, personal freedoms must often be balanced against the larger public interest.

There are many recent examples of urban residents pushing the limits of personal freedoms in pursuit of excitement and adventure (certainly qualities of urban life we want to encourage). In September 2019, residents of the Washington, DC, area were intrigued by a mysterious BASE jumper who was secretly jumping from tall buildings in the region, including the Lumen building, a thirty-two-story tower that was under construction. This extreme sport is not for everyone and is usually done in places like El Capitan in Yosemite National Park. But there is a certain thrill seeker to whom this hobby appeals (in this case, the main suspect was a sixty-eight-year-old former competitive runner).[1] BASE jumping is not illegal in Virginia, though trespassing is (and was necessary to reach the top of the Lumen building).

In September 2019, a group of BASE jumpers wore suits to blend in as they traveled to the roof of the forty-story Exchange Tower in Perth, Australia. No one was hurt or killed, and though the activity is not illegal in Australia either, the local police were not happy: "This type of behavior is reckless and irresponsible."[2]

Should society leave room for such exotic pastimes, especially given the dangers they pose in dense urban settings? Perhaps. Risk-taking and thrill-seeking are legitimate aspects of leading a full and interesting life, and though this is not my particular cup of tea, it is clearly very important to some. Should we not leave space for such activities, trying as best we can not to interfere with the unique and special ways that individuals find meaning and value in life?

This, after all, is the essence of what personal freedom is all about. But the exercise of a BASE jumper's freedoms is legitimately curtailed, perhaps, when the danger to others is significant or excessive. An article by travel writer Ed Grabianowski makes this point: "BASE jumping from buildings within cities is almost always illegal. The risk of pedestrian injury and traffic disruption are too great, although the vast majority of building jumps take place at night or at dawn. Police have promptly arrest [sic] jumpers who have leapt from the Eiffel Tower and the St. Louis Arch."[3]

It seems on the face of it to be an activity that does endanger the public, though it is hard to find news reports or much evidence of such outcomes in cities. Must we wait to impose restrictions?

Does it matter that outlawing such activities in cities does not or will not prevent a BASE jumper from enjoying this recreational hobby *somewhere* (just perhaps not in cities or in all cities)? "There are quite a few places to BASE jump legally," notes Ed Grabianowski. "Kjerag, on Lysefjord in Norway is a very popular location, and jumps remain legal there. Various natural formations throughout Europe are available for legal jumping as well. However, man-made objects with legal jumping are difficult to find, so anyone with a BASE number has probably had to break a law to get it."[4]

The ease and cost of the available alternatives (to jumping in a city) are valid considerations, of course.

Guns and Lawns

The freedom to own, carry, and use a firearm is yet another example that raises serious questions about the extent to which reasonable restrictions can be placed on individual rights and liberties. This freedom is a special case in the sense that it is enshrined as a right under the Second Amendment of the US Constitution. This fact could be used to argue for greater caution in undertaking public action that would control, moderate, or regulate this freedom—and perhaps for greater tolerance for the unintended public dangers and impacts associated with the exercise of this freedom.

In the case of guns, there is little question that the exercise of this liberty (and the acknowledgment in and firm protection of the Second Amendment) leads to significant negative impacts on the broader public. The "other-regarding" impacts of choosing to own and carry a gun are huge.

The public costs associated with gun violence, for instance, are significant and actually much higher than many realize. A 2015 article in *Mother Jones* puts the number of gun injuries over a single decade at an astounding 750,000 and the many medical, hospital, in-home care, and other costs associated with these injuries at nearly $230 billion per year. The vast majority of these costs—some 87 percent—are absorbed by the public.[5] Does this justify placing reasonable restrictions on this freedom, given the often-severe public impacts? Some cities have attempted to ban certain kinds of firearms. Other cities have sought to place restrictions on when and where it is acceptable to carry a gun, concealed or open carry. States and some cities place restrictions on bringing guns to schools, parks, or other public spaces and buildings, for example.

San Jose, California, has taken the novel approach of passing an ordinance requiring gun owners to take out liability insurance, in the same way motor vehicle users are required to carry such insurance. While cities have a hard time stringently regulating guns, there are other kinds of personal freedoms that seem easier to curtail. In many communities there have been significant debates and battles over how individual homeowners can use their yards and specifically whether they ought to have the ability to convert their conventional lawns to other uses, for instance growing vegetables or installing native plants that are better for birds.

If a homeowner simply wishes to allow their grass to grow and their yard to become a wilder kind of space, are they entitled to do so? In many communities and cities, they are not. Ordinances often forbid grass lawns over a certain height in order to prevent a sense of unkemptness and to protect the property values of surrounding homes.

A recent experience of a colleague, Nina-Marie Lister, a planning professor at Toronto Metropolitan University, is instructive. Lister converted her yard to a native garden, with extensive native plants, but a neighbor filed a complaint, and Lister found herself in violation of the city's tall grass and weeds bylaw.

The irony is that Toronto's bylaw is directly at odds with its stated intent to enhance biodiversity in the city, which has even adopted an official biodiversity strategy. Indeed, the city is an exemplar when it comes to conserving and protecting flora and fauna (a leading city when it comes to bird conservation, for example).[6]

Many cities' efforts to protect trees raise a similar question about the freedom of homeowners to make these kinds of decisions. Here the issue cuts a little differently. I believe there is a strong ethical duty to protect older trees, and I support the notion that cities can and ought to have the power and authority to limit a homeowner's or landowner's ability to cut down trees and to impose certain standards that limit this freedom (including requiring, when a tree is cut down, a mitigation standard that might force replacing it with new trees at a compensation rate of, say, three or five to one).

I do not believe a landowner has a God-given or constitutionally given right to cut down any tree on her or his property. Trees, especially older heritage trees, are profoundly imbued with a "publicness" that distinguishes them from other simple forms of property a person might own (such as a car, chair, or house). As an environmentalist I find myself siding with the city's ability to limit the unfettered cutting down of trees but against a city's limits on installing a native garden. Both protecting trees and encouraging a shift from turfgrass lawns to native gardens provides many important public benefits, especially for birds. But am I being ethically inconsistent by supporting the homeowner's freedom in one case but supporting a limit on his or her freedoms in the other?

My ethical reasoning, however, is not as inconsistent as it might appear. If there is a legitimate and substantial public purpose to limit "lawn freedoms," I believe a city has the power and authority to do so. However, the ethics of such an action should indeed turn on the merits of the reasons. At a time when we need to protect existing trees for the cooling benefits and carbon sequestration they provide, there seems to be a strong reason to allow cities to take reasonable steps and impose reasonable restrictions on homeowners' freedom to cut down trees. Equally true is that there are strong biodiversity conservation reasons to permit, and indeed encourage, homeowners to install native and wildlife-friendly gardens.

Are there other ways to effect a positive public outcome but with less interruption to personal freedoms? In many situations where a homeowner wants to do something that might affect or impact neighbors, there are often provisions to allow for neighbor input and acquiescence. Could this be another option? To convert my lawn to a native garden, might I legitimately be asked to consult my neighbors and obtain their consent or approval?

For native lawns, many cities have some form of financial incentive program that pays homeowners to take out water-intensive lawns (for example Los Angeles and Las Vegas, cities that face serious water shortages). There are also programs that encourage planting native plants, for example by providing the plant stock free of charge or at low cost. In Australian cities, it is common for city councils to run their own nurseries for this purpose.

We could also recognize and reward homeowners for the ecological services provided by the native gardens they install, for instance by reducing their property taxes. One idea is for cities to adjust their property tax assessments to take into account the net changes in the ecological services provided by one's lawn. Installation of a native garden delivers a number of ecological and community benefits—for instance by attracting more insects and birds—and in turn reduces demand for community services such as potable water. Part of this discussion hinges on what we believe the duties of landownership are or include.

Another way to look at this is to flip the perspective—recognize that what Lister and other want to do is simply allow the land around their homes to revert to what nature originally was, harboring and supporting the native birds and butterflies and plant life that has been there all along and that, by the way, is also good for humans. Perhaps the turfgrass lawn ought to be viewed as the interloper, as the thing that is out of place and needs a special permit.

How we treat the freedom of homeowners and developers to cut down trees raises similar issues, though different in some ways from the native garden case. Often, we collectively object when a developer seeks to cut down large swaths of existing forests to make room for homes and shopping centers. Many cities have adopted tree protection standards that impose at least some restrictions on these freedoms—requiring an inventory of trees, taking steps to ensure that trees are protected during construction, and, most controversially, limiting the number of trees that can be removed. This happens in some cities by imposing minimum canopy standards on new development, reached by both protecting existing trees and planting new ones (or paying fees in lieu of planting). This seems, on the face, a reasonable outcome—a balancing of the competing interests of landowner freedom and the larger public interest, but the result is often the loss of many trees.

Do (or should) landowners have the personal freedom to cut down trees located entirely on private property? The psychology of cutting down older trees has, for me, always been troubling. It is especially difficult to see older trees, which we now know sequester so much carbon and provide so many important ecological benefits, cut down by homeowners often for trivial reasons—to create more curb appeal in the process of selling a home or to reduce the extent of leaf raking that has to be done in the fall. A fear of often-healthy trees falling on a home or limbs falling on windows and roofs, bolstered by dubious advice from tree-cutting companies, seems a key driver (see sidebar 5-1). But at the core is the assumption that the decision to cut down a tree is a personal one, to be made by the homeowner at his or her discretion.

Sidebar 5-1 Tree Psychology
Some of the Factors Influencing Decisions to Remove Trees
The aesthetics and perceived beauty of the tree
The potential danger posed by the tree; will it, or a portion of it, fall on the house?
The perceived age and/or health of the tree; "it is an older, unhealthy tree that needs removing"
The salability of the home
The inconveniences created by the tree (e.g., leaves that have to be raked)
The darkness in the home created by the shading from its canopy
The decision to remove seen as a completely personal decision

Going Back to *On Liberty*

John Stuart Mill's famous 1859 essay *On Liberty* is often the consensus starting point for discussions about how to balance personal freedoms and social or collective goals. When is it acceptable, indeed required, for the government to intervene and interfere with individual freedoms to protect a larger public interest such as safety or public health?

Mill believed it was only legitimate for society to curtail these individual liberties when they had clear effects on others or the general public, and he laid out a now-famous principle for guiding public policy and for determining when actions or policies that restrict individual liberties are ethically valid:

> That the only purpose for which power can be rightfully exercised over any member of a civilized community, against his will, is to prevent harm to others. His own good, either physical or moral, is not a sufficient warrant. He cannot rightfully be compelled to do or forbear because it will be better for him to do so, because it will make him happier, because, in the opinion of others, to do so would be wise or even right. . . . The only part of the conduct of anyone for which he is amenable to society is that which concerns others. In the part which merely concerns himself, his independence is, of right, absolute. Over himself, over his own body and mind, the individual is sovereign.[7]

Interfering with BASE jumping or any other personal hobby or endeavor would be justified only in cases of other-regarding or public impacts associated with this behavior. There would seem to be many on the face, such as the chance that the BASE jumper falls directly on another person below. One can quite easily imagine the public hazards of this hobby, especially if societies (or cities) were to give free rein and general permission for people to engage in it.

A recent example from California vividly illustrates other potential public impacts connected with this hobby. In this case, the BASE jumper had a less-than-successful end to the jump when his chute caught the edge of a building and caused him to slam into the side of a parking garage and remain dangling dangerously in the air. Passersby called 911, and a fire truck had to come rescue the individual at no small public cost.

Whether it is a motorcyclist who incurs significant hospital costs (and EMT and other public rescue costs) because she did not wear a helmet or a driver who was ejected from a car because he failed to wear a seatbelt, important and sometimes quite large social impacts typically result.

Conservative economist Milton Friedman has famously argued for protecting the personal freedoms of Americans, referencing Mill's rule. However, Friedman applies this rule in a narrow way, recognizing the validity of government interference only in cases where there is a clear "third-party effect." He does not support mandatory helmet or seatbelt laws, for example, believing that they do not result in public-regarding impacts.

As Friedman asks provocatively, "But how can you justify safety requirements which are intended to protect the driver himself?"[8] "If I'm riding a motorcycle," says Friedman, "I may be a fool and stupid not to wear a helmet to protect myself but it's my life. What right does the state have to tell me that I must wear a helmet for my own good?" What are we left to do in a world where the government cannot legitimately require someone to use a seatbelt or wear a helmet when riding a motorcycle? Personal persuasion is still a possibility, Friedman believes, something *On Liberty* mentions as well.

Another difficult moral issue arising in cities is what to do in circumstances where individuals—often because of a mix of mental illness, drug abuse, and bad luck—end up living on the street and in various levels of personal distress. Such cases raise the question of when it is acceptable, and indeed necessary, for certain actions be taken for the individual's own good.

One recent case in Los Angeles (and described in the *Los Angeles Times*) was that of a homeless woman named Kristal, whose circumstances were apparent and alarming to many who encountered her.[9] She was seen by many in a dire situation—incoherent, unclothed sometimes, unable to walk, and often sitting or lying in unsafe locations near traffic. What duty does a city have to Kristal to intervene, to interfere with her life, with the purpose of essentially saving her life? There are legal procedures, of course, in such cases (in California and other states) that allow the government or another individual, often a family member, to request a person be placed in a conservatorship, typically someone who is not able to house, feed, or otherwise care for him- or herself. As Kristal's case shows, though, this is not always an easy process—there are legal and bureaucratic hurdles, including the need to petition a court and to present evidence of a person's inability to care for themselves, and Kristal and her boyfriend actively resisted help from social service agencies. These kinds of cases raise serious questions about the right course of action when one's personal desires and agency conflict with the larger function and purpose of government.

Mill's rule about protecting the ability of individuals to make choices, even bad choices, does not extend to children, and here he lays out a special exception to his framework. "Those who are still in a state to require being taken care of by others," says Mill, "must be protected against their own actions as well as against external injury."[10]

Why ought we to err on the side of allowing as much personal freedom as possible? It is likely to be the best single philosophy to ensure that individuals are able to pursue meaningful and flourishing lives. Mill writes about the importance of protecting "liberty of thought and feeling" but also "liberty of tastes and pursuits" and "of framing the plan of our life to suit our own character, of doing as we like, subject to such consequences as may follow, without impediment from our fellow creatures, as long as what we do does not harm them, even though they should think our conduct foolish, perverse, or wrong."[11]

Distinctive and unique life plans are a good thing and ought to be encouraged in cities. Indeed, cities represent the best possible route to encouraging many different satisfying and fulfilling lives. The very basis and benefit of a city is the ability to do things and to live one's life in ways different than would be possible perhaps in more conservative and staid rural areas. Tolerance of personal idiosyncrasy and difference should be the hallmark of a city.

If we can't or don't want to stop or curtail an individual's dangerous behaviors or practices, what else can we do, then, to ethically address a problematic or dangerous circumstance? If outright prohibition is too severe, there are other options, including time and place restrictions. If we want to preserve the right for people to BASE jump, it would be entirely legitimate to restrict this activity to times of day or particular places in the city (even particular buildings) that might serve to reduce the dangers (to both the public and the BASE jumper).

We can also divulge and disclose information about the personal risks involved. While it may not be ethically defensible in a Millian way to forbid a BASE jumper from undertaking this activity, it might be permissible for the government to require the BASE jumper to watch a safety video and read a statement that presents objective data about how dangerous or safe the practice is.

Risk disclosure and information dissemination have become common practices of local (and state and federal) governments. If you choose to buy a home in an earthquake or flood hazard zone, you will likely be informed about this. And although hazard disclosure provisions have been shown to have a limited effect on buying decisions, it is surely better that risks—whether from BASE jumping or flooding—are fully understood and disclosed.

We might also institute some measures to encourage or even mandate more responsible behavior, even as we permit these personal freedoms. "There are also many positive acts for the benefit of others which he [an average person in society] may rightfully be compelled to perform," says Mill, "such as to give evidence in a court of justice, to bear his fair share in the common defense or in any other joint work necessary to the interest of the society of which he enjoys the protection, and to perform certain acts of individual beneficence, such as saving a fellow creature's life or interposing to protect the defenseless against ill-usage—things which whenever it is obviously a man's duty to do he may rightfully be made responsible to society for not doing."[12] There are corresponding duties, then, that may be asked of citizens.

Ethically speaking, cities must more squarely acknowledge the many ways in which they serve to encourage or underwrite risky behaviors. Historically, the government has provided incentives (and eschewed disincentives) that naturally shape the decision calculus for individuals. Here the concept of "moral hazards" is relevant, referring to the many fiscal, financial, and other policies that encourage risky actions. Examples include highly subsidized and artificially low-cost flood insurance, and provisions of the US tax code that allow deductions for property losses from floods and other natural disasters. Federal disaster policy has encouraged rebuilding in dangerous hazard zones, moreover.

The problem of moral hazards can be seen as well in the devastating wildfires in California in recent years: here, housing developments have over time been encroaching on the so-called wildland-urban interface, where fire dangers are significant and where the new presence of suburban homes complicates the challenge of controlling and fighting such fires.[13]

There remain many open questions here. Does it matter, for instance, that restraints on freedoms in the city are made through democratic means, deliberated and voted on by duly elected mayors and city councils? I think it does, and to no small degree. A legal limit placed on an urban freedom—whether it be the right to camp on public land or to freely cross a street midblock (what might be considered jaywalking)—is more morally defensible where it has been openly debated and deliberated and where there are political means to object and perhaps to overturn such restrictions.

Conclusions

Cities are, in theory, places where personal ideals and aspirations and unique life plans can find full expression. We acknowledge that individuals are in the best position to decide how to live their lives to the fullest and what will bring them the most meaning, purpose, and pleasure. Personal autonomy is a value we hope cities will embrace and respect. That said, there are limits to the exercise of personal freedom, and cities have a legitimate right, indeed an obligation, to take steps to curtail or limit those personal freedoms when they significantly and negatively affect others and the larger public good. Cities should do everything they can to stand back and refrain from telling citizens how to live their lives but again are justified in placing limits in the interests of the larger public good. Without rules that all citizens are willing to abide by—whether traffic regulations or respect for the bodily integrity of others—daily life would be difficult or impossible.

There are many contemporary urban issues that raise conflicting interpretations about the extent and limits of personal freedom. Does one have the right to freely carry, and even display publicly, a gun, even though this behavior serves to frighten and arguably endanger others? Does a homeowner have the right to plant a native garden and eschew the conventional turfgrass lawn that a majority of her neighbors prefer? Even more controversial, does a homeowner have the right to cut down a large and old tree, even though it is a beloved member of the community and provides many public benefits, from shading and cooling to sequestering carbon? As the discussion in this chapter has shown, these are not always easy issues to resolve, and the line between legitimate exercise of personal freedom and infringement of public health and safety is often anything but bright.

Discussion Questions

What do you believe are the most important freedoms to protect in cities?

When is it okay or acceptable for a city government to interfere with a resident's personal freedoms? Under what circumstances is government intervention justified?

Are there more or less ethical ways a city can go about curtailing or limiting personal freedoms when this is seen to be justified?

6

Ethical Policing and Use of Force

The exercise of a city's police functions and authority raises some of the most difficult and serious ethical questions. The ability to arrest, detain, incarcerate, and sometimes even kill highlights the potential threat that police actions pose to the dignity and autonomy of citizens, and in turn a special duty to carefully determine when and under what circumstances such actions are ethically justified.

Almost every person by a certain age has had an experience with the police. As a white male I have had a few, mostly in connection with driving (several speeding tickets, for example), but they have not resulted in a violent confrontation or a threat to my personal health and safety. This is not the case for many others, especially people of color, who have endured the disproportionate force and impact of policing in American cities. The killing of George Floyd in May 2020, the result of a Minneapolis policeman placing his knee on Floyd's neck for more than eight minutes, was important in demonstrating this fact. It was a shocking episode; some have called it a wake-up call and a line crossed. But it was certainly not new and not unusual, as a startling number of other examples show how people of color have been treated by the police. The ubiquity of cell phone cameras has allowed us (collectively) to witness and experience this visceral violence; in the past, many of these conflicts would have been hidden from view.

Ethical Policing and Questions of Reasonable Use of Force

"Much like a doctor's Hippocratic Oath, police must first do no harm." That is what Camden, New Jersey, police chief Scott Thomson told *Washington Post* reporter Deanna Paul in an article about that city's new approach to policing that emphasizes de-escalation and efforts to avoid the use of force.[1] The

> **Sidebar 6-1**
> **Camden, New Jersey, Directive on the Use of Force**
> The department's core use-of-force principles are as follows:
> CORE PRINCIPLE #1: Officers may use force only to accomplish specific law enforcement objectives.
> CORE PRINCIPLE #2: Whenever feasible, officers should attempt to de-escalate confrontations with the goal of resolving encounters without force. Officers may only use force that is objectively reasonable, necessary, and as a last resort.
> CORE PRINCIPLE #3: Officers must use only the amount of force that is proportionate to the circumstances.
> CORE PRINCIPLE #4: Deadly force is only authorized as a last resort and only in strict accordance with this directive.
> CORE PRINCIPLE #5: Officers must promptly provide or request medical aid.
> CORE PRINCIPLE #6: Employees have a duty to stop and report uses of force that violate any applicable law and/or this directive.
> Source: City of Camden, New Jersey

comparison to the medical oath is a telling recognition of both the serious impacts and implications of the police and policing practices a city adopts and the trend that many cities are rethinking conventional policing techniques. Policing is an ethical matter, a matter of ethical choice, at both the episodic or case level (how a police officer chooses to deal with a specific issue or conflict) and the level of city policy, as the new Camden policy shows (see sidebar 6-1).

Evidence of the value of de-escalation was on display in August 2019, when police were confronted with how to stop a knife-wielding individual who was threatening patrons at a fast-food restaurant in downtown Camden. Much of this confrontation was captured on camera. As police arrived on the scene, there were the usual shouts to drop the weapon, but what was clearly different was the police officers' willingness to give the culprit more time to walk down the street, more time for all involved to calm down and perhaps for the culprit to tire. The scene of twenty or more police officers surrounding the individual and walking with him as he moved down Broadway was striking and unusual. Eventually the officers Tasered the suspect, but they could easily have shot and killed him (and endangered others) and most likely would have in just about any other American city. But here, with the police guided by a new eighteen-page directive, the culprit, perhaps suffering from serious mental illness, survived. It was an outcome reflecting humanity and compassion and a function of both ethical policy and the training needed to effectively implement the new approach.

Policies that seek to restrain the use of deadly force are often resisted by rank-and-file police officers, perhaps not a surprise. When mayors and police chiefs strongly support these policies, they are seen as courageous—methods and practices such as de-escalation are still relatively new and are often resisted in the prevailing culture. Shooting, and probably killing, the knife-wielding culprit in Camden would have been (and still is) standard practice in most cities—a practice often referred to as being "awful but lawful." It is the duty of a police officer to protect the public and take appropriate steps to protect him or herself as well.

When Is Deadly Force Justified?

Police confront a host of other admittedly difficult circumstances that may cause them to take serious actions to protect themselves and the general public. They may encounter a bank robbery in progress, requiring them to pull out and fire their guns in a public setting, where errant shots can further endanger the public. They are frequently called to deal with belligerent or dangerous individuals in the community, and increasingly (and sadly) when shooters appear at a school or other public setting.

A major ethical judgment call for a police officer is deciding when and under what circumstances the use of deadly force is justified. And what specific guidance, or rules of engagement, ought local governments to establish and impose on police to regulate these circumstances? And, as important, what kind of training should be undertaken and police habits instilled to ensure the policies and rules of engagement are followed?

Ultimately, protecting the public and minimizing loss of life are key goals in this calculus, of course. It is difficult to separate the question of reasonable use of police force, deadly or otherwise, from communities being disproportionately affected by these actions, especially African American and Latino residents. Evidence is overwhelming that both minorities and communities of color bear a disproportionate share of the burden of dangerous and deadly police tactics. For instance, Princeton University professor Jonathan Mummolo found that in Maryland, SWAT teams tend to be used disproportionately in neighborhoods of color.[2]

Even common police practices such as "stop and frisk," used extensively in New York City, ensnare a much higher percentage of the city's Black and Hispanic than white populations. While use of stop and frisk has been significantly reduced since former New York City mayor Mike Bloomberg's administration, it is still in use and (as before) disproportionately affects men and boys of color. As a recent report by the ACLU of New York concludes, "Young black and Latino males between the ages of 14 and 24 account for only five percent of the city's population, compared with 38 percent of reported stops."[3]

The evidence seems very clear that there are policing techniques that will result in happier endings, that police are ethically required to use them, and that cities require their use. The technique of de-escalation is now being used in a number of cities with impressive results.

Even drawing a police weapon and pointing it at a suspect or group of suspects is a serious matter, yet it seems to happen too frequently. Under what circumstances, though, should police even be permitted to take this step, recognizing that the pointing itself can inflict trauma and raises the chance that shots are fired, intentionally or accidentally? Recent examples show the kinds of trauma such an experience can result in, and often, the circumstances in which guns are drawn further deepen the sense of unfairness.

Phoenix is one city that has struggled with this problem, as illustrated by a recent case. A four-year-old girl was seen taking a doll from a Dollar Store, unbeknownst to her parents. This led to several police cars chasing the family and stopping and surrounding the car with guns drawn. The drawn guns were accompanied, as is often the case, by extreme yelling and rough treatment, all captured in this case by police body cams. The mom was pregnant and also holding a baby, which police demanded she give to them. The mayor of Phoenix, Kate Gallego, expressed her disgust about the outcome: "This is not who we are, and I refuse to allow this type of behavior to go unchallenged." she said.[4]

The extent to which police pull out and point their guns is an important metric of how well a city is doing, though in many cities, recording such incidents may not be mandatory. Gallego was able to institute a new city policy requiring a report each time a gun is drawn, and now the city is able to track (in theory) the number of times it occurs. Gallego describes these new reporting requirements as "an important step for accountability and transparency."[5] Undoubtedly there are many instances in which drawing one's weapon is prudential and justified, but it is also the case that when the gun is not fired, drawing and pointing it is not without lasting consequences and ought to be avoided if at all possible.

So now in Phoenix police officers must record and report each time they draw their guns and point them, resulting in a clearer sense of how often this happens and perhaps even creating an incentive to resist the temptation unless absolutely necessary. Data from the first month of compliance was sobering, though, as Phoenix police drew their guns some 318 times. The data shows that 450 individuals had, as a result, a gun pointed at them, though in only one case were shots actually fired.

How Can Force Be Reduced or Avoided?

Part of the challenge of ethical policing is developing policing techniques that are effective, humane, and safe. Many policies and practices are used widely, but American police departments are anything but this. One practice that has come under scrutiny is the use of no-knock searches, usually by drug enforcement units. The idea of such a search is to enter a potential drug house quickly and with an element of surprise. But increasingly this appears to be a grossly unwise practice and dangerous both for cops and for the occupants of the home.

One of the most shocking recent examples occurred in Houston in 2019, when the Houston narcotics unit initiated a no-knock raid on the home of married couple Dennis Tuttle and Rhogena Nicholas. An informant had supposedly told police the couple was selling black tar heroin, information sufficient to get a judge to issue a search warrant. Things went poorly as soon as the raid began, as officers killed the couple's dog and then, confronting an armed Tuttle, shot and killed him and his wife. But in the process, five officers were also shot. Later it was discovered that the two officers leading the raid had falsified the material submitted to gain the search warrant. A third officer was later indicted on a charge of murder.

About a year later, similar tragic circumstances unfolded in Louisville, Kentucky, when a no-knock raid led to the death of Breonna Taylor and brought the practice to national attention. Taylor's boyfriend, who returned fire as police broke down the door, has said that he had no idea what was happening. The brutality of the event was shocking, though perhaps not remarkable, as Taylor's boyfriend witnessed her death and feared for his own life as he frantically sought help for her. It turned out that the drug dealer the police were in search of lived at an entirely different address.

There is little to recommend these no-knock, or "forced entry," raids and many reasons to avoid them. Given that many of the no-knock searches are to enforce search warrants connected to drugs, it is a legitimate question to ask whether the stridency of the methods, and the dangers connected with things going wrong, are justified by the desired ends. Many of the drug-connected search warrants involve marijuana, leading one commentator to conclude that the aggressive raids are more dangerous than the drug use they aim to curtail. And there are certainly other, less risky methods for administering warrants (less risky for both the occupant or suspect and the police officers themselves, not to mention bystanders and others, including pets). Almost any other method would seem preferable.

In the aftermath of the tragedy of the deadly Houston raid, the police chief announced major changes in the city's policy concerning these types of raids. No longer would they be considered routine, but they would now require a special exemption from top administrators. Also, in the interest of transparency, the police chief announced that body cameras would be required in all such raids. In June 2020, the Louisville Metro Council similarly voted to ban no-knock searches.

The practice of employing no-knock searches in the first place emerged a result of a broader trend toward militarized police departments. The shift began in the late 1960s and accelerated in the era of the war on drugs and efforts to address terrorism. The very acronym SWAT—special weapons and tactics—conjures up a militarized setting. Watching any police department action in real time today gives the impression of a military action—with police officers wearing military-style helmets and uniforms and carrying military-grade weapons and equipment. There is often support equipment such as metal-hardened tanklike vehicles. Much of this military equipment comes from the federal government, which provided it free of charge through the Department of Defense's 1033 Program, beginning in 1990.[6]

What kind of visual impression must it give and what kinds of psychological effects must it leave behind to see police in this kind of "battle mode"? They can't be positive and may feed into doubt about whether police are there to help the community and create conditions for safe living or rather whether they are an occupying army to be feared.

Mummolo has done some interesting visual experiments to better gauge people's reactions to militarized police forces and police tactics. He developed and tested a series of "survey experiments," in which respondents are asked to read a scenario and react to photos that represent different levels of militarized policing. Where the images are more militarized (the most militarized including an armored vehicle with police officers in heavy battle gear), respondents expressed increased perceptions of crime and lower support for more police patrols (and lower support for increasing the budget of police departments). What police wear and how they look clearly affects what we believe about their virtues and behaviors. If we want a police force, and individual police officers, that citizens will trust and seek out for help, they may need to look less threatening.

A number of cities are now working to reform their 911 call response systems so that dispatchers have the option of sending a mental health professional to a scene instead of a police officer, often leading to a better, less violent outcome. Cities such as Eugene, Oregon, have had such systems in place for many years, while other cities are just now operating pilots. Albuquerque, New Mexico, created an entirely new stand-alone department for this purpose—the Albuquerque Community Safety Department.[7] With an emphasis on de-escalation, and without guns, badges, or the ability to arrest, these responders are much better suited to many calls that involve mental health crises or homelessness.

Much of this reform involves critically assessing where and when police officers need to be called and reducing the potential for circumstances to turn deadly. Taking police out of the enforcement of traffic laws would do much. Such circumstances—such as police stopping a motorist for a broken taillight or speeding offense or a pedestrian for jaywalking—account for the lion's share of the public's interaction with police.[8] These are interactions that often result in violence, disproportionately impacting residents of color. How police came to be an extension of, and at the service of, a burgeoning car-oriented society is an interesting history but lends greater support for car-limited and even car-free cities and for greater use, perhaps, of self-enforcing technologies such as intersection and speed cameras (though these technologies raise issues of privacy for some, as I discuss in the chapter to follow).

The Ethical Decision to Chase or Pursue

One of my first memories of giving much thought to the issue of how police exercise their judgments about when and where to exert force and apply their considerable authority was while I was campaigning for my father, who was running for mayor of the city I grew up in. I had returned from graduate school to man the polls on his behalf and found myself standing next to a city police officer who was campaigning for my father's opponent (something that struck me at the time as inappropriate). I'm not sure how but the conversation turned to the propriety of police chases. The officer felt strongly that to curtail such chases, even dangerous high-speed chases, would encourage lawlessness and boldness on the part of criminals. On that day I recall thinking how odd that position was for a policeman to espouse, someone whose primary job was to ensure public safety. But that conversation illustrates the disagreements that exist and the different ethical positions held by those involved directly in local policing as well as the many individuals and citizens (like myself that day) who feel we have the right to an opinion about these practices.

Engaging in a dangerous high-speed police chase to catch a potential drug dealer or even for something less serious struck me then, as now, as unreasonable. The costs in terms of public safety and possible collateral loss of life seem too great to justify. It is undeniable that police have significant freedom to make decisions on the spot, in the field, and according to circumstance, which is evidenced by many of the bad outcomes that populate news headlines. As important, though, is the fact that cities, and local governments, can and (hopefully) do establish clear limits and conditions for these actions. Ultimately the elected officials of a city or county will and should be held accountable.

In Louisville, the police chief loosened the city's criteria under which police chases could occur, resulting in seven deaths in such chases over the last three years. In 2019, a Louisville *Courier-Journal* editorial had already issued a plea to return to those earlier policies of restraint: "The cost still doesn't justify the risks. . . . People are being killed or injured as vehicles fleeing the police careen out of control on our busy streets. And more people will die if you don't restrict police pursuits and use safer methods to catch criminals."[9]

The statistics associated with these chases, as analyzed by the *Courier-Journal* in a study of the seven years after the chase policy was relaxed, show the impact. Half the chases resulted in crashes and some $3 million paid out to the victims of those crashes. Not only are chases excessively dangerous, but they represent significant monetary impacts for a city government. It is hard to appreciate the personal trauma associated with these chases, especially the ones that end very badly. And there is little doubt that when a police officer decides to chase a car and continue the chase even after the suspect has accelerated, the dangerous driving the suspect engages in, such as swerving around other cars and running red lights, is itself a result of being chased.

In one chase in Columbus, Ohio, in November 2019, both the escaping criminal and the police cars following traveled at speeds over ninety-five miles an hour through neighborhoods and along the city's surface roads, creating potentially deadly danger for pedestrians and other drivers. In a December 2019 police chase in Cleveland, the impact on bystanders was evident: a carjacking that began in a Target parking lot ended fifteen miles away with the death of a thirteen-year-old girl.

The outcome was horrific, even though Cleveland had in fact adopted a relatively strong policy limiting police pursuits and aimed at curtailing these kinds of terrible results. The policy changes were a direct result of a chase in 2012 that resulted in the death of two unarmed people who were shot 137 times, by thirteen officers, eventually leading to a $3 million settlement to the victims' families.[10]

Under Cleveland's new policy, implemented in 2015, police must receive approval from a supervisor to continue a pursuit, and pursuits are only allowed in cases of either a drunk driver or a person who has committed a violent crime. The Cleveland pursuit policy is seventeen pages long and embedded in a quite long and detailed policy manual, called obtusely *General Police Orders*. One of the most prominent elements in the manual that catches the eye is this one: "Officers shall err on the side of caution and interpret this policy in the more restrictive manner if, for any reason, this directive does not offer clear guidance for a specific set of circumstances."[11] It is an admirable attempt to sort out who has responsibility for making decisions and the criteria and circumstances under which a vehicle chase could begin and continue.

"Pursuing officers," under the Cleveland policy, are required to immediately break off a chase if "the level of danger to life outweighs the need for immediate apprehension." Even though the policy provides some examples of what might lead to this conclusion (a driver speeding through red lights or stop signs), this is highly subjective language, open to widely varying interpretations, and perhaps easy to ignore in the moment of an adrenaline-fueled chase. Nevertheless, the Cleveland policy, as subject to personal interpretation as it is, is still a very positive step forward.

Judgments about when to initiate and when to continue high-speed chases are a ubiquitous challenge to local governments around the country, and almost every day brings a new story with a bad outcome. Yet another sad episode with a terrible outcome was captured recently on the national news: Two men robbing a jewelry store in Coral Gables, Florida, near Miami, commandeered a UPS truck and driver, resulting in a twenty-three-mile chase and ending in a hail of gunfire aimed at the vehicle stopped on a highway in rush-hour traffic. With police firing from multiple directions, there didn't seem to be much concern for the hostage, and not surprisingly all three occupants of the truck were killed, as well as a seventy-year-old man in another car. The outcome enraged relatives of the UPS driver, with his father-in-law criticizing the chase and the decision to fire on the truck: "They disregard the hostage. They disregard the people around the scene. They went out there like the old West."[12] The police came under criticism in this case even from their own, with the former Miami police chief agreeing that the decision to fire into the truck was a bad one.

It is not clear at this point whether there were any efforts to slow down or call off the chase, and the controversy has been more about whether shooting at a stopped vehicle, one containing a hostage, was wise rather than whether the chase itself was a danger to the public. It is not evident whether the Coral Gables Police Department had any chase or engagement policy and, if so, how the decisions were made by the police on the ground.

Many rank-and-file police officers do not like the idea of setting out policies ahead of time that could prevent them from chasing a criminal. A common argument is that the simple knowledge of those policies emboldens criminals. These sentiments have been expressed in cities such as Cleveland that have considered new policies. There is no evidence that this is in fact the case, and it seems unlikely that any criminal's specific decision to speed away or take some other form of illegal or evasive action would be a result of this kind of thinking. Nevertheless, the criticism continues. "These criminals now feel empowered to do whatever they want because they know they're not going to be chased," says Cleveland city councilman Mike Polensek. "When you shoot at a cop, you're shooting at every one of us."[13]

Other Elements of Ethical Policing

In the immediate aftermath of the Houston no-knock drug raid, there was much ballyhoo about the merits and bravery of police. But there was also some remarkable grandstanding by Joe Gamaldi, president of the Houston Police Department Union, about the naysayers and police critics. He pushed back against this criticism and even seemed to issue a kind of threat to the public: fail to appreciate what the police do for you at your own peril.[14]

It is a remarkable thing for the representative of the police to say. Police work in the broadest sense for the public and report in a more immediate sense to a city manager and the elected mayor and city council of that jurisdiction. It is interesting that many key police policies are considered and adopted at the level of the police chief and don't seem to rise to the level of an elected city council. The Cleveland vehicle pursuit policy, for instance, became part of the police department's *General Police Orders* manual, and perhaps this is appropriate given the many, many detailed management and policy issues that police face.

Having a policy is one thing, of course, and a good thing, but faithfully implementing it is another, leading to the recognition that police training and procedures for reporting are also necessary. Practice applying the standards and criteria would also seem a requirement of ethical policing. Giving police the chance to think ahead of time, in perhaps a more controlled and educational setting, about how they should react and how they can exercise their judgments and decision-making in the most ethical way is another key aspect of ethical policing.

An important dimension of public frustration is the sense of a lack of full and complete transparency and accountability when tragic events happen and investigations are initiated. There seem often to be few repercussions from bad decisions or failures to follow a city's use-of-force standards. A recent study of the Los Angeles Police Department found that few sanctions or penalties were applied when officers used their firearms (often resulting in significant deaths) in violation of the city deadly force rules.[15]

Second-Chance Cities: The Ethics of Incarceration and Reentry

It is hard to discuss ethical policing without also discussing the larger criminal justice system and the ethics of incarceration. Especially troubling are the ways in which minority students encounter police early in their lives, much to their detriment. There are many difficult ethical issues here and many that are unresolved: Should police officers (often euphemistically referred to as "resource officers") have a presence in schools? Can we ever expect a fair and equitable criminal justice system in the presence of poverty and systemic racism? Does our private, for-profit prison system incentivize incarceration?

In many cities there are also questions of the ethical treatment of prisoners. Recently, New York City's jail complex, Rikers Island, has come under fire for the abysmal living conditions there. A recent delegation referred to them as rising to the level of human rights violations.[16] What level of care and safety and basic living conditions prisoners are due remains an open question, and in the case of Rikers, there is a special sense of indignation about subjecting individuals to these conditions for parole violations or other minor infractions.

Questions of ethical policing are also bound together with questions about what constitutes lawbreaking, when citizens deserve to be arrested and jailed, and what punishments are fair and equitable. These are difficult and complicated questions, mostly beyond the ability of this book to fully address. But this is another important set of ethical questions for cities. It is also tied up in a larger moral question about forgiveness and second chances, societal values we claim to support but often don't implement in practice.

It is commonly noted that there are more individuals incarcerated in prisons in the United States than anywhere else on earth. Cities have some control over this, by virtue of what we decide constitutes lawbreaking and warrants arrest. Some cities recognize the need to decriminalize certain kinds of violations as one way to reduce the number of people jailed. Systemic racism is reflected in the disproportionate rates of arrest and incarceration of individuals of color. The "funneling" of young Black men and women into juvenile detention and lives of incarceration has been accurately referred to as a school-to-prison pipeline. According to the ACLU, "Many of these children have learning disabilities or histories of poverty, abuse, or neglect, and would benefit from additional educational and counseling services. Instead, they are isolated, punished, and pushed out."[17] Ending this pipeline is a major challenge, of course, and there is no consensus on how best to do this. One continuing point of contention is whether to place police officers in schools, which many critics argue merely serves to exacerbate the problem.[18]

Partly motivated by a sense of justice and partly by a sense of wanting to reduce the societal costs connected with so much incarceration, a first step is to reduce the numbers of citizens arrested and to find ways to reduce fines for many violations that should not and do not rise to a serious level. Traffic violations, as we have seen, often escalate to more serious confrontations and arrests, so some of the alternative policing ideas mentioned earlier will in turn divert from incarceration.

Do individuals who have committed serious crimes deserve second chances and an opportunity at redemption and forgiveness, and what role should a city play in that? It is not an insignificant question, as an estimated 600,000 individuals need to transition each year from prison back into society. The Center for American Progress makes the important point that it is difficult to transition successfully from jail or prison back into American society. A criminal record (and a remarkable 30 percent of Americans have such a record) is a burden that makes it difficult to find employment, secure housing, and generally enjoy the second chance that ethically we feel individuals are entitled to. An estimated 80 million Americans have a criminal record (including misdemeanors), so the scale of these challenges is great indeed.

What can cities do? They can take steps to make it easier for those who served their sentences to find employment and housing and to successfully reenter society. The Center for American Progress has called cities who undertake such programs and efforts second-chance cities. An ethical city, I would suggest, acknowledges that giving individuals second chances is the right thing to do.

Cities like Seattle are taking steps to "automatically vacate" convictions for misdemeanor marijuana convictions. And Seattle has also, like a growing number of cities, adopted a "ban the box" standard that prevents employers (at least early in the process) from disqualifying job applicants because of a conviction. As the Center for American Progress notes, "Ban the box policies remove questions about criminal history from job applications and delay background checks until later in the hiring process, encouraging employers to focus on applicants' qualifications rather than their past mistakes."[19] Another problem is that returning inmates have often had their driver's licenses revoked because of unpaid fines or court penalties, making it even harder for them to find and hold down a job (several states, including Virginia, have now passed laws prohibiting this practice).

Other cities have established reentry offices and programs to aid in the transition from incarceration. Los Angeles' Office of Reentry has established a comprehensive program called New Roads to Second Chances, described as "an investment in the health and appearance of the Los Angeles community, but most importantly, it's an investment in Angelenos who deserve a second chance."[20] There is an Office of Returning Citizens in Boston, the Mayor's Office of Returning Citizens Affairs in Washington, DC, and the Office of Reintegration Services in Philadelphia.

A series of articles and an investigative study in the *Philadelphia Inquirer* further make the point that, in many cities, parole and probation set individuals up for reincarceration, often for small or technical legal violations. It is a "probation trap," as the *Inquirer* calls it.

One especially important thing cities can do is partner with businesses and companies to expand employment opportunities, the lack of which is a major impediment to successfully transitioning (back) to a normal life. There are some wonderful businesses that prioritize hiring the formerly incarcerated.

One example is Nehemiah, a manufacturing company based in Cincinnati that has emphasized providing employment for the formerly incarcerated, with some 80 percent of its employees having felony records. The CEO of this company, Dan Meyer, speaks eloquently and emotionally about how everyone deserves a second chance.[21] Recidivism rates for these employees are much lower, and the benefits to the company, including reduced turnover and higher productivity, are also considerable.

As Meyer says, there is "not only a moral case but a business case for doing it." More companies seem open to second-chance hiring, and there is now even a Second Chance Business Coalition that includes companies such as Deloitte, Dick's Sporting Goods, McDonald's, Target, and United Airlines. As Nehemiah discovered, wraparound services (and a social worker on staff) are required to make this model work, as the formerly incarcerated face a host of issues, from housing to transportation, that other employees may not face (at least to the same degree).

At the heart of this topic is the conception of the human being that we hold and believe to be true. Much of the traditional criminal justice system believes that once a felony is committed, no matter how young the culprit might have been or how long ago the crime, that human being is forever damaged and disgraced, beyond redemption or repair, forever headed down a criminal path. Proponents of second-chance cities suggest otherwise—that humans are flawed and make mistakes but can change and are capable of heroic acts on behalf of themselves, their families, and the larger community.

Conclusions

As this chapter shows, there are extensive and pervasive questions of ethics that arise in the practices and behaviors of police officers in cities everywhere. These judgments and practices involve serious questions about when use of force, especially deadly force, is justified and when it is not. This is an area of urban policy and a key aspect of what constitutes an ethical city. An ethical city is, first, a city that recognizes the inherent ethical dimensions of these decisions and is actively engaged in discussion and public debate about what constitutes ethical policing. More and more, it seems, cities such as Camden and Cleveland are developing policies that better balance benefits and costs and that steer in the direction of reducing, where possible, the use of deadly force and the unintended violent outcomes of, say, a high-speed police chase.

Ethical policing recognizes that lethal force should be avoided or used only as a last resort and that steps, policies, and practices are needed to lessen the often-bad outcomes that result from high-adrenaline, low-judgment circumstances. Policies of de-escalation seem especially justified, particularly given the likelihood that lethal force is exacted more often on minorities. An ethical city must also confront the broader causes and patterns of incarceration, as well as the fairness of reentry programs. An ethical city is a second-chance city that recognizes the importance and power of redemption and forgiveness.

Discussion Questions

When and under what conditions is it acceptable for police to use deadly force? When is it acceptable, if ever, to engage in a high-speed chase?
What are the most promising police reforms that cities can undertake?
What are the key changes that are necessary to bring about "ethical policing"?
What do you think of "second-chance cities," and what steps can we take to ease the way for the formerly incarcerated to integrate back into society?
What steps can cities take to break the "school-to-prison pipeline"?
What are cities duty bound to do to make second chances possible for the formerly incarcerated?

7

Panopticon City
Surveillance and Privacy in the Ethical City

In the modern digital era, privacy, it seems, is in short supply. By explicit or implicit consent, we have traded much of our personal data and information in exchange for the convenience of ordering books and shoes online or using an app to pay for a cup of coffee at Starbucks. Some describe this as surveillance capitalism, and there is a healthy debate about what we are risking or losing in these types of bargains.

But this represents an important set of ethical issues and dilemmas for local government officials as well. Increasingly we could describe the modern city as a "surveillance city" or "panopticon city," referring to nineteenth-century philosopher Jeremy Bentham's famous design for a prison, in which the inmates are continually in fear of being watched and monitored. To many, cities today feel a lot like prisons.

Around every corner in today's city, there is often a camera or other device monitoring our movements and behaviors, often with a legitimate public purpose or goal, such as preventing crime, behind its installation. As the technology of sensors and other digital devices that collect and monitor data further advances, along with the increasing deployment of drones and robots, there is further risk that we will compromise the privacy of citizens in the pursuit of public safety or private commerce. What are the limits we should place on the use of these technologies, and what are the essential elements of privacy that citizens are entitled to and that must be protected in this new world of potentially intrusive technologies?

What Is Privacy and Why Do We Need It?

According to the International Association of Privacy Professionals, privacy can be defined in this way: "Broadly speaking, privacy is the right to be let alone, or freedom from interference or intrusion. Information privacy is the right to have some control over how your personal information is collected and used."[1]

The ability to be left alone and the expectation that there are boundaries to one's life that create the opportunity to truly be alone with oneself are key elements of privacy. There is a sense that intrusion into one's private realm diminishes one's liberties, freedoms, and even the opportunity to shape one's own identity and sense of self. And intrusions into one's personal life may have the potential to shame, embarrass, and even cause the loss of one's job, so there may well be tangible economic impacts associated with privacy.

It is especially interesting and important to think about privacy in the context of cities. Cities, especially larger cities, are valued in part for providing a person the ability to be anonymous in a way that is not possible in a small town or rural community. Many people have a tangible desire to restrict the amount of information known or collected about them, and cities are a good place to do that. It is possible to live in one part of the city, recreate in another area, and work in yet another part, preserving the sense of restricted privacy among these different life realms. For this reason, a loss of privacy may be especially troubling for those who have chosen to live in a city in part to preserve some degree of privacy.

As Bruce Schneier argues, too much surveillance discourages humans from doing things or acting in ways that are different—in short, experimenting. As he says in a provocative essay in *Wired*, "People need to be able to read critiques of those norms without anyone's knowledge, discuss them without their opinions being recorded, and write about their experiences without their names attached to their words. People need to be able to do things that others find distasteful, or even immoral. The minority needs protection from the tyranny of the majority."[2]

The Benefits and Limitations of Panopticon City

We live in an era where the technology and means to monitor movements and life activities seem to be growing exponentially. There are benefits to this, of course, but there are also concerns and worries.

This is certainly not a new debate, as the idea of the panopticon goes back to the late 1700s and the ideas of utilitarian philosopher Jeremy Bentham. Bentham's panopticon was a prison with a circular design (though he saw it as a useful tool for other social structures) with a watchtower in the center. The guards in this prison could easily see and monitor the prison cells, but the prisoners could not tell if they were being seen. Bentham saw it as a design that could efficiently allow the monitoring and control of a prison and would also induce a kind of self-regulation on the part of prisoners. Prisons were rather nasty environments then, and Bentham thought his ideas would help improve conditions. In a famous quote, Bentham saw the outcomes of the panopticon prison as "morals reformed, health preserved, industry invigorated, instruction diffused, public burdens lightened . . . all by a simple idea in architecture."[3]

Bentham's prison was never built, though a close version was constructed in Cuba in the early twentieth century. But the idea of the panopticon is less a specific design and more a powerful metaphor of our times. CCTV cameras and other monitoring devices in the public realm are the new watchtowers, it can be argued, and the presence of cameras—and their very visibility to the public—is intended in large part to prevent bad behavior in a similar way. Along with the cameras themselves, just in case you didn't notice them, might be a sign alerting you to their presence, as if to say "Don't break that window or spray paint that wall, because you are being watched." Whether this psychology works is an open question, and whether the proliferation of cameras and other monitoring devices represents a worrisome infringement on privacy is also up for debate.

In my own city of Charlottesville, we considered for a decade or so the merits of installing a system of cameras along the Downtown Mall, a public pedestrian mall and the location of Main Street. The proposal morphed and changed and has not been without controversy. The initial estimates of the costs of installing cameras were deemed by some to be just too high. But the cameras are being installed, with four blocks of the Downtown Mall finished (and seven cameras installed). We have at least made a (somewhat) public decision to trade some of our privacy as a community—when we are enjoying a walk on the Downtown Mall or eating at an outdoor restaurant—for the benefits that such monitoring can provide.

Charlottesville is certainly not alone, as many cities around the country have been installing similar systems and then some. New York, a much larger city, has invested heavily in cameras and a comprehensive video monitoring system, aimed especially at larger public spaces, including in the Financial District in Lower Manhattan. Called the Domain Awareness System, it was developed by the city in collaboration with Microsoft (and as a result, the city reaps 30 percent of the profit from the sale of the system to other cities). This extensive network of public and private cameras—some 9,000 in all—is partly justified as an antiterrorist system and includes the collection of license plate numbers and radiation-detection devices.[4]

In Charlottesville, the camera proposal set off a series of objections, notably around First Amendment protections, from the local Rutherford Institute and its president, John Whitehead. "Imagining a camera trained on the free speech monument downtown is pretty scary," Whitehead says in the Charlottesville *Daily Progress*. "There's a lot of free speech that goes on there. . . . Some of it is pretty bad speech, but it's free and cameras would inhibit that speech."[5]

We can be recorded doing things that are embarrassing or worse, Whitehead warns. "Cameras record everything. They record people coming out of a psychologist's office and other places, and we don't want a permanent record available for review of someone coming from an [Alcoholics Anonymous] meeting." It turns us all into suspects, Whitehead fears.

The First Amendment monument is a unique element on the Downtown Mall—essentially a two-sided chalkboard where residents and visitors are encouraged to express their unfiltered thoughts. And they do, kids and adults alike. Would a nearby camera capturing someone writing something objectionable or inflammatory represent a serious infringement on personal privacy? It is not clear, but it would seem possible to address this specific concern by placing cameras in ways that might avoid the wall.

But the larger fear seems to be that the presence of cameras will alter behavior, and not in socially positive or constructive ways. Whitehead raises the specter of "lip-reading software" that might allow someone to listen in on a personal conversation ("People will be very careful about what they say in public spaces"), and he, like many others, believes the proliferation of cameras watching our every move will have a kind of "chilling effect."[6]

Proponents of the cameras on the Downtown Mall (or those installed in New York) will argue that the safety and crime-reduction benefits will more than outweigh privacy concerns. In 2014, Charlottesville endured a gut-wrenching demonstration of these benefits when University of Virginia student Hannah Graham went missing. Tragically, she was found dead, and police were able to piece together her movements on the evening she went missing, and eventually catch the killer, by accessing store security cameras. I think my own personal view of security cameras changed markedly that evening, seeing a small loss of privacy as a small price to pay in finding a killer, likely preventing a future attack, and making the larger city safer as a result.

But of course, the city is increasingly filled with new monitoring devices of various kinds, found in places expected and unexpected. It may be increasingly difficult to "see" these devices, though at an intellectual level we probably realize they are there. In an era of seemingly nonstop delivery of goods to our doorsteps and porches, there are countless stories about "porch pirates" appearing on the local news, accompanied by video imagery collected from doorbell cameras. Sometimes it feels like we are actively monitoring spaces in potentially intrusive ways. The rise in the number of homes that have installed Ring doorbell cameras raises questions about how we collect and share images of those who may innocently knock on a door or place a package on a porch.

Recently, a local candidate running for the Virginia Senate was caught taking away his opponent's campaign literature and replacing it with his own.[7] He was caught on a Ring camera and "outed" as a result, and the story made the local news, with the opposing side expressing due indignation. The candidate apologized publicly: "I'm not proud of it," he said, attributing his "lapse of judgment" in part to frustration over seeing some of his campaign signs damaged.[8] It was an embarrassing incident to be sure, and not good judgment on the candidate's part, but perhaps also not deserving of the public shaming that resulted.

Undoubtedly, Ring footage has the potential to capture some behaviors that are especially serious and even criminal, such as the stealing of UPS packages from doorsteps. But the ubiquity of these videos also raises a cautionary note.

Monitoring for Safety:
From Red-Light Cameras to Facial Recognition

Police and traffic safety advocates understandably seek to use some of this technology to reduce loss of life or injury from car accidents. Having witnessed firsthand a fatal intersection accident resulting from someone running a red light, using deterrents such as red-light cameras seems to me to be a valuable goal and a valid use of a surveillance technology.

Yet the use of red-light cameras has generated significant controversy throughout the country, with some eight state legislatures passing laws prohibiting local governments from using them. Those expressing opposition seem perturbed for several key reasons: one argument is that their use is unconstitutional because they simply assume a driver is guilty, sending a ticket in the mail (to be paid). There is no presumption of innocence and no ability to "confront one's accuser."

Some objections seem primarily aimed at a concern about the reach of government, and in some cases it appears the strongest opponents have personal histories of speeding. The latter include a prominent New York state senator

(Martin J. Golden), representing Brooklyn, who himself had been caught speeding on camera numerous times.[9] Opposition to these cameras has led to a tug-of-war between the state and the city of New York, and for a time the city lost authorization for the cameras, though they are now back in use.

The opposition to red-light cameras appears to fly in the face of most of the evidence that concludes they help make cities safer. Research by the Insurance Institute of Highway Safety, for example, concludes that "red light cameras are an effective way to discourage red light running."[10] And there are some 500 cities around the country using them. It is true that in some cities their use has led to an increase in rear-ending accidents, but even where this seems to be the case, it is worth noting that such accidents are less dangerous than those that can result from running a red light.

The Insurance Institute of Highway Safety has this to say about privacy concerns: "Cameras don't violate privacy. Driving is a regulated activity, and people who obtain licenses are agreeing to abide by certain rules. Red light cameras are a way to catch people who break those rules, just like traditional enforcement."[11]

The Rise of Facial Recognition and Artificial Intelligence

Facial recognition technology is perhaps the newest technology being tested and applied, famously as an instrument of oppression in China. It is at once one of the potentially most useful applications of artificial intelligence, or AI, and one of the most troubling. It is already commonly used in the United States in airports and ports of entry, and the technology has been available as a security feature on iPhones for several years. But its widespread use raises serious concerns, especially about the ways it might permit the government to track the movements and behaviors of citizens.

Because of these significant ethical concerns, some local governments have taken steps to curtail its use. In May 2019, San Francisco became the first locality in the nation to ban the use of facial recognition technology, including by the police department, with supporters of the ordinance arguing that this perceived center of the tech world had a special duty to take action. ACLU representatives came out strongly in support of the ban, with Matt Cagle quoted as fearing the technology's "unprecedented power to track people going about their daily lives" and noting that the technology is "incompatible with a healthy democracy."[12] Other large cities, including Boston and Oakland, have enacted similar bans. There is precedent to worry about the sinister ways the government might use such technologies: Veena Dubal points to the "nefarious surveillance activities" of the FBI in the 1950s and '60s aimed at undermining the nation's civil rights movement.[13]

Others have been more critical of the San Francisco's rush to ban a technology that may prove important in police work and crime prevention; perhaps a more temporary moratorium on its use would make sense. One very important concern is that there is evidence (from an MIT study) that the technology is inherently less effective in identifying faces of color, with the serious worry that widespread application of the technology would disproportionately impact citizens of color. Perhaps the technology will improve (it likely will), but for the time being it seems the prudent path to limit its use, as San Francisco and other cities are doing.

Facial recognition is one of the most ubiquitous applications of AI. It relies on a potentially limitless sourcing of facial imagery as well as complex algorithms and machine learning. We are now in a period of rapid rise in the use of AI, and there will be a growing number of instances where worries about privacy will need to be carefully balanced against public safety and other collective benefits. AI may help us better synchronize the flow of traffic in a city, for example, perhaps leading to fewer accidents and faster travel times—but it would first need to collect and analyze the individual movement patterns of thousands of motorists, which is a worry to some. The harvesting of cell phone data and cell tower pings to track and predict movement might be useful to local government service agencies, and certainly to law enforcement, but at what price to privacy (even when there are assurances that data will be anonymized)?[14] One new application aims to allow schools to identify potential shooters as they approach a school building by analyzing shapes and movements that can signal threatening actors.[15] But the price may be near-constant monitoring and surveillance of people around schoolyards and school entrances. Ethical cities will have an increasing role in managing the risks to privacy and collective trust that these AI applications present, as well as in judging when the risks and downsides are outweighed by the benefits. Cities are beginning to do this. An example is the newly released AI Action Plan for the City of New York, meant to allow the city to "carefully evaluate AI tools and associated risks, help city government employees build AI knowledge and skills, and support the responsible implementation of these technologies to improve quality of life for New Yorkers."[16]

Rethinking Our Zone(s) of Privacy in Cities

It is an established principle of constitutional law that in American society there are "zones of privacy" that must be beyond the reach of societal or commercial intrusion. Cameras are not allowed by law in many states (such as New York) in bathrooms or changing rooms, for example. In such places it is understood that there is a "reasonable expectation of privacy."

The emergence of new technologies such as drones has also raised serious questions about this expectation of privacy and the extent of the zone of privacy. Drones are now quite commonly used in selling real estate, for instance, as agents and others marketing houses and apartments want to capture and present the best shots of those properties. It is certainly a good practice that many drone operators follow to knock on neighborhood doors in the vicinity of where a drone will be used and to let residents know what is going on.

Controversy has surrounded drones in a number of cities, with people worrying about drones appearing at window level, compromising residents' privacy. Drones are increasingly suspected of being "peeping drones," with calls for greater regulation and scrutiny of their use.

Conclusions

Privacy and surveillance represent major ethical issues for cities. On the one hand, many of the ways that cities surveil and monitor—for instance through deploying cameras along streets and in public spaces—are standard and can do much to advance community safety. In such cases it seems that a nominal loss of privacy is more than compensated for by an increase in safety. But not everyone agrees, and the emergence of new technologies such as facial recognition raises many more difficult questions and has already been shown to treat people of different ethnicities differently. Especially worrisome is the rapid rise in use of drones by police departments, now in many cities serving as first responders to 911 calls and raising the possibility of near-constant surveillance and monitoring.[17]

Discussion Questions

Have cities gone too far in deploying networks of cameras along streets and in public spaces? Are we sacrificing too much of our privacy as a result? Or on the other hand, is this just what is necessary to ensure public safety and solve crimes more effectively?

What do you think about the concept of "zones of privacy"? Do we need to adjust these zones, either by expanding or curtailing areas where privacy is protected?

Should we worry about future technology making it harder and harder to protect our privacy?

What are some of the key ethical questions and concerns raised by the rapid emergence of artificial intelligence (AI), and what might cities be expected to do about them?

A City's Obligations to the Future

Decisions in and about cities always have a temporal dimension, though the time frame is usually short. Decisions occur in the contexts of annual budgets and instruments such as capital improvement programs that may last three to five years. Even a city's comprehensive or master plan (or general plan in California) typically spans only twenty or thirty years.

Cities (in contrast) have existed for 12,000 years or longer and will exist for thousands of years into the future. So it is surprising that there have been such meager attempts to broaden our planning and decision time frames. We largely think, and plan, in these shorter, perhaps more manageable time frames—but it is now time to challenge cities to drastically extend their temporal horizons. Indeed, an ethical city requires it.

From a philosophical vantage, an initial question is whether and how much we actually care about the future. Here a famous philosophical thought experiment is highly valuable and leads to some surprising conclusions about how important the future seems to us. Philosopher Samuel Scheffler asks: What if we lived a full life but knew that upon our death an asteroid would hit our planet, wiping out all life? Would such knowledge depress us and make us sad? Would the knowledge of this impending end of what Scheffler calls the "collective afterlife" influence the way we live our life?[1] The thought experiment, he believes, shows that we do deeply care about the future, about the continuation of life even after we die. I believe this, too, and that meaning and purpose in life depend in large part on the knowledge and reassurance that life will continue and that the deeds and work we engage in today will have meaning and import later, when we are no longer living. The collective afterlife matters psychologically and morally, and it matters to how we plan, design, and manage cities.

The future clearly matters to many of us, and there is quite a lot of it left. Thinking in human terms, most of the development of our civilization, the things we are perhaps proudest of as a species, have occurred in a geological microsecond, just a few thousand years in the more than 4 billion–year history of our planet. Most of our history is yet to be lived or made; there is a vast stock of time left, which will be influenced by the decisions cities make, if we consider the longevity of the sun, which sustains life. Most estimates suggest that the hydrogen fuel that supports the fusion of the sun will last at least another 5 billion years, though over time the sun will become brighter and life on Earth eventually impossible.[2] That's not likely to happen for another billion years, though there are some estimates that we are due for a devastating asteroid sooner (of the sort that caused the extinction of the dinosaurs 66 million years ago). A billion years is a long time; even 50 or 60 million years is practically an infinity. Yet the point is that the implications of our actions today can impact an incredibly expansive future; there is an incredible bucket of time remaining on the human clock and an unparalleled responsibility to ensure it is used wisely.

Longer-term thinking has (thankfully) been receiving more attention from theorists and practitioners alike. Geologist Marcia Bjornerud wrote a wonderful book on behalf of what she calls "timefulness" (which is also the title of the book).[3] As a geologist she is especially critical of just how little humans seem to know about deeper time. We are largely "time illiterate," she says, with implications for how effectively we manage the planet. "Like inexperienced but overconfident drivers, we accelerate into landscapes and ecosystems with no sense of their long-established traffic patterns, and then react with surprise and indignation when we face the penalties for ignoring natural laws."[4]

"Time denial," Bjornerud says, is built into a lot of our contemporary institutions and decision methods. Short-term consumption of resources is economically rewarded and even conflated with citizenship, she notes. Our prevailing economic reasoning and methods tend to tilt in the direction of the present—we prefer benefits that can be reaped and enjoyed as close as possible to the present; we prefer costs that can be postponed and delayed until a later point in time. The method of benefit-cost analysis explicitly seeks to convert economic values into "present value," and this practice of discounting, though rarely questioned, reflects a morally dubious view of the future.

Our political systems, moreover, are geared to reward politicians for short-term accomplishments and specifically tangible, physical achievements, such as building a new library or improving the quality of streets and public transit, all important undertakings. Rarely, though, are there rewards for a decision not to build something or for sustained efforts at conserving landscapes, nature, or biodiversity. These are on the list of the many things that elected officials work on that are harder to see, explain, or show as achievements to constituents choosing between different candidates.

Roman Krznaric's wonderful book *The Good Ancestor: A Radical Prescription for Long-Term Thinking* is a reference guide for how we might do it differently.[5] Even more sharply critical of our "pathological short-termism," Krznaric minces no words in condemning our moral failure to consider the interest and well-being of the "silent majority" who will occupy our world, and our cities, in generations to come.[6] "We have colonized the future," he writes, and "we treat the future like a distant colonial outpost devoid of people, where we can freely dump ecological degradation, technological risk, and nuclear waste, and which we can plunder as we please."[7]

Toward Timeful Cities

One goal that both Bjornerud and Krznaric advocate is enhancing our ability as a society (and as cities) to think and act longer-term. What Bjornerud calls "timefulness" she defines as "a feeling for distances and proximities in the geography of deep time." We can (and she does) live our present lives with an abiding awareness of how deep time has influenced the present, and to her that is a reassurance that comes from understanding that we live on a "very old, durable planet." It is also the basis for a shared global existence—we are all products of and dependent on this ancient planet, and we together share this "common heritage of geology."[8]

Ethical cities must acknowledge that there are many ways in which decisions today, whether building a highway or filling a wetland, will hamper or diminish life or otherwise negatively impact those living in the future. Equally true, there are many actions—investments in ecological restoration or in preservation of cultural resources—that require a long-term perspective and vantage point to guide and justify them.

Cultivating "time literacy" is an important goal for cities. This might involve, for instance, curricular changes that require kids in public schools to more fully understand the deeper geologic and ecologic histories of the bioregions in which they are situated. Developing (or rediscovering) rituals and urban practices that connect us to the past is another possibility on the way to developing "a new relationship with time," as Bjornerud notes.[9] Consider as one example the Mexican holiday of All Saints Day, which is mostly about making room to remember the important people who were once in our lives and to express gratitude and thanks.

> **Sidebar 8-1 Krznaric's Six Ways to Think Long**
>
> Deep-time humility   Cathedral thinking
> Legacy mindset   Holistic forecasting
> Intergenerational justice Transcendent goal
>
> Source: Roman Krznaric, *The Good Ancestor: A Radical Prescription for Long-Term Thinking* (New York: Experiment, 2020).

Failure to understand the true extent of change in a city is often the result of not assuming a long enough time frame. Fisheries scientist Daniel Pauly of the University of British Columbia coined the term *shifting baseline syndrome* to describe the phenomenon of each generation judging change by the conditions they know and circumstances they experience firsthand. Change that occurs over a single lifetime, while lasting and serious, may mask the much larger long-term changes that are occurring. As Pauly says in a popular TED Talk, "We transform the world, but we don't remember it."[10]

Krznaric rightly argues that we need to spend more time cultivating our long-term thinking skills. He offers an especially helpful set of six ways to think long-term (summarized in sidebar 8-1). These include deep-time humility, legacy mindset, intergenerational justice, cathedral thinking, holistic forecasting, and transcendent goal.

City planning departments represent the function of local governments that has perhaps the most explicitly to do with time and is in the best position to apply these new ways of "thinking long." However, the standard future-looking document, meant to guide the physical and social development of a city, is the comprehensive plan, which rarely takes the long view! That may be changing in many parts of the country, especially in coastal settings, where it is increasingly relevant to reflect on and strategize about the impacts of climate change and the effects of sea level rise.

Design and Planning for a Longer Time Frame

Few things in life are as vexing as time. For city officials and planners, time, and things that can and will happen in the future, is of paramount consideration. The temporal dimensions of city policy and planning raise serious ethical quandaries, such as how much of the future to take into account. Should officials consider the ways in which actions or decisions today may impact life in, say, 100 years? Or should our time frame be longer (say, 1,000 years or longer still) or, alternatively, shorter, recognizing the inherent limits in predicting what citizens will want and need in the future?

As Alexander Rose of the Long Now Foundation told me, the span of our thinking and planning ought to be much longer: "Both the last 10,000 years and the next 10,000 years. . . . We're placing ourselves in the middle of the story rather than at the end of a story." One key idea is that we must be ever cognizant of actions that will limit choices in the future. This is the principle of keeping options open and avoiding actions that will close future society avenues. We ought to avoid irreversible steps or outcomes (think extinction of a species or destruction of a complex ecosystem such as a coral reef).

"Fundamentally, if you're making choices that limit future generations' choices, you are making the wrong choices. If you're making choices that increase those choices, you're making the right choices," says Rose.[11] The Iroquois federation famously applied a seventh-generation principle—considering the impact of every decision on the seventh generation. If we think of a generation as thirty years, that rule provides a planning horizon of roughly 200 years—much longer than most cities currently think about or plan for but perhaps a more practical time frame to embrace.

One of the key ethical considerations is what moral status future inhabitants will have. Some ethicists say that because these people don't yet exist and don't have faces and names, they are not part of our moral community and thus not entitled to moral consideration in decision-making. This seems contrary to what an ethical city should be. And it denies several key assumptions about the future. One is that it is undeniable that our actions and decisions today will affect the quality of life and livability of cities and the planet for people in the future. And second, while we may not understand exactly what the wishes and desires of future residents will be, we can be fairly confident that they will want most of the things current humans want: clean air, a safe environment, shelter, food, and security.

Thinking in deeper time will also help us tackle environmental and societal problems that will require much longer time frames to achieve. Restoring ecosystems, for instance, or, say, fully replenishing global fisheries are ambitious goals for the future that will require concerted investments and actions over a long time frame. One example is Zealandia, an ecosanctuary in the heart of Wellington, New Zealand's capital city. Here, a predator-proof fence has been erected around a wild zone, with the goal of allowing native species, birds especially, to rebound that have been devastated by introduced, nonnative species. The stated goal is to "create self-sustaining ecosystems representative of the pre-human state that existed in New Zealand approximately 1,000 years ago."[12] This is a bold vision of restoration that is expected to take 500 years to achieve—and will require growing the large trees, such as the rata, that made up the canopy of this forest.

Cities are duty bound as well to invest in the civic infrastructures necessary to sustain livable and just places: from libraries and courthouses to walkable streets and social infrastructure, cities must pass along a built environment that is healthy and uplifting.[13] City infrastructure could be designed with longer time frames in mind. Renzo Piano is designing a new bridge for Genoa, Italy, his home city, to replace a viaduct that collapsed in 2018, killing forty-three people. In light of this failure, Piano is taking the approach of designing something that will be safe for a long time. He says: "It will be a beautiful bridge. One that will last one thousand years."[14] Efforts to design for longevity and durability are rare indeed.

A notable example of longer-term thinking can be seen in Norfolk, Virginia, which has adopted an impressive document called *Vision 2100*, a strategic plan for how the city will comprehensively adapt to a future with much more flooding and sea level rise.[15] This document is unusual because of its longer time frame—about eighty years but suitably pegged to estimates of sea level rise by the year 2100. There is already a lot of so-called sunny-day flooding in that city, and virtually no one there is in denial about climate change. The estimates for the future are daunting—predictions are that the city will likely see a meter of sea level rise by 2050 and around two meters (around six feet) by 2100. This is a real and serious threat to the future of this city, but not an unusual one today, as many cities in the coastal United States and around the world face a similar future. How Norfolk was able to engage its population to think about the future 100 years down the road is interesting and instructive. One lesson that Norfolk planning director George Homewood notes is that longer-term thinking may actually free us from some of the immediate biases and concerns about whether and how a law or policy change might impact us and our friends and neighbors.

Gifts a City Gives the Future

A legacy mindset advocate is someone who sees the value of passing on gifts from one generation to the next, and so much of what we do in planning, whether it's protecting biodiversity, setting aside large expanses of nature, or investing in social infrastructure such as a library or a network of low-carbon rail service, can and ought to be appreciated as legacies we leave, gifts we bequeath. Those living today, Krznaric reminds us, benefit from many such gifts given by people in the past.

Passing along such gifts is also a matter of intergenerational justice—the idea that we are duty bound to consider the rights and interests of those living in the future, especially on a planet as rich and flourishing as the one we have inherited. We should acknowledge that there is a kind of intergenerational golden rule, Krznaric suggests. And invoking John Rawls's "veil of ignorance," discussed in an earlier chapter, it is only fair for us to resist acting in ways that overly favor the current generations. As Rawls's framework implies (though he did not specifically address ethical duties to the future in his seminal book *A Theory of Justice*), putting on the "veil of ignorance" and thereby neutralizing potentially biasing information about which generation we are a member of would lead to much greater fairness in our deliberations about the future, since we wouldn't know whether we'd be alive at a specific point in time. Successful cities may already be defined by the legacies they leave behind; this is certainly true for mayors and others who have the chance to shape cities. It is a natural human tendency to want to leave a mark, to leave behind evidence of good works, and ideally to create a world (and a city) better than the one we inherited.

Krznaric speaks of the importance of gifts and gift-giving. We all benefit from the sacrifices previous generations have made and from the many gifts passed down from earlier times. This is certainly the case with cities: walk around any favorite city and you will understand that the things that make that city special, distinctive, and livable—parks, libraries, efficient transit systems—are all the result of investments and decisions made many years ago. The spatial layout of a city, its orientation, and the way it embraces topography, nature, and water are the result of many decisions made in the past. They are not always the best decisions, but they are often the result of many thoughtful and dedicated citizens, leaders, and organizations thinking and working on behalf of a larger good.

An ethical city, then, is a city that contemplates what it can and should leave to the future, what gifts it can pass along that will be loved and enjoyed by those not yet alive today. It should equally consider what problems can be solved today so they don't get heaped onto a future city and future residents who had no voice in the matter. An ethical city also nudges, supports, and encourages its citizens to do what they can to think and act in the longer term and to see what commitments to the future they can follow through on, what gifts for the future they can be inspired to leave.

I am often on the lookout for examples of cities that have taken steps and made choices with the longer term in mind. There are many good examples that cities can be proud of. Phoenix, Arizona, might seem like an unlikely example, but as anyone who lives there or has had the chance to visit knows, it is a city defined by the beauty of its desert and by the remarkable set of desert parks that have been set aside. These are not parks in the typical sense but large slices of remnant desert, largely unchanged over hundreds of years.

A case in point is South Mountain Park. The city was given the chance to buy the 14,000 acres from the federal government in 1924. At the time, it was a considerable distance from the city. Yet the city council took an action—creating this "pleasure resort for Phoenix," as it was referred to in news coverage—that 100 years later continues to deliver unusual benefits and value to current residents. And the precedent, in turn, has likely inspired efforts to set even more acreage aside (for example, the now 20,000-plus-acre Sonoran Desert Preserve in the adjacent city of Scottsdale).

Historic preservation in cities is another example of longer-term thinking and an opportunity to pass along buildings and landscapes that will be cherished for the history and perspective they provide. Saving a building often seems to turn on what we think of the beauty, aesthetics, or unique nature of the architecture rather than an explicit desire to preserve windows into the past.

Cathedral Thinking

Another of Krznaric's ways to think long is cathedral thinking: What big projects, big ideas, and big and important initiatives and challenges could the current generation take on, or at least begin, to make the future a profoundly better place in which to live? He provides a list of various examples of cathedral thinking in his book. These examples are provocative and at times curious, from an actual cathedral, Antoni Gaudi's still-unfinished Sagrada Familia in Barcelona, to public policies such as the New Deal; social movements such as the suffragettes; and planning and urban design concepts such as Hausmann's plan for Paris and Brasilia, Brazil's new capital built in the 1950s.

All of these projects took time and immense resources and energy to complete, and Krznaric admits that not all examples of cathedral thinking will be positive or viewed as successes by future residents. Years ago I had the chance to tour Brasilia, and while some of the architecture is wonderful, overall it is a sprawling, car-centric vision of a modern city that has not aged well.

Let's hope that we can invest in "cathedrals" that we have confidence will lead to profoundly better futures; we do seem to be faced today with so many cathedral-like and daunting challenges. What would be on our list for ethical cities? An end to systemic racism and conditions of spatial equality? A halt to climate change and the sixth extinction? Planetary restoration? Truly nature-immersive cities? There are many projects that cities with a long-term commitment can and should embark on, even if the fruits of this work will be enjoyed only or mostly by people living in the future.

The San Francisco Bay Area provides a series of examples of cathedral thinking in action. Some of them have to do with confronting and addressing climate change challenges, as the projections for future sea level rise there are daunting. Most impressive are the steps this urban region has taken to restore the wetlands and marshes around the bay. Most of the history of San Francisco has been related to degradation and loss—some 90 percent of the Bay Area's tidal wetlands have been lost to a combination of urban development, flood levees, and industrial salt production. But there are efforts underway to restore these wetlands, and in 2016, voters of the nine-county Bay Area overwhelmingly approved Measure AA, which created for the first time a climate parcel tax that will fund restoration. These wetlands are essential habitats, especially for birds, and are an important element in preparing for and mitigating the effects of sea level rise. One project receiving funding is the South Bay Salt Pond Restoration Project—which will restore more than 15,000 acres of "industrial salt ponds" and convert them to "a rich mosaic of tidal wetlands and other habitats." These are important bird habitats and key stopping points along the Pacific Flyway.

There is a specific nod to future generations in the criteria used by the San Francisco Bay Restoration Authority to make project allocations: "Priority is given to projects that . . . have the greatest positive impact on the Bay as a whole, in terms of clean water, wildlife habitat and beneficial use to Bay Area residents [and] have the greatest long-term impact on the Bay, *to benefit future generations*" (emphasis added).[16]

Growing up in Alexandria, Virginia, in the shadow of Washington, DC, I watched the region transform its transportation and mobility system by investing in an underground metro. It was a large and hugely complex undertaking, financially, politically, and from a design and engineering perspective. It is hard for some to believe there was a time not that long ago when Washington's metro did not exist. When planning began in earnest, I was a mere twelve-year-old, and by the time it opened in 1976 I was a student in college. The system provides remarkable access to a region where many can do without cars. A ridership of more than 600,000 per day (before the pandemic) illustrates how important the system is, and it has helped transform intensive development patterns along its routes. The system now includes 103 miles of rail line serving ninety-one stations, and while it has taken nearly half a century, the newly built Silver Line now reaches Dulles Airport.

But it is easy to forget just how audacious the metro system plan was— an engineering marvel and a huge challenge of how to build an underground metro in an already developed city. The deep tunneling and excavation and the steep escalators in the deeper stations are truly remarkable, as are the unique station designs. The cost to build the metro far exceeded estimates (eventually rising to $10 billion from the original projection of less than $2 billion).

Another example is San Antonio's effort to save the world's largest colony of Mexican free-tailed bats. In 2014, a proposed 4,500-unit housing project created a potential conflict with the bats at Bracken Cave, where 15 million to 20 million bats roost each summer. Each evening, they fly out of the cave in large numbers to feed, a process that takes three to four hours. It is a spectacle, and the Bracken Cave bat colony has likely existed for 10,000 years. Thanks to leadership from the city, which included then mayor Julián Castro and councilman (now mayor) Ron Nirenberg, a public-private coalition was formed to develop a plan and a funding strategy to buy out the project. The Nature Conservancy and Bat Conservation International were key partners in the plan and in coming up with the $20 million needed to purchase the 1,521-acre parcel.

Protecting the San Antonio bats is an example of a tremendous future-transformative action, though one that was accomplished in a roughly twenty-one-month time frame. There is undoubtedly more to do to ensure the bats' survival, but it shows that some conservation goals can be achieved even in short time frames: a cathedral outcome but not necessarily a cathedral timeline.

The Presence of Deeper Time in Cities

There is considerable value in being reminded that today's actions, individually important and cumulatively significant, can and do affect the distant future in profound ways. We have a moral duty to consider the interests of future generations, and visual and other reminders help us do that.

Natural features are some of the oldest things around us in cities, and trees are some of the oldest living organisms. We are already naturally drawn to trees—they affect us in deep ways, and we appreciate their beauty and grandeur. Many are hundreds of years old, and their age means they span multiple human generations and are a good example of community timekeepers. There are community and family stories and memories attached to many trees, and therefore they are also markers or reminders of a deeper historical record. Large older trees help maintain a visual reference to the past, and celebrating their age can help foster an attitude of timefulness. The conscious act of protecting older trees in cities helps cultivate and strengthen a culture of deep time.

In the words of English professor and nature writer James Canton in his book *The Oak Papers*, "You can stand beneath a grand oak and know that your more distant ancestors did so too. Oaks hold onto the memories of earlier generations. By touching the skin of the oak it is possible to feel some tentative trace of those that have gone before."[17] Such large, older trees evoke a sense of reverence and wisdom and deep time constancy that lends itself to reflections and memories.

Ensuring the protection of ancient trees, especially in cities, is a challenge, as local tree protection codes, if they exist at all, are often relatively weak. Increasingly, we recognize that cities have ethical responsibilities to protect and preserve these majestic trees as part of the essential natural heritage that must be passed along.

Buildings can make deeper time visible as well. In historic districts, older structures often sport a clearly visible date on their facades from when they were constructed. In the city where I live, there is the former Peoples Bank building constructed in 1875, and the exterior of Fargo Bank indicates its construction was in 1920. And there are many buildings, such as the Hardware Store building, that tell visitors and pedestrians (through its exterior signage and through its very name) what the original use of the building was. Perhaps architectural style is a sufficient indicator of the age of a building, but most of us are not architectural historians, so the clear date on a facade is helpful and adds special interest and meaning to the buildings around us. More recent buildings seem lack such clear and visible "time stamps," which is a shame and will make it harder, perhaps, for future occupants of the city to decipher and understand the city in a deeper, temporal way.

A culture of deeper time can also evolve, Krznaric argues, through art, music, and literature. A powerful example is the Future Library, a project in Oslo, Norway, that commissions an original book each year for 100 years, until 2114, at which point all the books will be printed on paper from trees planted specifically for this purpose.

How Can Future Generations Be Represented in City Decision-Making?

It becomes important to consider how we give real voice to those who do not yet live in our city or who perhaps are not even born yet. Do they have rights and any kind of moral status in the planning and decisions we undertake today? And how, as a practical matter, do we give future generations a voice in city decisions and design?

Wales has addressed this by creating the position of future generations commissioner through the passage of the Wales Well-Being of Future Generations Act of 2015. The act laid out a set of seven well-being goals and created a "well-being duty," requiring local authorities and other specific government bodies to indicate how they would achieve or reach these goals. The act required agency ministers to set national indicators and to publish an annual report showing progress made toward them. One of the most interesting and impactful results of the act was the creation of the future generations commissioner position, who is to "act as a guardian for the interests of future generations in Wales, and to support the public bodies listed in the Act to work towards achieving the wellbeing goals."

The commissioner can offer advice and recommendations to governments (which they must make reasonable efforts to follow), can conduct his or her own research, and can undertake policy and project reviews. The position has already had significant impacts and has changed the conversation in a number of ways. For instance, the commissioner had a major voice in a debate about expanding highways in Wales, specifically the M4 freeway. Sophie Howe, the inaugural future generations commissioner, did not mince words about this decision being shortsighted and antithetical to the purposes of the act she guided. "Building roads is an old-fashioned solution to addressing congestion and we should instead be seeking to invest in better public transport which would be a more useful solution for the 25% of Welsh families who have no access to a car whilst also supporting the obligations we have to reduce our carbon footprint."[18]

In June 2021, the Welsh government announced it was halting all road projects in the country, a bold step aimed at helping to reach greenhouse gas emission targets and undoubtedly influenced by the report of the future generations commissioner. Without a longer time frame, we fail to see the true extent to which important changes have occurred, most notably when it comes to diminution and degradation of the natural environments and ecosystems in which cities are embedded.

One of the most compelling and promising ideas for better representing future generations in city decision-making is the future design movement in Japan, which has devised new and creative processes for citizens to serve as surrogate representatives of the future and engage in negotiation and consensus-building with other citizens representing the present. One such process took place in Yahaba around devising a vision for the future of this town in 2060. This type of citizen assembly is happening more frequently and shows how giving the future an explicit voice helps change priorities and outcomes, leading to a consensus that includes more of the ideas and visions being advocated by the future group.[19]

Conclusions

There are few things that cities can do that will have a greater impact than making investments—ecological, social, and economic—in the future. This is a key premise in the field of urban planning: taking many steps today with the health and flourishing of future generations in mind. In this chapter I have attempted to sketch out some of the main (and compelling) ethical and moral reasons for why we have duties to the future and the many things that cities can do to acknowledge and give tangible expression to these duties. Taking the steps necessary to address (and potentially solve) climate change seems to be an especially pressing duty, as does generally maintaining the inhabitability of our planet; here cities have an essential role to play.

There are many ways that cities can engage in cathedral thinking and invest in the next generation of "cathedrals"—those immense and difficult tasks that may involve bringing native birds back from the brink of extinction, restoring large ecosystems, or protecting in perpetuity large and important natural systems that will sustain future populations (ecologically and emotionally). An ethical challenge for cities will be to make the future visible and front of mind. This can happen in many ways, but sharing our cities with ancient trees and working to preserve buildings and landscapes that reach across generations will need to be part of the answer.

Discussion Questions

Are future generations members of our moral community, and are we duty bound to take their interests into account when making decisions today?

In what ways could cities actively work on behalf of the future? What kinds of city decisions will have the most impact (positive or negative) on the future?

How can cities best incorporate the perspectives and voices of future generations into the decision processes of modern cities today? Should every city appoint a future generation commissioner or councillor?

What happens when the interests of future generations clash or conflict with important goals of the present generation, for instance the desire to eliminate poverty or to provide every current resident with affordable housing?

The Ethics of Local Democracy and the Need for Fair and Shared Governance

An ethical city is a democratic city, where every person has the chance to vote and to participate equally in the political and civic life of the city. Increasingly we recognize that citizens ought to have the chance to participate directly in the governance, design, and decision-making that happens in a city.

How can citizens be given a more direct voice and more direct control over some or all of the decisions made in a city? The encouraging news is that there are now many specific tools, ideas, and initiatives in use in cities today to ensure more democratic outcomes and the inclusion and engagement of all citizens.

"The open city is a demanding place. . . . Getting people to agree is hard work," says sociologist Richard Sennett.[1] But when we actually engage citizens, it is often through very imperfect means; they are given the chance to express their opinions through a three-minute open mic at the beginning of a city council meeting, for example, or by writing a letter, making a call, or responding to an online survey. And it may often seem that elected representatives are not following the larger will of the people but are motivated more by greed or ambition, swayed especially by the donations of the wealthy few. There are often conflicts of interest, real or perceived, that taint the fairness of the decisions that result.

Fair and Ethical Representation

Determining how city councillors and mayors (and other elected or appointed representatives) are elected, and the ethical standards we hold them to, is a good place to start. A big part of the equity and ethics of city decisions revolves around creating conditions for fair representation. This means fairness in the electoral process: maximizing the opportunity for citizens to vote and ensuring that elections are fair.

From an elected official's point of view, there will always be dilemmas in how to vote and how to act in his or her official capacity, and it is hard to minimize the ethical judgment that elected officials must engage in. There are competing notions of representation, for example. An elected official may feel that the ethically correct decision is not the popular option, perhaps because it affects future residents or future generations or residents of adjoining or nearby communities, and thus people who have no formal way to participate. In the presence of an angry and vocal group of citizens who have come to oppose, say, a proposed affordable housing project or a (needed) increase in taxes, it may be hard for elected officials to do anything other than vote as the crowd insists. But the more ethical position may be to support an important principle or an underheard voice or constituency. Not all ethical decisions are popular decisions.

And listening to constituents at a public hearing or city council meeting may also give an inaccurate picture of the true views of citizens. Studies show that attendees tend to be older and white. Setting meetings at times of day that make it difficult for working parents to attend without providing childcare services or adequate transportation to get them there means that meetings will be skewed in their representation. These are good reasons to look for more effective and equitable methods—for instance, by providing day care, shifting meetings to more convenient days and times, and even financially compensating attendees for their participation.

That said, many of the motivations of elected officials may be inappropriate, and often background influences are not transparent or clear to the public. Does an elected official support something because he or she benefits directly (financially or in some other way) or indirectly from it? Conflicts of interest remain a serious problem and a major impediment to ethical decisions. Conflicts of interest arise when one is in a position to take an action (e.g., vote on a proposed development project) that would provide direct or personal benefit. Members of a city council or a planning board have a moral, and often legal, duty to recuse themselves from discussions or votes in these situations. Even the appearance of a conflict, most would agree, is to be avoided, as it results in a loss of public trust and the perception that a decision was biased or unduly and unfairly influenced by personal gain.

We also expect our public officials, elected or not, to work primarily for the larger public interest, and when they don't, trust in local governance and democracy suffers. A recent example from Charlottesville, Virginia, is telling. The CEO of the publicly owned and funded transit company Jaunt came under scrutiny for lavish spending on travel and meals. There were trips to Paris, hotel stays at more than $1,000 per night, and meals with expensive bottles of wine. A Freedom of Information Act request uncovered the details, though the press was initially alerted by an anonymous whistleblower report. The CEO defended the expenses as normal and reasonable but later resigned. Technically a private company, Jaunt originally resisted responding to the Freedom of Information Act request, eschewing transparency and further undermining trust.

While this case likely doesn't cross a legal line, it could, as public officials may line their pockets or unreasonably benefit from the perks and benefits of the job. Of course, there are many instances of out-and-out criminality, many more than we care to think. Bribes and payments in exchange for favorable treatment or votes are remarkably common. Examples of this fill the pages of newspapers today.

Our elected officials often do not fully reflect the diversity of their urban constituents. Governance in American cities tends to tilt significantly toward white men, perhaps for obvious reasons. City councils must be more reflective of the constituents they represent. Some of the reforms mentioned above can help, but more active work is needed to ensure that women and minorities are better represented on every committee and board. A new generation of women mayors is encouraging, but more are needed to ensure that dependable political pipelines exist. A 2018 International City/County Management Association survey found that less than 18 percent of chief administrative officials (e.g., city managers) for local governments were women.[2] There can be little doubt that having a more equal representation of women in city government will lead to different planning and policy priorities.

Enfranchised Cities

Cities are (and should be) engines for democracy and inclusion. Cities are today's bulwarks of democracy and the anchors of a counternarrative to the disenfranchisement, gerrymandering, and voter suppression that has characterized much of the recent politics in the United States. Cities can take many steps to further enfranchise their citizens and to further strengthen the values and culture of a healthy democracy.

In the face of active voter disenfranchisement efforts, cities can and should take active steps to empower voters and increase access to, and ability to engage in, active participation in the local political process. Making it easy to register to vote and to actually vote must be a priority of cities. Cities like New York have been early leaders. Through New York's local agency registration program, city agencies are required to provide registration forms to (eligible) residents being served by those agencies. Some cities mandate that landlords distribute voter registration forms to their tenants. High school voter registration and preregistration are other innovative methods. The evidence is convincing that focusing on high school students can be an effective way to increase voting.[3]

There are a number of other steps cities might take to become more democratic. Increasing the number of elected representatives serving on a city council or other governing body is one possible action: with larger councils each council member represents a smaller number of constituents, in theory making it easier for constituent views and priorities to find their way into a decision. The City of Los Angeles is currently debating the merits of such an increase, though there is no consensus yet around this idea.[4] Who gets to vote is another open and contentious question. In some cities in the United States even noncitizens can vote. New York City famously gave its more than 800,000 noncitizens the right to vote in 2021, though this decision was later shot down by the state's supreme court.[5] In some cities, such as San Francisco, noncitizens have been able to vote for school board candidates, though this was recently struck down as unconstitutional as well. Proponents argue that noncitizens, even those in the country illegally, pay taxes, are members of the community, and are entitled to a political say.[6]

Cities can also make an effort to reduce the negative influence of money in campaigns by publicly funding elections and using innovative approaches like Seattle's Democracy Voucher Program, begun in 2015, which distributes coupons to voters, who can then donate them to (and thus help fund) participating candidates who agree to campaign spending limits. Cities are our engines of innovation in so many social and technological arenas, and it will be essential for them to find new, innovative ways to re-enfranchise their residents and thus reinvigorate local politics.

Who gets to vote is another important ethical question. Some people argue that we should actually reduce the voting age, allowing young adults, who have a significant stake in political outcomes, to exert some political influence. Many cities are even changing their voting systems to be more democratic. New York City has become the largest city to shift to a rank-order system for choosing a winning candidate in an election. The advantages of this system are many: such a system more fully accounts for the preferences of voters, overcoming the usual "winner take all" dynamic.

Beyond Pay-to-Play

One of the biggest threats to local democracy is the outsize influence of special interests, especially real estate and development interests that depend on favorable local decisions. These kinds of reforms are difficult even at the local level. A 2017 proposal in Los Angeles to ban contributions from developers with projects before (or that had recently been before) city council failed to garner much support. It has been called "pay-to-play"—the reality that funneling money to politicians and their campaigns is necessary to secure political access and attention—and every city should work to ban or severely limit this practice. As the *Los Angeles Times* opines, this is a hard sell: "Of course, many council members never wanted to move forward with such a ban anyway. Real estate interests are a reliable source of campaign contributions, and elected officials are loath to turn away money they could use not just on their reelection bids, but also on office expenses and trips. Besides, city politicians insist, they *never* let campaign contributions influence their vote on a development."[7]

Denver voters passed a major voter reform package in the November 2018 election, showing what is possible at the local level. Measure 2E (also known as the Democracy for the People proposal) forbids corporations and unions from giving to council campaigns and created a voluntary Fair Elections Fund that provides matching funds for candidates (at a rate of nine to one for contributions up to fifty dollars). Plus, the law created a total per-person cap on candidate donations—$1,000 for mayor and $400 for most city council candidates.[8]

It is time to expect and demand that public officials, elected and nonelected alike, adhere to rigorous ethical standards. Many cities have ethics commissions and ethics regulations that lay out often strong requirements for reporting gifts, avoiding conflicts of interest, and taking mandatory recusals in cases where officials have financial and other interests.

Cities from Philadelphia to San Diego have adopted such provisions, but they are rarely stringently enforced. Pay-to-play is especially insidious and undermines the larger public interest; cities should clamp down firmly on this practice. Los Angeles, for example, has been rocked by a series of such conflicts, most recently the case of a city councillor who, according to allegations in the *Los Angeles Times*, "had asked companies that do business with City Hall to donate to a private school where his wife was working as a professional fundraiser, and that he assigned his staff to help with the effort."[9]

Episodes of self-dealing, sometimes subtle and often hidden, seriously undermine good decisions as well as confidence in the public institutions. The answer to this is in part vigorous enforcement of a city's ethics laws but also the inculcation of a deeper culture of public service that understands the need to avoid conflicts of interest and assigns disapprobation for any form of self-dealing.

Sharing Authority and Power:
Co-planning Cities and Tactical Urbanism

Part of the agenda of inclusive cities is about placing more of the decisions about one's street, block, and neighborhood in the direct hands of those who live there to improve those spaces, make them more responsive to the desires and needs of residents, and foster a sense of ownership. And we must invest in a culture of political engagement and participation. There is an increasingly robust set of tools that cities around the country are using to bring about this renaissance in urban democracy.

Grassroots engagement of citizens in the running of a city and the shaping of a city's environment is an important goal. There are many steps cities can take to share power and authority and to give those in the best position to make judgments about what they need and want in their neighborhoods and communities the chance to act directly. In urban planning circles, much attention has been given to the idea of "tactical urbanism," the many small-scale urban interventions that can be undertaken in cities, from guerilla wayfinding to DIY painting of bike lanes and traffic calming.[10]

Many cities have moved from tolerating such interventions to encouraging and legalizing them. Portland's experience with a project called Intersection Repair is instructive: neighbors did not ask permission before dramatically painting and pedestrianizing key intersections (essentially taking them back), but over time the city adopted an ordinance creating a legal process for initiating new intersection repair projects. The more citizens can empower and facilitate these kinds of hands-on projects, the stronger and more democratic these neighborhoods and cities will be.

Open democratic societies require abundant public spaces. One can describe the public spaces of a city as profoundly democratizing; that is one of their key functions. These are the spaces and places where citizens can congregate to discuss, protest, celebrate, and make their discontent or support physically and visibly evident. They are ideally "sticky" spaces, where residents want to linger, watch and participate in public life, and see and be seen.

Cities should explore new processes and legal instruments for engaging citizens directly in their management. In Bologna, Italy, it is now possible for the city government and citizens to enter into collaborative agreements under its innovative Regulation on Public Collaboration for Urban

Commons, which creates a legal mechanism for allowing various forms of coproduction in the city.

There are many different and creative tools and decision processes that can foster more direct engagement in one's city. Another category involves crowdsourced funding platforms that allow citizens to conceive of, create, and directly fund neighborhood and community projects, ideally sourcing funds for such projects directly from friends and neighbors. One impressive example of this is the organization IOBY—which stands for "In Our Back Yards," meant to be a direct retort to the NIMBY (not in my backyard) movement, which tends to be the dominant dynamic in many cities.

IOBY was cofounded by three Yale graduate students, one of whom, Erin Barnes, until recently served as its CEO. She is proud of what they have accomplished, and the stats are telling: more than $13 million has been raised through the platform, supporting more than 2,800 projects in many different cities around the United States.[11] Most significantly, these are small-scale and neighborhood-based projects, with an average donation a mere fifty dollars (and an average funding goal of around $4,000)! These are small projects but impactful for their neighborhoods. Especially impressive is the statistic that more than half of a given project's donors also volunteer for the project.

San Francisco gives neighborhoods the option of creating a so-called green benefit district; the Dogpatch and Northwest Potrero Hill Green Benefit District is the first and so far only one in the city. The process requires a relatively modest annual charge for home and condo owners (around five dollars a month for a small condo), which is used to fund things such as landscaping, rain gardens and parks, street tree planting, and neighborhood art.[12] It has been described by some as an example of "hyperlocal democracy." "It is a city-sanctioned institution with elected board members and transparent goals," says *San Francisco Examiner* columnist Robyn Purchia.[13]

New funding in Dogpatch is being used to support a variety of collectively determined green improvements. One of the most interesting is something called the Eco-Patch: a pilot project to create and fund an experimental native plants garden on spare land close to a nearby highway. San Francisco has really been a pioneer when it comes to giving residents the power (and supporting them with resources and technical assistance) to take ownership over small but significant spaces in their urban surroundings.

Participatory Budgeting and Citizen Assemblies

Cities should explore new processes and legal instruments for engaging citizens directly in the management of the city and in decisions such as budgeting. The tool known as participatory budgeting was pioneered in Latin

American cities; Porto Alegre, Brazil, is often identified as the first place it was used. It is now being successfully used in some 6,000 cities around the world, according to the Participatory Budgeting Project. The Participatory Budgeting Project describes the idea as "a democratic process in which community members decide how to spend part of a public budget. It gives people real power over real money."[14]

In most cases participatory budgeting allows citizens direct control over a relatively small portion of a city's overall budget. Participatory budgeting in New York City dates back to 2011, when it was started by four city council members. A citywide participatory budgeting initiative was created through a 2018 citywide referendum, which also created the Civic Engagement Commission to run the program and to more generally seek to "enhance civic participation, promote civic trust, and strengthen democracy in New York City."[15]

The New York City approach allows city council districts, and the council members elected from them, to decide whether they want to allocate a portion of their discretionary budgets specifically for capital or infrastructure expenditures. The process usually starts with a brainstorming or nominating process, soliciting community ideas for expenditures. New York City's program was suspended in 2020 because of COVID but returned in 2021 on a smaller scale in four council districts.

New York City residents can nominate an idea, which is then uploaded to an online map, which becomes a kind of comprehensive record of these ideas. Hovering over one of these map points gives additional information about the proposed idea.[16] In New York the process involves several stages, from "idea collection and voluntary recruitment" and "proposal development" (with so-called volunteer budget delegates, who with the help of city agencies develop full-fledged proposals) to a nine-day period when the public votes on the proposals.

In the 2021 participatory budgeting cycle, more than 100,000 New York City residents voted on the allocation of $39 million to 145 projects.[17] This is at once impressive and, given the size of New York City's budget and its population, underwhelming. Yet it is one potentially important tool for engaging residents and for them to give voice to projects and priorities that might otherwise be overlooked or steamrolled by other demands. Interestingly, one only needs to be fourteen years old to vote in the New York City process, and individual council districts can lower the voting age even further. This holds promise on several levels: making it possible to hear directly from young people about their budgeting priorities and cultivating civic competency and voting habits early, which will enhance overall democracy in a city over time.

In the fall of 2020, New York City's Civic Engagement Commission initiated a participatory budgeting process specifically aimed at youth ages nine to twenty-one called It's Our Money. It focuses on youth in neighborhoods that were especially impacted by the pandemic and culminates in voting on projects that will allocate $100,000.[18]

In Hartford, Connecticut, participatory budgeting efforts are run by a volunteer-based organization called Hartford Decides. A citywide vote there has led to funding for planting trees at schools and repairing sidewalk damage along an important city bridge.[19] In a Grand Rapids, Michigan, pilot program, potential projects to be voted on by residents are generated at the ward level (about $2 million in city funds were allocated to be spent in the city's three wards) and must address specific priority areas (housing affordability and reduction of violence, for instance). A citywide steering committee oversees the process and helps refine and select the projects that will ultimately be voted on.[20]

Studies suggest that participatory budgeting offers many benefits, including direct civic engagement of residents, transparency in budget decisions, and the shifting of city expenditures to better reflect citizen priorities. One recent New York University study shows that participatory budgeting has indeed led to different funding outcomes, shifting expenditures in the direction, for instance, of schools, public housing, and street improvements.[21]

One especially promising application of participatory budgeting is in a city's public schools, where students are able to voice their ideas and vote for projects and changes that will directly improve schools. It's also part of what can be done to cultivate a sense of civic engagement early on by young people and will likely pay dividends for a city and society later in their adult lives. The City of Chicago, which uses participatory budgeting citywide through its ward system, started a pilot project in schools, now including sixteen schools. The project grants that are allocated through student initiative and voting are relatively small, only a few thousand dollars each, but the program seems successful. A review essay in *Chicago Reader* reaches this conclusion: "Students who were previously distracted in class or hesitant to participate started coming to class excited to work on their participatory budgeting project and kept up their engagement after the program ended."[22]

Citizen assemblies represent yet another emerging tool to more fully and more accurately take account of constituents' opinions and judgments. The idea is to randomly select a certain number of citizens who then study and deliberate about a specific issue or set of issues, reach conclusions, and offer recommendations. These participants are meant to better reflect the interests of the broader city; in theory they are not beholden to any existing establishment, power structure, or political party; and they should be more deeply representative of the community than elected officials generally are.

Such assemblies are used in cities around the world to address a variety of policy issues, from climate change and urban green space to gender equality. They typically meet over several consecutive weekends, in person or online, hear from speakers and experts, and reach agreement on a set of recommendations that hopefully make their way into the plans and actions of the municipal government. In Bristol, United Kingdom, a citizen assembly of sixty randomly selected residents was formed to address the question "How do we recover from COVID-19 and create a better future for all in Bristol?"[23] After thirty hours of meetings over four weekends, the group issued its final report in 2021, presenting some seventeen recommendations and eighty-two specific action items.

A clear advantage of citizen assemblies is that they can serve to correct for a less-than-fully representative city council. There is also the assumption that posing policy questions to a group of citizens with the time and ability to discuss and deliberate them will lead to different outcomes and will help overcome the polarization that characterizes much of politics today.

It is an open question as to whether deliberation really does change perspectives and choices, but there does seem to be some evidence that suggests it does. James Fishkin and his team have been experimenting with a variation on citizen assemblies—what he calls deliberative polling, in which citizens come together in person or virtually to deliberate on an issue but are not expected to reach consensus. Their research suggests that after the group deliberates, there is a shifting in the views of participants and a "de-polarizing" that occurs as a result.[24]

The methods and techniques for selecting participants for citizen assemblies have not been without controversy, with some noting the need to take into account different rates of participation (once selected) and abilities of different groups in the community to participate. An article recently published in *Nature* suggests ways to address this problem and to achieve a truly more representative group of participants.[25]

One intriguing idea is to form a standing citizen assembly in a city. It would in essence become a truly representative countercheck on a city council's votes or actions. Use of citizen assemblies is a positive step and a useful tool, though it is important to point out that even as careful as the algorithms for selecting participants might be, they will undoubtedly fail to capture the perspectives and voices of all impacted parties, especially the many nonhumans affected and the many millions of humans living in the future. How to modify or reform these assemblies to better account for these interests is a challenging question, but perhaps some selected participants could be asked to assume the point of view of the city's official bird or its urban forest; as discussed in the previous chapter, the work in Japan to include future generations in such processes suggests it is possible to make citizen assemblies more temporally diverse and representative (but how to ensure that every generation, or most generations, is represented is perhaps an impossible challenge).

There are many ways that cities can organize and facilitate other means of coproduction, where citizens are empowered to collaborate on and design and produce their urban futures. Bologna, Italy, as mentioned earlier, pioneered the idea of collaborative agreements between citizens and the city. Bologna's Regulation on Public Collaboration for Urban Commons is one example of a legal tool to make coproduction easier in cities. There are undoubtedly others, and ethical cities committed to providing meaningful ways to share power with citizens should develop and explore new tools to allow this to happen.

Digital Democracy

One large ethical and practical subject for cities today is how to best take advantage of new digital technologies and platforms to make local decisions more democratic. Participatory budgeting is one idea, certainly, but there are many others. Many of the ways that data are currently collected and used in cities are troubling, and part of the natural response is to be cautious and concerned about the ways that our digital presence and behavior are being recorded and monitored—whether our online purchases or the digital fingerprints we leave when we swipe a transit card or use an app to purchase a cup of coffee at Starbucks. It is not clear what responsibilities cities have here or what role they may play. Part of the discussion centers on who has ownership or control of digital data and how it will eventually be used. There is an immense amount of such personal data, and for the most part, as individuals, we have little to no control over it. Especially in the United States, such data is understood as the domain of companies and corporations, something they get to capture and use to sell us more products and to generally make more private profits.

An alternative view can be seen in Barcelona, where then-new mayor Ada Colau pushed to expand digital democracy and rethink who owns and controls digital data. Barcelona pioneered an online platform for facilitating democracy called Decidem (meaning "we decide" in Catalan), which is now in use in a number of cities around the world (including New York). Citizens can do many things and be engaged in many different ways through the Decidem platform. In Barcelona, it was initially used to facilitate public discussion of the municipal action plan.

Through the platform, some 40,000 individuals submitted a remarkable more than 10,000 specific proposals for how to improve the city. Many of them—more than 8,000—actually found their way into the plan.[26] These efforts were led by Francesca Bria, the city's first chief technology and innovation officer. Bria referred to the Barcelona approach as a "hybrid" form of participatory democracy, blending online and in-person offline forms of engagement.

A particular concern is how the digital data collected by the city gets reshaped and reframed. Barcelona collects a lot of data through Sentila, its municipal network of sensors, and makes this data—relating to everything from transportation and mobility to air quality and waste collection—available for citizens to see and use. As many cities aspire to become "smart cities" and use similar sensor networks, a concern is raised about who benefits and how such data is collected, analyzed, and stored to ensure privacy.

Barcelona is moving toward a view that some might consider radical: that data generated by citizens should be owned and controlled by citizens. Bria believes we should see this data as a "common good and a public infrastructure like water, electricity, roads, and clean air."[27] In an op-ed in the *Financial Times* calling for greater digital sovereignty, she describes the important idea of "data trusts," "where the underlying data, once anonymized, might be shared in the name of the greater public good."[28] "We want to move from a model of surveillance capitalism," Bria says, "where data is opaque and not transparent, to a model where citizens themselves can own the data."[29] An important step has been to modify contracts for vendors doing business with the city, requiring them to share the data they collect so it can be used by citizens and local companies.

Citizens should themselves be able take direct steps to generate useful digital data—measuring heat or air pollution levels in their neighborhoods, for instance—and in so doing add to the knowledge base of a city and its ability (and political will) to take action (e.g., planting trees or reducing emissions). In this way, the many hundreds, and perhaps thousands, of cities' citizen science projects and initiatives are examples of coproduction and grassroots participatory democracy.

Other cities have experimented with ways that digital technologies can help foster greater awareness of, and connections with, the larger moral community, including the many nonhuman species that tend not to be heard or considered in most city decisions. There are many promising examples. In Melbourne, as part of a community engagement strategy, the city gave each existing tree its own email address and asked residents to send a loving email to their favorite tree. The trees would even write back. It was a highly successful campaign, and many expressions of love and care were received even from individuals far beyond the borders of Melbourne.

Still, emerging digital technologies raise new challenges to local democracy. The rapid rise of artificial intelligence (AI) and chatbots such as ChatGPT has already led to the spread of fake photos and misinformation in local campaigns, further threatening to erode confidence in how we judge and elect our city representatives. There are growing calls to place limits on the use of AI in campaign materials, for instance requiring disclosure when synthetic or AI-created images have been used or banning them entirely, issues cities will increasingly grapple with as the use of AI spreads.[30]

Conclusions

This chapter has raised some critical questions about the fairness of the political processes and mechanisms by which decisions are made. An ethical city is a democratic city that strives to be fair and equitable in the way representatives are elected and in the ease with which constituents can directly and effectively express their opinions and perspectives. In an ethical city it should be easy and effortless to vote, and there should be effective restraints on the influence of money and wealth. We should hold our elected officials to high ethical standards and put in place rigorous standards and processes to uncover and prevent conflicts of interest. Every city can begin to invest in and utilize the emerging mechanisms of direct democracy; tools such as participatory budgeting and citizen assemblies, among others, are beginning to be widely and successfully used in cities around the world. A city is ethical in part when it makes decisions that are deeply inclusive, participatory, and democratic, and cities must begin to better harness and leverage digital technologies to strengthen local democracy.

Discussion Questions

How democratic are local politics? In most cities, are citizens able to effectively convey their opinions and preferences and exert influence on political outcomes?

How ethical would you say our elected representatives in cities are today? Are there ways to make them more responsive to constituent opinions and less beholden, perhaps, to special interests?

What is the role of money today in influencing how democratic local politics are?

Which new tool for participatory democracy is most promising?

What is the potential of digital democracy?

10

The Ethics of Public Spaces and the Public Realm

There is little question that the physical environments around us—the shape and design of cities and urban spaces—have a great impact on and connection with our values and ethics. Sociologist Richard Sennett, in his 2018 book *Building and Dwelling: Ethics for the City*, makes a case for the "open city," a place that is tolerant and accepting and can contribute to making us better people and better citizens.[1] The open city, Sennett believes, provides the context for humans who otherwise don't know each other and have no connection to walk, meet, and talk. Sennett invokes the famous German saying "City air makes you free" (*Stadtluft macht frei*). He wants a city to be a setting that can "embrace difference, a place of porous membranes and spatial invitation."[2] We want and need "spaces of encounter and friction."[3]

The open city is a place that accommodates differences and diversity. And it is a place that should be designed to allow for exposure to and interaction with these differences in terms of income, ethnicity, sexual orientation, and political views; it should be a place that celebrates diversity and difference, actively seeking or overcoming sameness in people (and in space). "Ethically, an open city would of course tolerate differences and promote equality but would more specifically free people from the straitjacket of the fixed and the familiar, creating terrain in which they could experiment and expand their experience," says Sennett. In arguing for the open city, Sennett distinguishes it clearly from the inverse: the closed city, which is rigid, fixed, and "over-determined." Such cities are "frozen" and unable to effectively change and adapt over time. "As uses change, buildings have to be replaced, since form-function relations make them so difficult to adapt. . . .

> **Sidebar 10-1 What Are Some of the Values We Want to See Expressed in Public Spaces?**
>
> Anonymity
> Belonging
> Experimentation
> Quiet and solitude
> Dignity
> Diversity
> Connectivity
> Complexity
>
> Adventure
> Wildness
> Ecology and richness of nature
> Safety
> Exploration
> Beauty
> Equality and respect

The over-specification of form and function makes the modern urban environment a brittle place."[4]

An open city should, Sennett believes, be "both dense and diverse, either in the form of dense streets or packed squares; such physical conditions can prompt the unexpected encounter, the chance discovery, the innovation which is the genius loci of cities."[5] Sennett argues for "ambiguous edges" and makes the important distinction between "boundaries" and "borders," the former being an overly fixed edge and the latter a more fluid zone of interaction and overlap.

The most rigid form of boundary can be seen in the emergence of gated communities, which create a city of isolated enclaves with little social or physical interaction. Ethical cities seek to take away these sharp and exclusionary stopping points. Borders, on the other hand, represent positive areas where social connections can be fostered and spontaneous interactions encouraged. Gridded, open streets in a city can facilitate movement through its different neighborhoods, strengthening a sense of connection and cohesion and working to resist or overcome isolation and separation.

As this example shows, the physical design of spaces in cities can help to foster or strengthen certain values (social connection, interaction, inclusion) while perhaps undermining others. Cities, in planning public spaces especially, but also in their spatial organization more generally, should keep in mind a variety of important values and collective ends (see sidebar 10-1).

Public Spaces and the Ethical City

Among urban planners there is strong agreement that public spaces—parks, plazas, and pedestrian spaces—are essential elements of a good city and critical preconditions for democracy. It is hard to overstate the essential value of actual physical spaces where individuals can come together for social and political activities of various kinds. In an era of email and text messages, of high dependence on digital and social media, there is no substitute for actual physical spaces in which face-to-face communication and exchange can occur. Providing such abundant, easily accessible, and safe public spaces becomes a hallmark of a democratic city and a major goal for city designers. It is the very publicness of spaces in cities that helps make them more democratic and inclusive—places where we see and experience people and points of view we would not otherwise encounter.

Cities must work hard to both protect the public spaces they have and secure new spaces and new public rights to spaces. Inspired by the High Line, cities have innovated new forms of public space and new notions of parks, especially over the last decade. There is New York's Lowline, Miami's Underline, and Toronto's already highly successful Bentway park, which converts 1.75 kilometers of space below the Gardiner Expressway "into a new gathering space for our city's growing population."[6] It is a vibrant space for community events, art, music, and festivals of various kinds, and during the winter months it becomes a skate trail.

Abundant public spaces are essential for democracy. They are the physical manifestation of an open city—the places where people who may look different, have different economic means, and have different opinions can come together. We want streets and neighborhoods that are walkable and parks, plazas, and community gathering spaces that encourage engagement, are interesting and stimulating, and provide venues and opportunities to express dissent, safely protest, mourn but also celebrate, and come together to help each other during difficult times.

It is important to recognize that there are many private spaces in cities that seem public but do not allow for the full expression of political and civic values. Years ago, one of my faculty colleagues in the Department of Urban and Environmental Planning at the University of Virginia, Richard Collins, was running for the Virginia House of Delegates. While campaigning, he handed out campaign brochures in the parking lot of a local grocery store (a good place, it seemed to him, to reach sympathetic voters). The parking lot was part of a private shopping center called Shoppers World. Collins and the shopping center's owner got into a verbal tussle and Collins was arrested, a shocking escalation from what seemed to many of us a reasonable exercise of his First Amendment rights. Albemarle circuit judge Paul Peatross agreed with the shopping center and fined Collins fifty dollars, concluding that "under the Virginia Constitution, there is no general right to engage in political speech in privately owned shopping centers."⁷

While the laws vary, there is no guarantee that citizens are able to use privately owned or controlled spaces as places to speak their minds or to protest or demonstrate. This case and many others like it show the essential democratic role served by truly public spaces such as a public squares or plazas.

The Special Importance of Mixing in Cities

There is an important set of benefits that cities, and especially public spaces, provide in helping to facilitate mutual understanding and to overcome fear and suspicion of the "other." We need ramblas, plazas, and public squares in part because these are spaces that, if they work in the right way, bring people together, bring them in close contact, and help normalize diversity and overcome prejudice. This is referred to as the "contact hypothesis" or "contact theory," and as Jesse Singal notes, "It's the simple, inspiring idea that when members of different groups—even groups that historically dislike one another—interact in meaningful ways, trust and compassion bloom naturally as a result, and prejudice falls by the wayside."⁸

Creating the kinds of public spaces that will truly bring diverse residents into contact with one another is a major challenge for cities, of course, and one that requires careful and thoughtful design and planning. There is now a large body of literature and case studies about public spaces that function very well and the qualities and design attributes of the most successful of these spaces. Good public spaces are safe and physically attractive, with seating, food, and other amenities, and perhaps most important, they are interesting places and spaces where people want to be.

We could also apply the contact theory at the neighborhood level. We have already discussed the history of spatial segregation in the United States, and an ethical city must aspire not simply to diversity in public spaces but to diversity in neighborhoods as well—and this is an even greater challenge. The rise of gated communities, as mentioned above, throughout American cities especially, represents a threat to connections and connectedness, through the lack of public streets and sidewalks, and risks creating a city where there is little physical or social contact between people of different socioeconomic, racial, or other groups.

But would all active and well-attended spaces result in the kind of social mixing results that the contact theory predicts? It depends. Do these spaces feel safe and welcoming to all members of the community? That depends on an even larger set of factors, for instance whether there is a (potentially menacing) police presence or whether there are shops and restaurants that are affordable and cater to a wide socioeconomic clientele.

Are there sufficient facilities for young children and for families? The lack of adequate public bathrooms especially hinders the use of public spaces by families, particularly those with young kids. And if the only food available to visitors of a public space is at high-priced sit-down restaurants, these spaces will not be very hospitable or accessible to everyone. All cities must be cognizant of the many ways public spaces can encourage or discourage a diversity of users and visitors.

Alexander Garvin, in his book *What Makes a Great City*, makes a strong case for the importance of public spaces in "nurturing and supporting a civil society."[9] Positive examples for him are Hyde Park in London and Grand Central Terminal in New York City. "It is not enough," Garvin says, "just to avoid doing anything that might harm others. People also need a place where they can express themselves, do things together with others, protest against what they consider inappropriate or destructive of a civil society, and advocate societal improvements to their fellow citizens."[10]

Hyde Park was the site of Women's Sunday, the first major suffragette march, in 1908. Organized by the Women's Social and Political Union, some seven processions of women marched through the city, each perhaps 30,000 in number, converging dramatically on Hyde Park, where some have estimated the attendance at half a million. Public spaces are essential venues for such social movements and public protests, and a city can be judged on how easy or difficult it is to find spaces to accommodate such events.

John Parkinson, in his book *Democracy and Public Space*, makes a strong case for the essential democratic functions provided by such physical spaces.[11] "Democracy depends," he says, "to a surprising extent on the availability of physical, public space, even in our allegedly digital world."[12] In these spaces we have opportunities for civility and face-to-face interactions, allowing for "all the non-verbal cues to be transmitted and received."[13] Such abundant spaces enhance a sense of "inclusions and membership" and ensure that public decisions are more likely made in public.

Parkinson evaluates capital cities around the world for the quality of their democratic physical spaces and finds many wanting. He suggests, interestingly, that physical space is about abundant public plazas, certainly, but also about cheap and extensive public transit to easily reach these spaces (and to this he might add investments in even more egalitarian modes of mobility such as bicycles or scooters). Don't forget "footpaths and streets," he adds. Such public spaces are also important to a democracy ("not to be controlled by private security guards, business associations, or residents' associations, regardless of ownership").[14]

Jane Jacobs was a major advocate for vibrant streets and their civilizing effects: "Safety on the streets by surveillance and mutual policing of one another sounds grim, but in real life it is not grim," she says. "The safety of the streets works best, most casually, and with least frequent taint of hostility or suspicion precisely where people are using and most enjoying the city streets voluntarily and are least conscious, normally, that they are policing."[15] The "basic requirement" for our cities, Jacobs says, is "a substantial quantity of stores and other public places sprinkled along the sidewalks of a district; enterprises and public places that are used by evening and night must be among them especially. Stores, bars and restaurants, as the chief examples, work in several different and complex ways to abet sidewalk safety."[16]

We need to design and build (and require) more housing that includes semipublic spaces where residents can socialize and interact. This is certainly part of the answer to our epidemic of loneliness. In Australia, Nightingale Housing is a new apartment model that emphasizes carbon neutrality, less dependence on cars, and design for spaces where social interactions can occur.[17] One component of such design is shared rooftop space in apartment buildings, where instead of washer/dryers being placed in each unit, they are located on the roof, creating an opportunity for regular social interaction among residents. Of course, part of Nightingale's goal must be to overcome social, economic, racial, and age segregation by ensuring that its affordable flats accommodate a diversity of residents.

The COVID pandemic resulted in a newfound appreciation for balconies, another especially helpful design element in cities. During the pandemic, balconies were places where residents applauded and affirmed the value of health-care workers, where evening concerts occurred, and where conversations and connections of all sorts were made possible. If balconies are large enough, they also provide essential outdoor space to enjoy fresh air and watch and listen to birds and other restorative aspects of nature.

I am reminded of New York City residents at the height of the pandemic. At 7:00 p.m. every evening, they would stand on their balconies and clap, yell, and whistle as an expression of tribute and thanks to the many doctors, nurses, and other health-care workers taking care of COVID patients. It was an act of collective solidarity and an example of the unique ways we can come together in the less conventional public or semipublic spaces around us. In Italian cities, residents would sing together each night from their balconies!

As former Vancouver planning director Brent Toderian notes, not all balconies are big enough or deep enough to effectively serve such functions. He tells of efforts in Vancouver to adjust zoning rules to encourage bigger balconies by extending the amount of square footage exempted from density limits, allowed under certain circumstances such as when balconies can be shown to shade a structure, reducing energy consumption and greenhouse gas emissions (which would generally be the case).[18]

The Civilizing Effects of Nature

There are many examples of leftover or underutilized spaces in cities being converted into "secret gardens." William Drayton wrote about one such secret garden in Greenwich Village (more than twenty years ago in an article in the Atlantic): the MacDougal-Sullivan Gardens Historic District.[19] Here, space behind a block of twenty-one row houses was converted into a wonderful communal garden space. All of the units on this block open onto the garden, which has trees and is wrapped around by an English hedge. The conversion happened in 1920, though the row houses date to 1844. Once home even to Bob Dylan, these row houses have become quite valuable in large part because of the garden.

Drayton writes that cities could create more such gardens if they chose to. "Thousands of blocks with hollow centers could renew themselves—and in the process strengthen their surrounding neighborhoods." It has been estimated that in New York City alone, there is room to create some 3,200 gardens in the centers of urban blocks.

Few cities have done as much as San Francisco to repurpose smaller spaces for public or social uses. The city has become famous for its promotion of "parklets"—small public parks converted from two or more on-street parking spaces. A green alleyways initiative and an innovative sidewalk gardens permit also allow residents to replace some of the pavement in their neighborhoods with biodiversity-enhancing flowers and greenery. These are opportunities for neighborhoods to recapture space, take control, and create new places to meet, relax, and talk.

One innovative space-repurposing program is San Francisco's Street Parks Program, which allows residents to repurpose leftover spaces owned by the city's Public Works Department. Many of the spaces are median strips in the middle of busy roads, many of which are impossibly small or awkwardly shaped. Neighborhoods propose a plan for such a space, and one or more volunteer stewards must agree to tend and look after the space over time. The program has been a success, and there are now more than 200 such street parks. Every city has opportunities to shift some, and perhaps a significant, amount of the space devoted to cars, including car parking, to spaces that could be public or semipublic. In doing so, cities will make more space for trees and nature. Evidence is mounting that nature is a potent civilizing force. In the presence of nature, experimental psychology tells us, we are more likely to be generous, for example. Nature softens the edges of human conflict.

There is also evidence that working on behalf of trees and engaging directly in the work of planting trees in cities leads to other forms of civic engagement. The best evidence comes from the work of Dana Fisher, Erica Svendsen, and James Connelly, who provide one of the few comprehensive empirical studies analyzing the ways in which engagement with nature can carry over into many other forms of community and civic involvement.[20] Specifically, they analyzed the participation of volunteers in New York's MillionTreesNYC program, which involved some 13,000 volunteers in a collaborative tree-planting effort. The researchers found, among other conclusions, that participating in the tree-planting program served, for volunteers, as a "gateway for more environmental participation and civic activity" and "was an essential part of their path toward more heightened democratic citizenship."[21]

Some research has shown that in the presence of nature, people are more likely to be generous and cooperative.[22] It follows that the more urban spaces are able to include trees and abundant nature (as they increasingly must to address urban heat), the more likely they are to play a role in strengthening the values of an ethical city in ways similar to the contact hypothesis. I am reminded of an interview I conducted years ago with the then mayor of Lancaster, California, about the city's unique crime-reduction strategy of broadcasting birdsong (through a string of speakers in the commercial district). The mayor's idea was that birdsong (recorded, in this case) would soften and civilize the city. The results, he told me, were positive and led to a reduction in crime.

Spaces That Stitch the City Together

Another important aspect is the extent to which physical forms and features that permit movement through and across a city and across different neighborhoods help underpin civic values. An interesting category of semipublic spaces is the many different kinds of trails, pathways, pedestrian bridges, and other spaces that allow one to travel around a city on a bicycle. Could such pathways and trails help build trust, overcome differences within and between neighborhoods, and help bind a city together?

One example of the power of urban trails can be seen in San Francisco's relatively new Crosstown Trail. It extends seventeen miles diagonally across the city, from Candlestick Park to the Pacific Ocean. One can use the trail to traverse the city and in so doing be exposed to the diversity of neighborhoods and people living there. Do such trails help weave a city together and create a kind of collective understanding that would be hard to bring about without the walking space to allow it?[23]

Part of what can bring people together to enjoy trails are the public events that can occur on and through them. In New York City's northern Manhattan, the annual Hike the Heights event, for example, is billed as a "community hike and celebration." The path of the hike connects several parks and the number of walkers (and partiers) grows along the way (in what has been described as a "snowball-like effect"). The trail's route takes the shape of a giraffe, so it has become known for this, with giraffe signs and sculptures all along the way.

In more hilly cities, there are extensive systems of stairways and steps that can provide similar perspectives. Pittsburgh and San Francisco are two cities with impressive networks of such steps. The care and repair of these steps has been a challenge, but they are widely recognized in both cities as something unique and special and a mobility resource that opens up spaces, nature, and vistas otherwise not available.

The creation of democratic and inclusive spaces also requires cities to reckon with the ways in which parks, green spaces, and nature can displace existing residents. This is sometimes called ecogentrification or green gentrification. The gentrifying effects of the High Line in New York are a clear example, where sharp rises in housing prices have been seen in areas close to the park.[24] Some have argued for an approach of "just green enough," providing new parks and nature but just enough to improve quality of life in a neighborhood and not enough to gentrify or displace.[25]

A better approach is to anticipate and mitigate such effects ahead of time, for instance through programs aimed at protecting and expanding affordable housing and jobs for residents. The 11th Street Bridge Park under development in Washington, DC, is a positive emerging story. Here, many actions are being taken in advance of building the park, including the creation of a new community land trust, the establishment of neighborhood buyers' clubs, and other measures to help reduce displacement as part of a comprehensive equitable development plan.[26]

Weapons in Public Spaces

For many Americans, the decision about whether to go for a walk, stroll, or jog is a mental exercise in weighing risks, with the prevalence of guns and gun violence being a significant and completely valid consideration. Almost daily mass shooting incidents again raise real worries about spending any amount of time in public spaces. The chances for an argument or altercation are high, and the normal functioning of public spaces as places for spirited discussion, debate, and counterprotesting becomes difficult and can even lead to a deadly outcome.

The widespread prevalence of guns is a special threat to the exercise of one's First Amendment rights (so say constitutional legal scholars such as Mary Anne Franks of the University of Miami School of Law), and in this way gun violence and gun safety issues must be a primary concern for urban planners and advocates of robust democratic cities. Some states and cities restrict the ability to carry (concealed or open carry) guns in parks and other public spaces, but the restrictions are anemic, rare, and subject to lots of troubling exceptions.

Against this backdrop many cities have sought to better control and contain guns. Indeed, this is essential if cities are to preserve their roles as places of social mixing and cultural integration. There are many design strategies cities can employ to make public spaces more inviting, of course, and there is an extensive literature and knowledge base about what makes public parks and plazas successful. A feeling of safety is one such quality. If one feels unsafe or threatened, including by the presence of an individual with a visible handgun, the value of using public spaces for protest or expression is lost. The presence of armed troops seems to be one very effective approach to stifling dissent, a common practice (together with actively harassing and arresting peaceful protesters) of authoritarian regimes such as the one in Belarus.

In US cities right-wing groups and militias, often toting high-powered automatic rifles are equally concerning. The explicit intent is often to intimidate, for instance at a Black Lives Matter rally. Many states do not have explicit authority to ban open carry of weapons, but in some states (e.g., California) guns are banned at permitted demonstrations. And in some states, cities have the power to impose their own bans.

This is a clash between constitutional rights—our First Amendment rights to free speech and assembly and our Second Amendment right to bear arms. It seems absurd on the face to think that the public-oriented functions of public spaces—for protest marches, political rallies, parades, and other similar events—could prevail in the intimidating presence of military-grade weaponry. Cities should have the power, and indeed should exercise the power if they have it, to prohibit or severely limit guns.

The Washington State legislature is on the verge of adopting a law that will impose such limits—a positive move. The legislation would prohibit the open carry of guns within 250 feet of protests or anywhere on the state capitol campus in Olympia. As Senator Patty Kuderer, a cosponsor of the bill, explains, "The purpose of bringing a weapon to a public demonstration is not to protect yourself; it's to intimidate."[27] Restricting guns in these most important public spaces helps ensure that residents will see them as safe. Participating in a protest march or political rally or even just picnicking at a local park will seem dangerous and risky in the presence of people wielding military-grade weapons.

Whose Public Spaces Are These?

The benefits of social mixing in public spaces are clear. But how truly inclusive and accessible are public spaces? Are there easy and abundant ways to travel to public spaces without a car, for example? Are there clean and adequate bathrooms, which is very important to visiting families? Are there places for kids to play and use the space in fun ways (e.g., fountains they can splash around in)? Are the spaces physically accessible if you are in a wheelchair? Will there be restaurants and food outlets that are affordable (and not just high-end restaurants)? These are a few of the important questions cities need to ask (and confront) when designing and planning major parks and public spaces.

There must be a greater effort in cities to represent all members of the community equally and fairly in their governance and to tell their stories fairly and equitably. We need parks and public spaces that tell the more inclusive, deeper history of a place. Cities are beginning to take away statues and symbols that are racist, hurtful, and divisive, while at the same time giving fuller voice and fair attention to all voices and perspectives in the community.

Trillium Park in Toronto is an example of how essential spaces in a city tell more inclusive, deeper stories. The park was designed with the extensive involvement of the Mississauga of the Credit First Nation, upon whose traditional territory Toronto is located. This engagement led to significant design elements that make this deeper history visible, such as stone carvings of traditional moccasin designs and marker trees, grown and shaped in the same way the Mississauga did hundreds of years ago to guide their seasonal travel and movement along the trails that crisscrossed Toronto.

Giving more visibility to Native peoples in the normal course of urban life is important and acknowledges the long-standing ownership of the land on which a city sits. Cities should strive to ensure that public spaces of all kinds tell a full and complete history, not a sanitized or romanticized version. And the stories and faces that are privileged and celebrated in the signs, statues, names of buildings, and streets should reflect the diversity of a city. The history that is usually visible and celebrated is white and male; many cities are working to change this.

Public spaces clearly reflect what we think is important. In many cities, such as Atlanta, rainbow crosswalks have been painted as a way to highlight and celebrate the LGBTQ+ community and to promote solidarity with its cause. They have not been without controversy and objection, however; in several instances, US highway department officials have argued that rainbow crosswalks represent a safety concern, potentially distracting motorists.

Black Lives Matter Plaza in Washington, DC, is an inclusive public space that was created by Mayor Muriel Bowser in the aftermath of the brutal clearance of protesters in the park immediately across from the White House, itself a demonstration of how forces of authority can take away safe and prominent places for protest. Black Lives Matter Plaza was quickly painted and blocked off from car traffic and became a center of protest activity in the city. In July 2021, it became a permanent public space, with the ground mural repainted onto brick pavers (with thirty-five-foot-tall letters) and a permanent pedestrian plaza created in the center. While creating new spaces like Black Lives Matter Plaza and making efforts to take down racist statues are positive steps, they are criticized by some people as simply not being enough and even sometimes distracting from efforts to instill deeper, more systemic change in a city or society. Some people in the Black Lives Matter movement called Bowser's creation of the plaza "performative."

The Stories We Privilege and Make Visible in Cities

A city's commitment to equity and equality can be judged by the diversity and inclusiveness of the stories and narratives conveyed in its spaces and buildings. Which historic buildings do we choose to protect and shore up; which ones do we allow to be lost to development, be razed, or fall down over time? What does that say about the fairness and equality of a city? An ethical city should feel like a place where you belong as a resident, where you are not invisible, and where the accomplishments of your ancestors and leaders are represented in the spaces and built environments around you.

More cities, for example, are making room for important buildings, spaces, and symbols related to the LGBTQ+ community. San Francisco's recent designation of the Lyon-Martin House as a historic monument is one example; for more than five decades, it was home to iconic lesbian leaders Phyllis Lyon and Del Martin. As Christine Morris of the National Trust for Historic Preservation says, the designation is an important step in preserving this history: "This house may be small, but it has outsized significance stretching far beyond San Francisco or California. Phyllis and Del's lifetime of activism battling discrimination against the LGBTQ+ communities and violence against women has changed thousands of lives. This is a place where women had a national impact on LGBTQ+ civil rights on a par with Stonewall, and it deserves that same level of respect and recognition."[28]

There are other potential LGBTQ+ landmarks under consideration in San Francisco, including the camera shop of the city's first gay elected public official, Harvey Milk, who was assassinated by a fellow council member.

The Values We Convey through What We Build

The design of our built environments reflects particular values, whether consciously or not. Architects have always been aware of this, and specific kinds of buildings convey clear cues, messages, and priorities. A courthouse is meant to convey, in its pillared form, a sense of authority and power, a prison a sense of security and safety (and perhaps dread, through its walls and razor wire). Modern libraries, it could be argued, seem to emphasize values such as curiosity and inquiry, and an open airy interior with expansive views of the city seems to suggest the life-enriching benefits of knowledge.

Sometimes the symbolic meanings of the built environment are more accidental or unintentional, for instance the way New York City's tall, skinny skyscrapers have come to symbolize the excessive wealth and inequality in that city. There are good and important discussions to have in an ethical city about the values and priorities reflected in what we design and ultimately build. A recent essay in *Architizer* questions the need to have built the Burj Khalifa tower in Dubai, the world's tallest building. It "should never have been built," says Pat Finn, who views the structure as nothing more than a reflection of the city's "bragging rights."[29] The building's height reflects hubris and waste. "The world needs more functional architecture," Finn says, especially housing. "It does not need more monuments to the power of capital."

Values are also implicit on other scales: gated communities convey exclusion (you are not welcome here), for instance, while many public spaces are designed to explicitly convey a sense that you are welcome, indeed encouraged, to visit. Cities should at least be more aware of the values conveyed by their physical environments and spaces and more ideally design and plan in ways that support and strengthen the values of an ethical city.

Could buildings be designed in ways that make us kinder or reinforce other important values and prosocial behavior? The psychological concept of "priming" is useful here: visual and other stimuli in the built environment keep certain things front-of-mind and may predispose us to think and act in certain ways.[30] Does the steeple on a church predispose us to think more about God? Perhaps a life-size mural of a blue whale in a coastal city might encourage us to scan the seascape each day looking for a glimpse of this large creature—or, even better, to take actions to support whale conservation. A mural depicting an important piece of community history or a building renovation that makes visible or prominent something important from the past might help us to keep that past in mind or to have a stronger sense of our collective history in our daily lives. Many kinds of public art challenge us to look differently at the world and inspire creativity and open-mindedness.

Cities are also the setting for thousands of monuments and commemorative signs that celebrate events, people, movements, and epochs in time. Our collective understanding of many of these (and the depth of our knowledge about events and people) changes over time. A monument that may have seemed appropriate in 1910 may in today's awareness and context seem wrong and even racist. Especially in the aftermath of the Unite the Right rally in Charlottesville, Virginia, in August 2017, many cities have rightly reconsidered these monuments, as well as the names attached to buildings, schools, and plazas.

Cities have taken a variety of different approaches to addressing Confederate monuments: some are studying and discussing the issues and moving slowly, and others are taking more immediate steps to banish these symbols from the public realm. In Baltimore, then mayor Catherine Pugh decided that several Confederate statues would be taken down overnight. These included the dual equestrian statue of Robert E. Lee and Stonewall Jackson erected in 1948. She defended her action as necessary and "in the best interest of my city." Pugh concluded that she had the emergency power to take this bold and decisive action, believing that the statues were a "security threat" and there was a need to "quickly and quietly" remove them "to protect her city."[31]

As we know, seeing and experiencing Confederate flags, statues, and other tributes in the public realm is painful and gut-wrenching, and to most African Americans they are offensive and racist, sending signals that are embedded in the physical space of the city that they are lesser citizens and lesser humans.

What we name or call the many spaces and buildings that occupy our cities is an ethical choice as well, fraught with moral underpinnings, assumptions, and choices. In 2014, Taos, New Mexico, changed the name of its Kit Carson Park (named after an individual with a history of cruelty to Native

Americans) to Red Willow Park, derived from the Tiwa word for Taos. At once this new name is more respectful and more inclusive of the deeper history of this place. Other communities have followed suit, renaming parks, streets, and neighborhoods that celebrate individuals who were racist or exploitative.

Few cities have been more active in grappling with the history of names of public buildings and spaces than Boston. Recent steps have included renaming Dudley Square, originally named after a colonial governor known to be a racist and a supporter of slavery. The renaming was the result of an extensive campaign that included a referendum and approval by the Boston Public Improvement Commission; the square is now known as Nubian Square, a name referencing a beloved neighborhood gift shop with African connections. The fact that the neighborhoods directly surrounding the square are mostly African American made the original historical name that much more galling. As Sadiki Kambon of the Black Community Information Center, which organized the name-change campaign, says, "Surely all would agree this is a much-needed campaign as it makes no sense to have the primary commercial shopping district in our Black/Brown community to be named in honor of the slave owning Dudley family."[32]

An even higher-profile renaming effort was in the case of the historic Faneuil Hall, named after Peter Faneuil, a slaver and supporter of slavery, who gave the market and civic building to the city of Boston in 1742. He became the city's "wealthiest merchant" on the back of buying and selling humans. As Kevin Peterson says in a compelling opinion piece arguing for the need to rename the hall, the devastating ills of slavery are not just historical facts but explanations for the present conditions people of color experience: "Names, in and of themselves, are neutral. But within the social world they gain meaning that can be uplifting or degrading, depending on the context. For many African Americans names and icons like Faneuil Hall have dismissive connotations. They serve as memories of hatred. They are reminders of the evil of inequality. They are manifestations of inhumane intention. It is essential to denounce such names in the effort of moving forward."[33]

Then mayor Martin Walsh opposed the renaming and opposed even a public hearing to discuss it. Peterson believes that much of this resistance was due to a sense that slavery, while evil and despicable, is something for which current living residents bear little direct responsibility. In this view, our collective "racial sins," as Peterson says, have been "washed away over the course of time," including through the civil rights movement of the 1960s.[34]

Should a city comprehensively examine and change its street names to better reflect social justice and the stories and people who define a city? In my own home city of Alexandria, there have been efforts to comprehensively address the names of streets and lanes named for Confederate leaders and generals. Dating back to the 1950s, a local law even required north–south streets to be named after Confederates, but the law was later little known and mostly ignored. The largely hidden story behind these street names feels to many of us like deceit and harm inflicted by the city's earlier leaders.

But new awareness of the people and histories behind many of Alexandria's most prominent street names has led to a move to rename them. The city has lowered the threshold for renaming—only 25 percent of residents of a street need to sign a petition (down from 75 percent), before it goes to a renaming committee and is ultimately voted on by the city council. This long-overdue reckoning has been aided by a local organization called Reconstruction Alexandria, with volunteers going door to door to collect signatures in support of the renaming.[35]

It is telling that as a child growing up in Alexandria (or even as an adult today), I didn't know the origins of the names of streets. One street name currently in contention is Van Dorn Street, a street I spent much of my high school years traversing. I would have been horrified to learn that the street was named after a Confederate brigadier general, Earl Van Dorn. It is a curious choice for a street name in Alexandria, because he had absolutely no connection to the city and was a lesser-known cavalry officer who did not live to see the end of the war. There is a proposal to rename the street Keckley Street, after Elizabeth Keckley, dressmaker and confidant to Mary Todd Lincoln.[36]

Conclusions

There are many ethical dimensions to the many decisions we make in the design and planning of buildings and public spaces in cities. There are questions of equity and fairness in the very size and distribution of parks and public spaces, of course—and much evidence of how such spaces are smaller and less accessible to people of color, for instance. We need public parks and plazas, and the many smaller and more semipublic spaces, from porches and balconies to alleyways, to provide opportunities for residents to socialize, come together, and (hopefully) build an important degree of understanding and trust. The contact hypothesis holds that such spaces can do much of the work of helping residents of cities see "others" as inherently similar to themselves and to develop empathy and caring. Jane Jacobs makes a compelling case that the physical design of neighborhoods, and specifically the critical qualities of street life, are absolutely essential for creating conditions for public trust. There is a growing recognition that parks and public spaces in cities must tell a more inclusive and deeper history. Cities are beginning to take away statues and symbols that are racist, hurtful, and divisive, while at the same time giving fuller voice and fair attention to all voices and perspectives in the community.

Discussion Questions

In what ways does the design of public space serve to reinforce particular values?

Think of a specific public space in a specific city: What value or values do you believe are reflected or conveyed by those spaces? Are they welcoming to all? Are there particular stories or people that are privileged in these spaces?

How might we use the design of public spaces to bring about a more ethical city?

The Ethics of a Healthy and Flourishing City

The promotion and protection of public "health and safety" have historically been key goals and motivating values for cities. Much of what a city, agencies, and staff do is directly aimed at ensuring the safety of residents, such as fixing holes in city streets to ensure that sidewalks are level and safe, regulating traffic speeds and intersection lighting to prevent auto accidents, and inspecting restaurants to ensure health codes are being followed in the preparation of food. There are many responsibilities a city assumes to ensure that citizens can live their lives without undue worry about danger and harm.

Cities have an ethical imperative to protect and enhance health, but there are many ways to do this and different ways to think about health. In many respects, the health and healthfulness of a city's residents are determined by things that are mostly out of our collective control. They include, for instance, personal decisions to smoke (or not), the kinds of food we choose to eat, or whether we choose to be physically active. Does an ethical city seek to influence these personal choices?

Cities increasingly understand their roles as more than just working to prevent illness or disease (e.g., reducing particulate air pollutants) or eliminating immediate dangers in the urban environment (again, that sidewalk hole or dangerous intersection). Here, the concept of flourishing becomes an especially good way of thinking about cities' broader health-advancing goals. Corey Keyes, a professor at Emory University in Atlanta, has done much of the important writing on this and has devoted much of his work to fleshing out the more specific conditions that make for a flourishing life. Flourishing, he believes, includes such things as positive affect and satisfaction with life, personal growth, purpose in life, trusting personal relationships, and a sense of belonging to a community, among others.[1] It is more than the eradication of dangers or the prevention of disease.

What Are Acceptable Levels of Risk?

In many ways, cities shape and moderate the kinds of risks their residents face and make explicit decisions about the extent of risk we believe it is acceptable for individuals to assume. One role of a modern city is to work systematically to reduce the kinds of serious risks encountered in urban life. But there remain questions about what levels of risk are acceptable and who ought to have the responsibility to decide.

The rise of dockless electric scooters has highlighted some of these ethical challenges. Start-ups such as Lime, Skip, and Bird took the approach of rolling out a product—dockless scooters—very quickly and without permission or appropriate permits, garnering the ire of many city officials. There have been concerns about the safety of these scooters, as many cities noted a dramatic uptick in emergency room visits when scooters appeared on their streets. A news report describes how injured scooter riders were "pouring into emergency rooms," presenting with injuries that look more like the kind that would result from automobile accidents: "broken noses, wrists, and shoulders, facial lacerations and fractures, as well as the kind of blunt head trauma that can leave brains permanently damaged."[2]

Such safety concerns led one mayor, Jenny Durkan of Seattle, to ban the scooters. What should cities (such as Seattle) legitimately expect to ensure safety? Should cities require mandatory helmets? An adequately trained maintenance crew might be another reasonable expectation—sufficient to ensure that all scooters are collected, inspected, and maintained and that accelerator sticking and faulty brakes are not a concern.

It might be argued that cities sometimes go too far in protecting residents from dangers. If I want to venture into a slippery-edged swimming hole for an invigorating dip on a hot summer day, I ought to be able to assume this risk. It is fair to point out that our overly litigious American society leads to extensive lawsuits and legal action when, for example in this case, the swimmer slips and injures himself. But more generally we believe that an important function of a city is to protect citizens from risks to health and safety and that the small loss of freedom or choice is outweighed by the achievement of a safer urban environment.

Worries about overreaching to protect health and safety take on a special dimension when children are involved. There is an active debate about the extent to which kids should be allowed to walk and bicycle on city streets without adult care or supervision. Some parents and advocates of the concept of "free-range kids" believe, for example, that parents should be complimented when they encourage their children to develop life skills to walk to the store unaccompanied.

And that that is in fact the way to raise kids who will, in the end, be safer because of the skills and experience they develop through this independence.

A Precautionary Approach

The health of a city's population is impacted by many things: air and water pollutants, the presence of toxic waste and other potentially carcinogenic substances, and excessive levels of traffic and other noise, among many others. These are all things that cities (in combination with federal and state environmental laws) seek to moderate and curtail. There are extensive ethical quandaries here—for instance, how far to regulate a dangerous substance and the extent to which a city ought to adopt a precautionary principle or approach. The City of San Francisco, for example, has formally adopted the precautionary principle. This approach holds that the city need not wait for definitive science on the danger of, say, pesticides but understands a responsibility to be proactive and to seek alternatives where dangers are likely or suspected. The precautionary principle is the first chapter in San Francisco's environment code and "requires the selection of the alternative that presents the least potential threat to human health and the City's natural systems."[3]

One result is that, in comparison to most other cities, San Francisco works hard to limit the use of chemical pesticides and herbicides. They are mostly prohibited and are not used in parks or public green areas in the city, though some use is permitted as a last resort. Park managers must exhaust other nonchemical options first, for instance controlling invasive vegetation with blowtorches or sheep or goats, an increasingly popular option in many other cities.[4]

A city's duties of care increasingly include natural hazards and disasters, as well as adaptive responses to climate change. Climate resilience is a goal now commonly espoused by cities and calls for a wide range of actions including addressing rising urban heat and responding to a variety of climate-related emergencies and disaster events, such as by preparing for an approaching coastal storm or hurricane. Few events create more ethical dilemmas for elected officials than a large storm. When does the mayor call for an evacuation? Too soon and perhaps the evacuation was unnecessary, but waiting to confirm the storm's path means residents may be caught in a car on a causeway mid-evacuation or be unable to evacuate in time. Should such evacuations be mandatory or voluntary? There are many different points of view. And there are clear social equity dimensions to this, as the ability to evacuate seems to depend in part on one's wealth and resource levels. During Hurricane Harvey, Corpus Christi mayor Joe McComb called for only a voluntary evacuation even though it could have been mandatory. "We could mandate it, but people need to make a decision of their own. . . . I'm not going to risk our police and fire people going to try to drag somebody out of the house if they don't want to go," McComb said.[5]

A city's building codes and construction standards, and its system of building inspections and inspectors, are some of the most important means by which the public can be kept safe. The collapse of the Champlain Towers South in Surfside, Florida, in June 2021 has become a learning moment on this topic and a compelling example of how building occupants (and housing consumers) simply lack the expertise and knowledge to know if their building is safe or prone to a catastrophic collapse. While the precise causes of the collapse remain unclear, it seemed at least in part the result of a lax and underfunded inspection system. Needed repairs had been delayed—not a surprise when left to the voluntary timeline of building owners without a full understanding of the dangers.

The duty to keep citizens safe in the face of natural hazards intersects alarmingly with the implementation of building codes. In many cities, such as San Francisco, Tokyo, or Istanbul, there is a serious seismic danger, and codes can prevent structures from collapsing even in large earthquake events. This is an important function of city government, recognized even by conservatives such as columnist George Will, who decades ago wrote about the importance of government's role in reducing these kinds of risks. A good society, Will says, is one where the "take-for-granted quotient" is high. Here, he says, citizens don't have to continuously wonder about the safety of restaurants or elevators. "To keep modern society flowing, government must act in many small ways to take large amounts of hesitancy out of life," says Will.[6]

Building safety similarly falls into this category and is a safety consideration for the larger community as well. There is a public interest, for example, in ensuring that buildings or parts of buildings don't fall in an earthquake. A remarkable example of this can be seen in the aftermath of a major earthquake that struck the New Zealand city of Christchurch in February 2011. On a personal note, the daughter of a close colleague was riding in a bus traveling through downtown Christchurch when the earthquake occurred. On Colombo Street, a building's heavy parapet fell to the ground, hitting her bus and killing twelve inside as well as four pedestrians nearby.

She was lucky, the only passenger on the bus to have survived, though with a serious leg injury.[7]

The victim, Ann Brower, a professor at Lincoln University, became an impassioned advocate for more stringent building standards. She was incensed to learn that building owners were allowed to keep certain reinforced masonry buildings, such as the one whose parapet fell on her bus, in dangerous condition (both before and many months after the earthquake, it turns out), rather than required to secure and attach their dangling parapets. Even more serious, she believed, was the moral hazard created by the national government assuming all legal liability for these buildings, precisely the wrong step to ensure their repair and the safety of the public. Due to her diligent advocacy and passionate voice, changes were made to significantly accelerate the required retrofitting of these kinds of buildings.

To be sure, there are difficult questions about acceptable risk here. The costs of bracing the parapets on the building that struck Brower's bus were high, likely more than the value of the building. At a personal and societal level, when is the cost of mitigating or reducing the risk too high and thus the risk is deemed acceptable? Of course, there are important equity dimensions, too, to consider—the economic benefits (of being relieved from making the repairs) fall entirely to the building owner, while the risks and dangers are externalized and assumed by the larger public (including those, like Brower, who never set foot inside the building). As Brower observes, "Allowing the parapets to persist unattached benefits only the owner. It transfers all the risk on to the public, and the future costs on to the public health system. This privatizes benefits and socializes costs."[8] And the risks to the public are largely hidden—members of the public like Brower did not even realize they were assuming these risks.

Few issues are more vexing today for cities than addressing the ravages of addiction to opioids, especially the recent fentanyl crisis. According to the Centers for Disease Control and Prevention, there were more than 80,000 deaths due to opioid overdoses in the United States in 2021 alone.[9] What can and should cities do in response? There are difficult conversations underway in many cities about the benefits and limitations of decriminalizing drug use, as well as the necessity of public health steps to prevent and respond to rising drug overdoses. Many cities now implement a range of so-called harm-reduction techniques (something that started with needle exchanges during the AIDS epidemic). Some, such as making overdose-reversal drugs, including naloxone (also known by the brand name Narcan), more widely available, are relatively uncontroversial and have proven effective at saving lives. Others, such as safe injection sites (also known as supervised consumption sites), where addicts can use opioids and other drugs under close supervision, have also saved lives but have been highly controversial. New York City established the first of these sites in the United States in 2022.[10] Some believe they encourage drug use and do little to promote treatment or long-term recovery.[11]

Can a City Be a Nanny State?

Collectively our notions of health have been changing, and the ethical obligations and moral commitments of cities have been shifting. There is a growing importance of shifting from a disease-based approach to health, with an emphasis on medical treatment, to one that recognizes the moral duty to invest in prevention and the many "upstream" conditions and strategies that will avoid the need for medical treatment in the first place. This means a city can and must concern itself with the behaviors and habits of its citizens (empowering good and health-enhancing habits such as getting sufficient exercise, designing the physical environment of cities to encourage active lifestyles, and discouraging bad habits such as smoking and eating salty foods).

Many of the things that lead to bad health are activities, behaviors, and practices that have largely been the domains of personal choice: how much and what to eat, how much to walk or exercise over the course of a day or week, or whether to smoke. In recent decades these have also become behaviors that city officials have taken aim at, and it is clear that cities have a variety of levers and tools at their disposal to encourage healthy behaviors and lifestyles and discourage the opposite. But many such policy interventions have been controversial and raise questions about the reach of local governments and whether it is acceptable or desirable to seek to influence these behaviors. Can a city do too much, take too many steps to influence behavior and lifestyle, and ought these things be left mostly to the considered judgments of individuals? In short, can a city act too much like a nanny state?

It is possible to influence individual behavior, for instance through education and public service announcements or through pricing, while still leaving the ultimate choice about lifestyle decisions to the individual. Transparency, and the full disclosure of risks and hazards, can also simply be understood as something owed to a city's residents, an ethical duty, and such information could also lead to better decisions and more proactive risk-reducing behaviors on their parts.

But in many cases cities have a legitimate right, and indeed an ethical duty, to take steps that prohibit a dangerous product or activity and that take away an element of choice. One example is New York City's 2006 decision to ban trans fats.[12] An unusual step, but there was little doubt that foods high in trans fatty acids were associated with elevated levels of heart disease. Eventually—in fact, about a decade later—the FDA enacted a similar ban at the federal level. But New York's early action undoubtedly saved many lives, as a 2019 study in the *American Journal of Public Health* concludes.[13] Similarly, there are strong public health rationales for cities to take steps to curtail smoking, which is addictive, has truly gruesome and deadly health impacts, and has serious public impacts (e.g., secondhand smoke).

New York City took the bold step two decades ago to ban smoking in parks, restaurants, and bars. Such steps were mostly about protecting the health of those not choosing to smoke, of course, and protecting the enjoyment of urban spaces for the larger general public. But the regulations also send a strong moral signal about the city's attitude about smoking. In 2017, then mayor Bill de Blasio expanded many of these measures, including significantly raising the minimum cost of a pack of cigarettes to thirteen dollars, limiting the number of places tobacco products could be sold in the city, and banning the sale of tobacco in pharmacies, among other measures. Especially when it comes to young people, there is a compelling argument to support strong actions cities can take to prevent the countless deaths and suffering that result from kids getting hooked on smoking.

Some believe that efforts to raise the cost of unhealthy behaviors just penalize those who have few real options for change and, in the case of cigarettes, are motivated by a physical addiction. A pack of cigarettes "could be $50 and people are still going to smoke," said one New York smoker interviewed at the time for a *USA Today* story about the laws. The addiction is hard to deny, yet raising the price does have an impact and may be especially important in discouraging kids from starting to smoke. Raising the price can't be the only strategy a city pursues though; education is another important category of policy. For many years New York City has invested in extensive efforts at antismoking education through TV spots and an ad campaign.[14] In 2019, the city started a new campaign called "Smoking = Suffering: Three More Reasons to Quit Smoking," highlighting the long-term health impacts. The media segments are difficult to watch, with graphic views of open wounds, surgeries, and amputated limbs.

Perhaps more controversial still are New York's mandates in the area of healthy food. Most restaurants in the city now must post calorie counts and full nutritional content information on their menus. Calorie labeling is required by the federal government, but New York City was many years ahead of this standard. New York City imposed the first requirement that mandated that chain restaurants (restaurants with fifteen or more outlets in the United States) place a saltshaker icon next to all menu items that contain 2,300 or more milligrams of sodium; the Centers for Disease Control and Prevention indicate that 2,300 milligrams is a healthy daily intake. Given the fact that one would be consuming the recommended daily amount of sodium in just one menu item, during one meal, 2,300 milligrams seems likely to be an overly high threshold for the menu icon. But nevertheless, it's a good start.

One of the ethical reasons for setting a standard for sodium intake is the inherent informational problem that comes with eating at a restaurant. Just as with the sanitation requirements restaurants are required to adhere to and the inspections that usually generate a visible health grade, calorie and sodium data provide the consumer with information he or she would otherwise have no way of collecting or compiling. In supporting the New York requirements, a representative from the American Heart Association said this about the sodium standard: "Americans are consuming dangerous levels of sodium, most often found in processed or restaurant food. This rule will help to increase transparency."[15] Transparency is a key aspect here: consumers are entitled to know what they are ingesting and should be given sufficient information to make an informed decision about their health.

Cities can influence the availability of healthier food in other ways. In the last several decades, healthy food issues have begun to embrace the questions of access to and availability of healthy food and the ways in which urban residents may be food insecure. Long lines of cars at food banks during the pandemic were a vivid reminder of how many citizens have been (and currently are) food insecure, with significant implications for health and well-being. Cities can help address food security by supporting new grocery stores in neighborhoods that need them and by working to make it easier to grow (at least some) food in urban neighborhoods.

Guns and Gun Safety as a Public Health Issue

A dramatic recent rise in gun violence raises yet another important public safety issue in cities and one that is even more controversial because of strong and unyielding support from gun owners who feel that any restrictions will (now or eventually) take away their constitutional "right to bear arms" under the US Constitution's Second Amendment. Increasingly, cities are treating guns and gun violence as a pressing public health problem and taking steps to impose sensible safety regulations and requirements on gun owners.

The United States has more guns than any other country, an estimated 390 million (almost half the world's guns, though we are only about 5 percent

> **Sidebar 11-1 What Steps Could Cities Take to Address the Public Health Risks of Guns?**
> Ban assault rifles
> Ban high-capacity magazines
> Ban bump stock attachments
> Institute mandatory background checks
> Enact red flag laws, allowing police to confiscate guns from especially dangerous individuals
> Impose gun storage and locking requirements
> Prohibit guns in or near schools
> Prohibit guns in parks, places of worship, and public buildings
> Require guns in cars to be locked and concealed from view
> Require that shopkeepers lock up their gun wares at night

of the world's population!).[16] We have more mass shootings than anywhere, and gun deaths amount to nearly 40,000 each year. More than half of those deaths are suicides, and there is a strong correlation between availability of guns and suicide rates (which are higher in states with higher levels of gun ownership).[17] This is not surprising, given the lethality of guns. Better controlling access to and availability of guns would do much to address the problem of suicide.

One-third of American households with children have at least one gun, putting many children at risk of injury or death. The presence of loaded guns in a house represents a serious health threat to children and other occupants, and many are accidentally killed or injured each year. A 2018 study estimated that 4.6 million children live in households where guns are being stored in unsafe ways (loaded and unlocked).[18] The authors observed the "high prevalence of children exposed to unsafe storage" and noted that these circumstances rebuke the myth gun owners commonly perpetuate that a gun in the house means greater safety (in fact, the reverse seems to be true).[19]

What can and should cities do? As sidebar 11-1 suggests, there are many commonsense safety requirements that cities can impose, from background checks to red flag laws that allow police to take guns away from high-risk individuals. Requiring gun owners to lock their guns is one especially sensible requirement. Oakland, California, requires gun owners to store their guns in a "locked container," defined as a "secure container that is fully enclosed and locked by a padlock, key lock, combination lock, or similar locking device."[20] Some cities have gone further. Denver has banned assault rifles (and Boulder tried, though Colorado has adopted a preemption law preventing other cities from doing this). Littleton, Colorado, requires gun shops to lock up their wares at night.[21] St. Louis has enacted an ordinance requiring gun shops to notify the city's police when a buyer fails a background check.

Mandating safe storage of a potentially deadly device would seem the very minimum of what we can expect and what would be ethically required of a city. When kids find loaded guns around the house, the results are often heartbreaking. Some options cities have tried, such as gun buybacks, have been less successful. St. Louis tried this approach, and while substantial numbers of guns were taken out of circulation, most agree this was but a drop in the bucket and unlikely to result in the reductions in gun deaths and gun violence that cities need and want to see.

Prohibiting guns in certain places of the city can be another important strategy. The Giffords Law Center provides a comprehensive listing of these restrictions by state and vividly demonstrates that so-called location restrictions are extensive and common.[22] In the District of Columbia, for example, guns, either concealed or open carry, are prohibited on public transit, in day-care and childcare facilities, in bars and restaurants serving alcohol, at places of worship, at stadiums and athletic events, and at demonstrations and protests. There are already, then, significant restrictions on where and when one can have a gun, though one wonders about effective enforcement.

Healthy Buildings and Neighborhoods

As humans we spend more than 90 percent of our time inside. This is unfortunate; a goal of an ethical city should be to propel and entice residents to spend more of their day outside. But it is undeniable that health and well-being are heavily influenced by the interior spaces of the homes, offices, and other buildings where we spent the lion's share of our time. For these spaces to be healthy, we increasingly realize, they must be places of abundant natural daylight and have visual connections to the outside and, where possible, views of trees and green spaces. Operable windows have been rediscovered in architecture, allowing occupants an important measure of control over their environments, as well as (hopefully) inviting in natural breezes and the sounds of birds and nature. Interior spaces should include as much actual nature as possible, and there are now many off-the-shelf interior green walls and green wall hangings.

Hospitals and health facilities have been leaders when it comes to biophilic design, naturally recognizing the need to enlist nature and the design of a hospital itself in the healing of the patient. Incorporating shapes and forms of nature is another important design strategy. One dramatic example of this is the cancer center of the Credit Valley Hospital near Toronto, whose atrium lobby is designed to mimic a forest.[23]

Historically, our approach to community design has not made health and physical activity very easy at all. The iconic single-family detached home in a conventional suburban development, embedded in a larger sprawling land use pattern of car dependence, represents a threat to public health as well. We have, as a culture and society, become too dependent on cars and are living lives that are simply too sedentary. "Sitting is the new smoking," the popular health line says. Rising rates of obesity and a rising percentage of Americans being overweight carry severe personal and societal health burdens.

Getting people outside should be another health- and life-enhancing objective. An indoor environment can be nature-rich and healthy, to be sure, but that is no substitute for spending time out of doors. An outdoor city is also a healthy city. Richard Louv wrote especially compellingly about this problem in his clarion call of a book *Last Child in the Woods*. Kids today are anything but free range and, for a variety of modern reasons, spend too much of their time inside, attached to video games, iPhones, and televisions. But there are many positive steps cities can take to overcome this problem, from sponsoring "walking school buses" and "safe routes to school" to rethinking the designs of schools and the school day to provide more nature time and time outside.

There are many ways a city can facilitate greater physical activity. The City of New York prepared a set of "active design guidelines" to identify the many ways the built environment of a city can make it easier to be physically active and thus enhance one's health. "Your city should be your greatest ally in health and well-being," declares the New York City Department of Design and Construction's active design web page.[24] The guidelines provide a wealth of ideas about what a physically active city would look like: mixed-use land use patterns and developments, high street connectivity, good access to public transit, abundant children's play areas and public plazas, and bicycle infrastructure, among others. We should also design all office and residential buildings to foster greater physical activity, such as by including exercise rooms, showers, and lockers (which will make bicycling to work easier) and "appealing and supportive walking routes" through the building. The New York City guidelines suggest that buildings should be designed in ways that stimulate walking and encourage movement: "Incorporate interesting views along paths of travel, within a building, including natural and designed landscapes, nearby architecture, interior views of people-oriented activities and visually appealing interior finishes."

The New York guidelines are meant to be advisory, but perhaps just as a city's building and fire codes aim to ensure safe egress and protect occupants from various hazards (e.g., earthquakes and high wind loads), active building codes could aim to protect against less immediate but no less lethal risks, such as type 2 diabetes, a major and devastating result of physical inactivity.

Social Infrastructure and Health

In recent years there has been a growing appreciation for the many ways our mental health is affected by the design and structure of cities and their streets and neighborhoods. In the United States there is what some have described as an epidemic of loneliness. We also know that evidence is mounting that the more friends and social connections you have, the healthier you are. We need cities that help foster these essential social connections. One metastudy found a 50 percent increase in longevity when individuals had an extensive social support network.[25]

The journalist Eric Klinenberg, in his book *Palaces for the People*, argues for the importance of investing in "social infrastructure" in cities. He defines social infrastructure as "the physical places and organizations that shape the way people interact."[26] For Klinenberg, the stock of things that fall within the definition of social infrastructure is extensive, including parks and playgrounds, schools, public swimming pools, libraries, community gardens, and of course, the streets and sidewalks themselves.

If enhancing health is an ethical obligation of cities, then investing in social infrastructure would be an effective means to achieve this. More parks, community pools, and community gardens would all be helpful, but it's also important to change the ways we use existing facilities and spaces—schools, for example, can be redefined and reprogrammed to accommodate a larger set of community functions and activities. In park-deficient neighborhoods, schoolyards can be redesigned to provide contact with nature and space for contemplation and gathering beyond what is needed for school kids during the normal school day. Community gardens can be places where many things happen besides the growing of food. Alice's Garden in Milwaukee is a good example. Here one can find a plot to grow some food, but the space also serves as a community gathering site and a place where a diverse set of social activities occurs, such as cooking classes, yoga, and many other health-enhancing activities.

A Life of Healthy Delights

A flourishing life is more than simply the absence of disease or illness. It is also about purpose, meaning, and deep connections. It includes art and creativity, literature, and sensory experiences of all kinds. A healthy city is a city that maximizes experiences of delight. One way this happens is through public art. Philadelphia is known as the City of Murals, drawing thousands of tourists to see these outdoor works through guided and self-guided tours. Many of the murals are biophilic or nature-based in content and tell important stories about people and events.

Cities can support beautiful design and vibrant art everywhere. Many cities support investments in community art through some form of "percent for art" standard, requiring new public buildings and development projects to commission or otherwise include public art. In Fremantle, Australia, a "1 percent for art" standard is required for all development, including private as well as public projects. This means developers must spend at least 1 percent of the total cost of the project on public art, a sizable commitment of resources indeed. These funds have been used recently, for example, to allow the artist ROA to create a dramatic and beautiful mural depicting a numbat, an endangered mammal, on the side of a downtown building.

The importance of beauty, more generally, should not be forgotten in cities. Beauty is an essential element in urban design that may be difficult to adequately capture, and to be sure, there is an important subjective or "eye of the beholder" aspect to this. But few would deny the value and uplifting effects of buildings and streetscapes designed to be distinctive and characterful and that tell stories and pass along the history of a place.

Art is increasingly an important element of new buildings and can take many forms. Perhaps cities should promote a rediscovery of the floristic and other architectural flourishes that were so common in the past (and that were largely extinguished with the emergence of modern architectural styles). We see the value of such ornamental architectural traditions in buildings old and new. Consider, for example, the 1936 Lincoln Theatre in Miami Beach, with its elaborate "floral reliefs," or newer examples such as the Ronald Reagan National Airport's "window tracery" designed by Kent Bloomer, a newer practitioner of biophilic building ornamentation.[27]

Cities are sensory places, and sound plays a special role. Birdsong, for example, can induce calmness and reduce stress, and many other natural sounds, from cicadas and katydids to the rustling of leaves and the sounds of flowing water, are soothing, reassuring, and place-embedding and help elicit strong memories from our pasts. While we have (rightly) viewed noise as a negative condition that we need to control and minimize, we have tended not to appreciate or emphasize the positive qualities of natural sounds. The rise in sound maps that seek to record and inventory the many largely positive sounds in a community is an important step in seeing such sound as a positive health-inducing asset that we need to protect and cultivate.

There are a variety of planning and policy steps cities can take to redouble efforts at controlling noise, a significant urban health concern. Already cities have established quiet zones in parks (as in Central Park in New York City) or nature walks away from traffic. Reducing car dependence and car mobility would certainly help, along with placing noise limits on tires. New York City has sought to require a shift from pneumatic jackhammers to newer, quieter, electric jackhammers. In 2019, Washington, DC, took the bold step of banning gas-powered leaf blowers in an ordinance introduced by councilwoman Mary Cheh. There were, as expected, different perspectives on the ban, with the local Sierra Club representative pointing out that those most affected from a health point of view were low-wage landscape workers who were not likely to be in a position to complain or adequately protect themselves from the noise.

Noise and light pollution negatively affect sleep, with serious health implications. Bad sleep—both in terms of quantity and quality—has been associated with a variety of illnesses, according to the Centers for Disease Control and Prevention, including diabetes, cardiovascular disease, obesity, and depression. If health and flourishing are key goals in the future, planners and designers must pay more attention to conditions that generate good sleep. Light pollution has effectively deprived a large percentage of the population of the world from seeing the night sky with the naked eye. Part of the answer to that is adopting dark-sky lighting codes, which can at once reduce light pollution and reduce energy consumption. Lights-out programs in cities such as Chicago and Toronto significantly reduce the disorienting and fatal effects light pollution has on birds.

Cities That Invest in Mental Health

Significant numbers of people today suffer from social isolation, loneliness, and depression. Cities can also do many things to address these problems, including by facilitating social interactions and connections. This partly entails creating more physical spaces and places to be and to socialize in the city but also includes ways in which cities can encourage and make it easier for residents to join clubs, participate in hobbies that deepen friendships, and generally enjoy the company of others while also mastering a skill or engaging in a fun and rewarding activity.

Some examples include community sailing centers that exist in cities such as Milwaukee and Cambridge, Massachusetts. There has been a national decline in sailing, in part because of the cost involved and the paucity of mentors who can introduce and teach the next generation of recreational sailors. In Cambridge, the nonprofit Community Boating tries to address this by making it very inexpensive and easy to learn to sail and to rent a sailboat. A city's financial underwriting of such programs would be a very good investment in the mental health of its residents.

Another example is the effort in many cities to make it easier to host a block party and close one's street to typical traffic. Port Phillip, Australia, created a program called Street Life to make it easier for residents to organize block parties, recognizing this as an important step in the direction of good mental health. The city makes it easier to put on such social events in several ways, including providing insurance through the council and loaning out equipment such as large barbecues needed for such events. Programs that foster greater "neighborliness" pay health and economic dividends to a city and ought to be seen as a legitimate area where a city can promote health.

There are ethical questions here about how far a city can or should go to underwrite and/or nudge residents to become more socially active. For many, these kinds of actions may simply go too far and intrude too much into decisions made by individuals and families about what hobbies and social activities to pursue.

Conclusions

Health and safety continue to be key values and primary ethical requirements for a modern city. But the extent of these duties and the portfolio of actions and conditions that influence health and well-being, over which cities are understood to have some level of shared responsibility, have been growing. The chapter began with a discussion of some of the traditional ways that cities are expected to protect the safety of their residents but then considered a broader agenda of ways a city could enhance and support health and well-being. There are numerous and intersecting ways that the design and management of a city can affect health and well-being—from streets, sidewalks, and urban density that make walking more or less possible to the social infrastructure, such as libraries and parks, where citizens can meet, discuss, and socialize. It is not just managing the more obvious risks that daily urban life poses to residents (such as keeping sidewalks safe or managing traffic dangers) that an ethical city must be concerned with but increasingly dealing with a variety of other concerns that affect the long-term health and well-being of residents: working to create an urban environment that allows and encourages walking and bicycling, making healthy eating habits and food choices, and enjoying health-enhancing contact with friends and neighbors, among many others.

Discussion Questions

Are cities ethically responsible for the health and well-being of their citizens?

Are there at least ethical responsibilities to ensure citizens are adequately informed about the risks and hazards they face?

How and in what ways can cities influence the health and flourishing of their citizens?

Is it possible for a city to go too far, and be too overzealous, in promoting and championing good health?

To what extent and in what ways can a city be designed to foster a more active (and thus healthier) lifestyle?

Is it okay for cities to take steps to encourage health-enhancing behaviors while discouraging (or even prohibiting) behaviors that are destructive or serve to undermine good health?

Should cities worry about the social lives of their residents?

The Ethics of Biophilic Cities

Rita McMahon is the founder of the Wild Bird Fund in New York City, essentially a rehabilitation hospital for injured birds, many of which have flown into a glass window in this skyscraper city. Much of her and her staff's work entails responding to alerts of injured birds around the city, especially during peak migration times in spring and fall. Birds fail to see windows as barriers and often see reflections of trees or clouds. An estimated more than 200,000 birds die each year from building and window strikes in this city alone. The national estimates are upward of a billion.

Should a city care about birds? Does a city have a duty to take steps to minimize this death and suffering? My answer is a definitive yes, especially because there are clear and effective (and cost-minimal) steps that can be taken, particularly the installation of bird-friendly glass. Several North American cities now mandate the installation of bird-friendly glass in the construction of new buildings and for major renovations of existing structures. New York City is the largest city to have adopted such a requirement, mandating bird-friendly glass on surfaces up to a height of seventy-five feet, the most dangerous zone for birds, as well as above green rooftops.

Cities have the ability to make a huge difference: both to protect animals that bring delight and joy to so many residents of cities and to profoundly reduce the pain and suffering of so many sentient species. Taking steps to make buildings and cities safer for birds is certainly done in part out of human self-interest, but it also reflects compassion for the many other living creatures with whom we share cities. McMahon, in commenting on the passage of the New York City bird-safe ordinance, makes this point: "What the Council did today is going to save thousands of lives, and hopefully, other cities, builders, and architects will follow New York City's compassionate lead."[1] How we treat animals and plants in cities is a major category of ethical question and is an important dimension for judging the ethics of cities.

The Moral Vision of Biophilic Cities

The fact that we have coevolved with nature and retain an innate connection with it is the key insight of biophilia (a love of nature and all living things). Biophilic cities are cities that seek to place nature at the center of their design and planning and that acknowledge the need for coexistence and the many benefits of having birds, trees, and nature all around us. Ethical cities are biophilic cities.

It is about the moral consideration of animals but also plants. I love birds and believe that cities are made profoundly more interesting and enjoyable because of their presence. But perhaps there is some truth to the observation that we tend to pay more attention to the animals that move through and around our cities than to the much more abundant plant life that exists. Biophilic cities aspire to protect and expand the living greenery—plants, flowers, shrubs, and trees—we see and experience all around us. Many cities already have extensive urban forests and tree canopies, and most have set goals and developed plans to further expand the trees and greenery.

Much of the way cities have looked at green nature in the past (and still today) is very utilitarian and instrumentalist: What are the benefits that investing in nature can provide us? We often speak in terms of green infrastructure, recognizing (importantly) that when we plant trees and forests in cities, they provide many direct benefits and beneficial ecological services—helping cool and moderate urban temperatures, retaining stormwater, and ameliorating urban air pollution, among others.

Nature in cities is a powerful antidote to many modern maladies, including depression, anxiety, and the epidemic of loneliness. One recent Australian study published in the *International Journal of Epidemiology* found that residents of neighborhoods with green spaces nearby reported substantially lower levels of loneliness.[2]

It is now a common practice in urban planning to map distances to nearby parks and green spaces and to set a goal, as New York and other cities have done, for every resident to live within a five-minute walk of a park or green space. This is a reasonable target, though in many cities not sufficiently bold. Urban forestry expert Cecil Konijnendijk van den Bosch recently proposed a more ambitious target that he calls the "3-30-300 rule": every urban resident should be able to see at least three trees from her home, live in a neighborhood with at least 30 percent tree canopy coverage, and have a park or green space within at least a 300-meter walk.[3] I like this rule, in part because it is catchy and can be remembered; some localities have officially adopted it.

We need nature around us and near to us, and a vision of immersive nature requires us to break free from the bifurcated notion that nature is somewhere else, to be visited and enjoyed, but that to be legitimate and authentic it can't occupy the common living and working spaces around us.

Nature in cities should not be understood only or exclusively as a kind of health pill—something we take a dose, or multiple doses, of over the course of an urban day to improve our mood or enhance our cognition. These human benefits are important to recognize but so is the inherent moral worth of other nonhuman life: living creatures of all kinds have a good of their own and a right to exist. Biophilic cities must be biocentric as well.

There is little doubt that we are largely governed in judgments about nature by a clear mental hierarchy—one that tends to put humans at the top, separate from and superior to other forms of nature; followed by animals, who exhibit sentience; and further down, plants. Plants are ever-present in cities but often seen to have a lowly ethical status. "We have constructed a simple vision of plants as lacking in intelligence, agency and sentience," notes forest ecologist Suzanne Simard.[4] Simard's groundbreaking research on trees show how they communicate and are connected in a complex network of mycorrhizal fungi. Mother trees share carbon and nutrients and can even alert offspring to impending danger. Other researchers such as Monica Gagliano have shown how plants learn and remember. In one experiment, she discovers that plants are able to find water by sending roots in the direction of the sound of water. These plants, she concludes, are "constantly making a myriad of choices about where to go, when to go, and how quickly to go."[5]

We are lucky to be able to share space in cities with such mysterious and complex living creatures. Plants represent the largest body of living creatures on earth in terms of number and biomass, dwarfing humans. So much so that Stefano Mancuso describes them as a "nation of plants." Mancuso believes that making space for plants in cities is a special opportunity and obligation. Cities, he says, "should be totally covered with plants. Not just in designated green spaces: parks, gardens, flower beds and so on, but rooftops, balconies, terraces, sidewalks, chimneys, traffic lights, and guardrails."[6]

Beauty, Wildness, and Awe

An ethical imperative to design and bring about beautiful cities is rarely discussed in urban planning circles yet is of remarkable import. Much of what we gain from seeing and living closely with plants in cities—ideally immersed in a sea of plant life, living as parallel citizens in the city-state of plants (to build on Mancuso's idea)—is the remarkable beauty they bring to our lives. There are many potential sources of beauty in a city, including buildings and public art, but there is something profoundly powerful about majestic trees and colorful flowers, things biophilia would argue are deeply pleasing to us because we have coevolved with them and their presence signals abundance and survival. Ethical cities must strive to be beautiful cities of nature. And as the late Stephen Kellert argues, "The moral imperative of biophilia is that we cannot flourish as individuals or as a species absent a benign and benevolent relationship to the world beyond ourselves of which we are a part."[7]

There is little question that living in a nature-rich and multispecies city can deliver different kinds of benefits that may be difficult to quantify or express in the usual economic metrics of our society. I have argued elsewhere that we need a new set of metrics for judging the goodness of cities that emphasizes important qualities of nature, such as the ability of residents in every neighborhood being able to see and hear native birds. A biophilic city, moreover, might be judged by the extent to which residents over the course of a normal day might be able to experience awe and wonder.

Judging a city according to the extent to which it maximizes opportunities to experience awe is an interesting proposition. For me, this presents an important chance to distinguish between cities that are enjoyable and pleasurable, working toward the idea of "happy cities," and ethical cities that seek and acknowledge more. We want and need to work toward cities that provide deeper meanings and experiences, even when seen through an anthropocentric lens: we want cities that provide opportunities for meaning and purpose, deeper connections, and commitments to place, to each other, and to a larger public.

Where does awe enter into a city and our urban lives? There are many places and experiences where this can occur and many possible unexpected feelings of vastness: I turned the corner in my neighborhood recently and saw the first blooming flower of a southern magnolia tree. Or consider the remarkable and physically improbable antics of urban birds, such as the white-breasted nuthatch moving up and down trees essentially upside down or the northern mockingbird showing off its vocally acrobatic singing skills. Many experiences of wonder require urbanites to stop, look, and listen with an intensity that opens them to seeing nature; often this nature is quite small, such as ants on a sidewalk or the subtle pulsating glow of fireflies on a summer night. Cites can invest in awe and wonder by, first and foremost, planning and designing in ways that make nature a priority: providing trees, native plants, and landscaping; controlling lighting and light pollution (urban sky glow is notorious in cities and makes it especially difficult to see the night sky); and taking strides to protect air and water quality, among many others. Improving the water quality in New York City resulted in a chance for residents to catch a glimpse of marine wonder, as humpback whales and dolphins have returned to the waters of New York.

Toward an Ethic of Coexistence

A city is a place for humans, a living, working, and recreating environment, but we must remember that cities are also habitats for and inhabited by a complex array of living things. A biophilic city, then, is a multispecies city, one that acknowledges and plans for the diversity of life it inevitably harbors and recognizes a duty to actively make room for these many other lifeforms. There are few spaces in cities that are not occupied by life—look up from where you are standing and you will see treetops and clouds, each a home for life; look down and imagine the subterranean habitats that exist for burrowing critters, ants and other insects, and the remarkable diversity of microscopic life in the soil. Look around and what you see is a biodiverse, three-dimensional city, where life occupies the many spaces, vertical columns of air, rooftops, storm gutters, and interstitial spaces around us.

Much of this nature may be hard for urban residents to see and thus to imagine; much of it is nocturnal, still other forms of life are moving and, depending on the time of year, migrating through the city. Still other species are in places—underwater, for example—where firsthand viewing may be hard. An ethical city is one that not only acknowledges the inherent worth of these many, often hidden forms of life but works hard (and creatively) to unveil these mysterious creatures and habitats and connect the residents of cities to them emotionally (and so also enhance and deepen the quality of our human existence). Ethicists such as Peter Singer, moreover, argue strongly that we must take into account the pain and suffering of all other sentient life-forms, wild or domestic.

It is especially significant to think about the ethical obligations of cities in light of the massive deforestation and habitat loss underway in the larger world. The fact that we are in the midst of a human-caused global sixth extinction adds special duties and obligations. Cities must consequently work to protect biodiversity and can in many creative and meaningful ways strive to maximize the positive role they play. What might this mean in practice? The possibilities are limitless: designing bridges and infrastructure for bats and birds or restoring wildlife habitats in cities, even in highly developed areas (as one positive example, consider the conversion of a sterile, chlorinated water feature in Perth, Australia, into a biodiverse, native wetland!).[8]

The status of many other life-forms that we share the world with is tenuous—at least their legal status and certainly their moral status. There are federal and state endangered species lists that attach certain legal protections to listed species, and this can sometimes limit or curtail cities' actions. But for the most part there are few cities with their own endangered species lists, though some cities protect certain kinds of rare or endangered habitats. For the most part, though, discussions about the ethical status of nonhuman creatures are haphazard and erratic, to say the least, and few of our official plans explicitly take into account animals and plants.

There are exceptions, however, that help show the way. Edmonton, Alberta, for instance, has developed a planning system with an emphasis on ecological connectivity. The city developed a set of civil engineering standards that now require design and installation of wildlife passages whenever a road or other infrastructure project is built, serving a human end in reducing automobile-wildlife traffic collisions. For Edmonton, this is just part of a larger strategy of planning and design through ecological connectivity. One of the tools the city has been using is so-called circuit theory: a way to see the city through the lens of a bird or other animal. Ecological pathways are like an electric circuit, where there will be blockages in many places—for instance, where the tree canopy stops—and where it will be difficult for a bird to safely cross a road or other humanmade structure in the city.

Investing in such passages may be required to ensure survival for some species, such as mountain lions. When animals have to cross highways and even major streets, the outcome is often disastrous. But successful wildlife passages are now in use in cities and communities around the world. Some years ago, I had the chance to visit a very successful wildlife passage in Brisbane, Australia. It was designed with multiple layers of features aimed at allowing different species to cross above (and below) the highway. There were rope ladders for opossums and poles placed at strategic places so sugar gliders could easily make it across. Some complain that the costs are just too high, especially for designs such as the crossing along Highway 101 in Los Angeles (which cost into the millions). But what is also true is that such passages prevent human-wildlife car collisions, as found in Edmonton, which leads to major economic savings.

There are of course many other actions that cities can take to advance the interests of their wildlife and reduce their pain and suffering. Several cities in Canada have recently decided not to display fireworks because of the clear negative impact the noise has on animals. In their place, the cities plan to display a kind of rock-concert "pyrotechnic display." Most of the things cities can do to minimize impact on wildlife won't in turn inconvenience or significantly reduce enjoyment for humans, though that is often the worry. Some believe that the shift to "low-noise fireworks" may actually deliver more colorful fireworks.

Cities face a variety of specific wildlife coexistence challenges, including perceived overpopulation of white-tailed deer, overabundance of Canada geese, and perceived nuisance species such as racoons that are effective at raiding unsecured urban garbage cans. The Humane Society of the United States advocates for a position of tolerance and the ability, in most cases, to minimize conflict without inflicting a fatal outcome on the offending animals. John Hadidian, for many years the head of urban wildlife with the Humane Society, used to frequently say that cities do not have a racoon problem but a garbage problem—the moral onus or fault is not with the animal, who after all is simply trying to exist, but rather with the failure to take adequate steps to secure trash receptacles.

There is heated debate in many communities in the United States about whether deer populations need to be controlled and how aggressively this needs to be done. Some communities have undertaken urban culling efforts, often by employing bow-and-arrow hunters to reduce the risks to urban residents. Others question whether this is necessary and, if necessary, whether this is the most ethically defensible approach to controlling the population.

There is little question that coexistence delivers special benefits for urban residents, and the occasional glance or prospect of encountering a wild animal in the course of daily life provides layers of richness and delight. Efforts by city planners and elected officials to make room for many other species is biologically and ecologically important but also simply adds a level of pleasure and delight to urban life that from utilitarian calculus more than justifies the planning and actions necessary.

Several years ago I had the enjoyable task of searching for the now-famous smooth-coated otters of Singapore (and making a short film about the story).[9] There are now more than eighty of these otters, in ten or so distinct families, living in this dense city-state, and wherever they appear, there is a human commotion and a frenzied positive reaction. For the most part coexistence has been relatively successful (though the otters occasionally snatch koi from ornamental ponds) and a positive outcome of the investment made to restore ecosystems such as the Kallang River that runs through Bishan-Ang Mo Kio Park. The Kallang has been miraculously transformed from a flood-control channel to its current condition today as a meandering, biodiverse river, supporting birds, dragonflies, and much other nature. And as heavy recent rains have shown, the restored natural river has also provided extensive benefits in floodwater retention and flood mitigation.

Some wild animals in cities represent an element of danger, for instance the now-healthy populations of coyotes that exist in virtually every American city today. This is one species that has actually benefited from proximity to humans, and evidence suggests that coyotes have adapted well to urban life. Yet the secret to coexistence is educating urban residents and making proactive efforts to engage in coexistence practices, especially including efforts to ensure that coyotes remain afraid of humans (noisemaking and hazing seem especially effective).

Caring about the Many Other Lives

Love, care, and respect for sentient animals in cities extends as well to nonwild inhabitants, or more domesticated creatures that co-occupy our homes—including, of course, cats, dogs, and other pets. How we balance the responsibilities we have toward our pets with the duties of care we have toward wild animals in the city is one of the most difficult and often contentious issues leaders and citizens alike will face. We love our cats and dogs—and there are more than 48 million dogs and 31 million cats in the United States alone.

Few American cities have undertaken any kind of systematic effort to give voice and consideration to the many other forms of life. New York City took the exemplary step in 2019 of creating a new Office of Animal Welfare, with a focus on four areas: "companion animals; wildlife; working animals; and human dimensions of animal welfare." This is an impressive step for a city to take; only one other city, Mexico City, has done something similar. The city also adopted a package of animal welfare laws that address a wide-ranging set of animal issues, from banning wild bird trade, including pigeons, to restricting when carriage horses can be used and under what conditions.

There has been a gradual and rising interest in returning chickens, goats, and other traditional farm animals to cities, and many city codes have been amended to make raising and keeping farm animals, at least up to established limits, possible. This may be helpful from an ethical perspective if it helps keep the animals' plight and interests in front of mind in a way that our mostly distant, industrial food chain works against. And it does raise the possibility that these animals could be treated more humanely as a result of this awareness. Concerns have been raised about the suffering of urban livestock at the hands of inexperienced (nonfarmer) urban residents.[10]

More visible than the plight of animals in industrial farming, but still concerning, are the many animals that labor daily on behalf of city residents and visitors. In many cities, for instance, horse-drawn carriages labor to carry tourists around the city, a strenuous and, in the heat, dangerous labor for these animals. New York City has 200 horses registered to work pulling carriages, and there are city requirements for their care, such as limits on the number of hours the horses can work and minimum square footage requirements for stables. But many residents think the correct path is to ban the practice outright, something former New York City mayor Bill de Blasio promised during his campaign but was not able to accomplish.[11] Partly due to opposition from the Teamsters union (despite plans to help these carriage workers transition to driving green taxicabs), de Blasio sought instead to take steps that reduce the horses' exposure to traffic and heat (such as moving the location where horses are allowed to line up).[12]

Opponents of such bans argue that the horses are domesticated animals that have served in cities for centuries, and they point to the humane and productive use of horses by police departments. Matt Bershadker, writing in favor of the ban, takes on this argument: "Police horses serve a public service. Carriage horses exist for personal profit. That's the difference between necessary and unnecessary."[13] Carriage rides may be beloved and iconic but are not essential to the health and safety of New Yorkers.

Other cities have been able to bring about such bans. Montreal banned horse-drawn carriages in 2018, and Barcelona did in 2017. Catalonia also banned bullfights in 2011: "Now the 20,000 seat bullring . . . has been converted into a megamall and popular tourist attraction."[14] Other cities have banned circuses that use live animals, and a growing number of cities, including Mexico City, have banned dolphinaria and other facilities that keep dolphins, penguins, and other animals in close quarters. It is increasingly viewed as cruelty to keep highly intelligent and social cetaceans in captivity, where, in the service of entertainment, their quality of life and life expectancy are sharply reduced.

These are some of the many nonhuman "souls" that cities have some level of purview over and some ability to reduce their suffering and pain. In such discussions, ethicists often distinguish between basic and nonbasic interests. Rarely if ever does the nonbasic (nonsurvival) interest of humans trump the basic interest (survival) of another sentient form of life.

A basic interest (life) of an animal is justifiably taken when it conflicts with a human life (another basic interest) but not when the goal or purpose is "nonbasic," for instance fashion. Here we find yet another category of sentient life affected by urban life, as many animals are raised and killed for their fur. There has been an active discussion about the ethics of this for many years (I can remember as a child having heated debates about this with friends and family). Recently some cities have started to take strong positions on this, notably in California; San Francisco, Berkeley, and Los

Angeles all adopted bans on the sale of animal furs. Most recently, California adopted a statewide fur ban, preempting the city laws.

The debate in Los Angeles over its proposed fur ban was illustrative of the different perspectives and voices that surround this issue. City councillors were swayed by arguments about cruelty and about animals' pain and suffering. Opponents noted the impact on jobs and livelihoods and worried about the slippery slope of banning leather and other animal products. The ordinance, while a ban, did allow for certain exemptions, including the sale of secondhand furs. And the ban did not apply to the wearing of furs. One city councilman called for a study of the economic impacts of the ban, but others mostly expressed the view that the economic impacts were largely irrelevant in the face of the egregious and cruel practice: "Animal cruelty is animal cruelty," noted councilman Paul Koretz, "and if we lose a few jobs, that's life."[15]

Yet another ethical dimension to how other forms of life are treated in cities arises when considering the pest control industry. Millions of urban mammals—from raccoons and opossums to field mice and voles—are indiscriminately killed by so-called pest control companies at the behest of urban homeowners, inflicting untold levels of pain and suffering. A homeowner complains of the sounds of a raccoon family that has managed to enter an attic, and a pest control company is called. The result is often gruesome, as animals are captured using an array of pain-inflicting methods. An ethical city must be judged in part by the steps it takes to minimize this pain and suffering and the methods it mandates (or prohibits). In 2010, Washington, DC, adopted the progressive Wildlife Protection Act, laying out requirements for pest control professionals and companies and banning certain practices, including the use of sticky, or glue, traps, as well as the use of leghold traps, inhumane methods still in use in many cities.[16]

Cities are also places where there are many species of animals in some form of captivity in zoos and aquaria. There continues to be an active discussion—with an extensive literature—about the value and virtues of zoos. The general trend has been to directly provide more humane conditions for animals in zoos, more space, and more naturalistic settings. Yet, as Emma Marris recently argued in the *New York Times*, while zoos and aquaria do provide some educational value, they are mostly places that entertain us. She also makes a strong case that even with additional space, the experience and treatment of animals in zoos is dismal and mostly negative.[17] This is true especially for larger animals, such as elephants, because it is difficult to provide the space and conditions they need that would approximate their habitat conditions in the wild.

Counterarguments about zoos and aquaria often have to do with their conservation activities and missions, and it is true that zoos undertake important research and conservation work. The San Diego Zoo's captive-breeding efforts have been largely responsible for saving the California condor from extinction, for example. Many aquaria, such as the New England Aquarium, undertake extensive and important research and advocacy and conservation efforts, and these are not to be underestimated or understated. But it remains an open ethical question whether the conservation benefits justify the harm, pain, and suffering of the animals in captivity. For aquaria there is an important new operating model that seems much more ethical: collect and release, where marine organisms on display are released back into the wild in a matter of a few months.

Can we also judge a city by what it eats and how it treats the animals that become food? What we eat clearly raises some serious ethical concerns, especially about the ways in which sentient forms of life are used and treated. Most of the animals that are raised and killed to support a city's food needs are invisible because they are raised, killed, and processed far away from the city. Ethicist Peter Singer's groundbreaking book *Animal Liberation* argues for an ethical duty to reduce the suffering of all sentient life and holds considerable implication for how we feed current and future urban populations.[18] Fifty years after the publication of *Animal Liberation*, Singer is generally optimistic and encouraged about the status and condition of sentient life. Some of the worst factory farm conditions for animals have been addressed in many places, especially the European Union and California (which set minimum standards for animal confinement, for instance).

New York City, as part of the package of animal welfare laws adopted in 2019, waded provocatively into this question by banning the sale of foie gras.[19] This practice involves force-feeding ducks and geese through tubes for long periods of time to produce the enlarged liver that makes up this food product. On its face there is little doubt that the production of this food makes these animals suffer tremendously. Nevertheless, and predictably, there was considerable opposition from restaurants—some 1,000 in New York had it on their menu. To soften the economic impact, including to upstate farmers, the ban did not become effective until 2022.

For many in the animal rights movement in New York, the foie gras ban, and the comprehensive package of laws, is a wonderful sign of progress, "evidence," says Allie Feldman Taylor of the organization Voters for Animal Rights, "that New York City is becoming more compassionate." Restaurateurs and the farmers supplying them were not happy, of course. One restaurateur was quoted in the *New York Times* as pondering: "What's next? No more veal? No more mushrooms?"[20] Production of veal is, yes, equally troubling and equally unethical—another example of a sentient life-form forced to suffer to produce a luxury product. Mushrooms, on the other hand, as far as we know do not feel pain and do not raise questions about humane treatment.

Until I had the chance to interview Singer several years ago, I had not thought much about the human treatment of fish or seafood, though I knew that the industrial-scale global fishing industry behind the harvesting of seafood was unsustainable, and I was aware of initiatives aimed at supporting local, more sustainable fishing practices, which is an encouraging trend (though not motivated so much by a concern about the pain and suffering of fish). Many cities have indeed nurtured small-scale fisheries, as well as more local and sustainable models such as community-supported fisheries (in the vein of community-supported agriculture), and these are positive steps.[21]

Crashing global fisheries suggest, Singer thinks, the need to explore other sources of protein for a growing population. That seems clear, but Singer adds another important dimension to this debate: he believes that as we've learned more about the psychological complexity and sentience of fish, shifting production to other sources of marine protein may be required. Both harvesting wild-caught fish and using aquaculture to raise large predator fish species, such as salmon, involve tremendous suffering. There is now good research showing the psychological and emotional complexity of fish, something not heretofore given much attention. This research shows, Singer says, that "fish are individuals. . . . Some are quite intelligent, good at problem-solving. . . . They have emotions and feelings and relate to others as individuals."[22]

By contrast, filter-feeding species such as mussels and oysters can be cultivated without this immense suffering (Singer believes the sentience line is somewhere between an oyster and a lobster or a shrimp, a speculation he included in *Animal Liberation* and that is now being validated, Singer believes, by science). Their production and harvesting also do not impose the same degree of environmental damage and, indeed, are actually ecologically restorative (e.g., they filter and cleanse water). Cities will not be able to avoid the ethical dimensions of the many ways they choose to facilitate, subsidize, or regulate food production and the ways they, in turn, frame and influence individual food choices.

The Ethical Status for Urban Ecosystems

Perhaps as important as the pain and suffering of individual animals in a city is the integrity and health of the larger ecosystems that sustain and support them. Perhaps we must begin to see the urban ecosystem as itself a living entity, with inherent value and worthy of respect, protection, and repair. This connects well with the global trend in assigning moral and legal rights to rivers, forests, and other ecosystems. This idea was pioneered by law professor Christopher Stone in a provocative law review essay (later published as a book) entitled "Should Trees Have Standing?"[23] A half century later, there are now working examples of ecosystems that have been given legal personhood. They can sue parties that have harmed them (with the help of legal guardians) and they can seek and receive damages that are used to repair and restore the harm.

In New Zealand, this notion builds on the Māori philosophy and view of the world, and legal personhood has now been granted to a forest (Te Urewera), a river (Whanganui Awa), and a mountain (Taranaki Maunga). In North America there is also movement in this direction, with a recent announcement that the Magpie River in Quebec will be granted legal personhood (and nine specific rights). The announcement was made by the Muteshekau-shipu Alliance, which includes the Innu Council of Ekuanitshit (the Innu are the original First Nation inhabitants of the river, known to them as Muteshekau-shipu in the Innu language).

Few of these examples are urban in nature, but that will likely change in the future. One notable urban example is the Lake Erie Bill of Rights, a popular referendum to grant Lake Erie legal personhood through an amendment to the city charter of Toledo, Ohio. The text of the Lake Erie Bill of Rights does indeed read like a legal bill of rights, establishing the lake's rights but also establishing the human rights of residents to nature and natural environments. The bill of rights states that Lake Erie and its watershed "possess the right to exist, flourish, and naturally evolve. The Lake Erie Ecosystem shall include all natural waters features, communities of organisms, soil as well as terrestrial and aquatic sub ecosystems that are part of Lake Erie and its watershed."[24] The city or its residents would, under the charter amendment, be able to institute legal action on behalf of the lake. Damages are calculated by the costs of repair and restoration, and they flow to the city, to be used "exclusively for full and complete restoration of the Lake Erie Ecosystem and its constituent parts."

How this will work in practice is hard to know. A federal judge struck down the charter in 2020, concluding that (because of its vagueness) it violated the Fourteenth Amendment of the US Constitution. There is at the time of this writing still some hope it can prevail legally, but there is little doubt that similar mechanisms will be used in and near cities in the future. It may be that the ultimate expression (and implementation) of the vision of biophilic cities is to be found in assigning legal (and political) rights to urban ecosystems, or at least portions of these ecosystems, such as a river, forest, or harbor. We will see, but given the historic inability to preserve and restore the natural systems and environments around cities, exploring these kinds of ideas makes a lot of sense.

Conclusions

Biophilia is the idea that we have an innate connection to nature, have coevolved for millennia with nature, and consequently are hardwired to need and want that connection. The evidence for this grows weekly, it seems, with new research coming out from disciples of environmental psychology, public health, economics, and other disciplines. While much of the research remains correlational (rather than causal), it seems hard to deny that nature makes us feel better, improves our cognition and mood, and helps heal and restore us. And when we have trees and greenery around us in cities—if we are ideally immersed in nature—we live healthier, better, and of course, more interesting lives. More nature-immersive cities are possible, as we shift from a view of cities that have pockets of nature (the park down the street) to a view of a city *as* nature. Nature is all around us, and it is three-dimensional, above us (birds singing in trees, rooftop meadows), below us (the tremendous biodiversity of soil), and all around us. Plants make up the bulk of nature in cities, as they do on planet Earth, but cities also harbor abundant animal life. Many of our personal and collective decisions in cities directly affect nonhuman life: what we choose to eat, how we design the buildings in which we live and work, how we recreate, and even how we commemorate important events. We must do a better job at taking into account the interests and welfare of these many nonhuman "souls" that live with us and around us. It is a challenge but ultimately a joy to discover, learn about, and care for the many forms of life with which we coinhabit urban spaces.

Discussion Questions

What kinds of nature can we find in a city, and where would we look?
Which plants and animals are most important to city residents, and what is the extent of our ethical duties to protect and care for them?
Are there special obligations when it comes to the sentient lives we share space with in cities? What about our many domestic pets, such as cats and dogs? We clearly love them, but are they more important than the wild animals such as the birds, squirrels, and ants that we see all around us?

What Is a City's Duty to the Larger World?

As singer-songwriter Jackson Browne says in his reggae-style song "It Is One" (one *world*, that is), "We don't decide where we are born."[1] That single insight is very important from an ethical and moral standpoint, with important implications for cities. Cities can choose to act in ways that take into account people and environments far away and far beyond their legal borders or boundaries. The actions of cities and their inhabitants, we know, often have serious global effects. From the discharge of sewage into our oceans to the effects of our urban consumption patterns on global biodiversity loss, we know that our decisions in cities have serious extralocal repercussions. Are we duty bound to work to reduce or eliminate such impacts? And should cities seek to offer aid and assistance, when they can, to address problems such as global poverty, hunger, and disaster relief? If we are truly "one world," in a moral sense, then cities must do what they can.

Philosopher Peter Singer, in a now-famous essay called "Famine, Affluence, and Morality," originally published in *Philosophy and Public Affairs*, argues that we have a moral duty to address starvation, calling out the international response to the deaths in East Bengal during the early 1970s movement seeking Bangladesh independence. Singer uses the example of encountering a drowning child: "If I am walking past a shallow pond and see a child drowning in it, I ought to wade in and pull the child out. This will mean getting my clothes muddy, but this is insignificant, while the death of the child would presumably be a very bad thing."[2]

Proximity encourages a response: we are more likely to act on behalf of that individual, Singer admits, but it doesn't change the moral duty—saving the child is something we ought to do regardless of proximity. For him, if we are indeed able to make a difference, regardless of how indifferent others

Sidebar 13-1 What Can Cities Do to Reduce Poverty and Raise Living Conditions beyond Their Borders?
Support (financially and otherwise) charities and nonprofits doing work in other cities and countries
Direct financial support to projects in other cities that reduce poverty and enhance living conditions
Direct financial or technical assistance in emergencies and disasters
Take steps to educate and activate citizens to directly contribute or otherwise address global poverty
Advocate for greater assistance from the federal government

around us are, we are duty bound to try. Singer states the ethical principle very clearly: "If it is in our power to prevent something very bad from happening, without thereby sacrificing anything morally significant, we ought, morally, to do it."[3]

Taking any kind of action runs the risk of unintended results, of course, and "do no harm" remains a central tenet in decision-making on the global scene. If we fear that our actions to help will inflict more harm, then we should think twice about doing them. But cities, especially affluent and politically influential cities in the Global North, have the opportunity and the resources to make a difference and help in big and small ways to address global problems of hunger, instability, natural disaster response, and of course, climate change.

But do cities have the mechanisms and means to take meaningful action on behalf of the world's poor, for instance? Certainly they can and must take steps to address poverty among their own citizens, within their own boundaries, but what can be done to effect change in faraway locales? The short answer is that there are many ways cities can help, many things they can do, and many forms of influence they can exert (see sidebar 13-1).

While cities may be able to take direct actions themselves, they are increasingly able to operate in nonunilateral ways to address poverty and other serious global problems. The age of global networks is upon us, and a typical city is a member of several, perhaps scores of, networks that typically emphasize specific issues. Global networks are one important avenue through which cities can exert a global influence.

Twenty-first-century cities are global, to be sure, and they have to be more engaged on the global scene. Democracy requires it. Some would use the neologism *local* instead, in the sense that many cities today creatively blend

> **Sidebar 13-2 Some of the Many Networks Cities Belong To**
> C40 Cities
> Global Covenant of Mayors for Climate and Energy
> Global Network of Learning Cities
> Carbon Neutral Cities Alliance
> ICLEI–Local Governments for Sustainability
> Cities4Forests
> Circular Cities
> Resilient Cities Network
> Biophilic Cities Network

the local (including the regional) with the global. Many forms of grassroots or DIY urbanism, some of which I discussed earlier, emphasize the importance of the local economy and provide more opportunities for city residents to, for instance, buy directly from local farmers or fishers.

Partly given the vacuum at the federal level, cities around the world have been organizing and networking to an unusual degree. We now have many more global networks than a decade or two ago. According to researcher Michele Acuto, there are now more than 200 global networks (compared with fifty-five in 1985), ranging from large and well-resourced networks (e.g., Resilient Cities Network and C40 Cities) to smaller, more nascent ones such as the Biophilic Cities Network (see sidebar 13-2).[4]

Cities gain much from networks, which can magnify cities' power and influence. Networks allow cities to share information and best practices, to inspire and learn from each other, and to embrace common targets and leverage global commitments to accomplish meaningful actions at home. Through such networks cities can take collective stands on the global stage that would be difficult or impossible individually.

Climate Mayors is a network that was formed in 2014 and now includes 470 US cities committing to the Paris Climate Accords. It is described as "a bipartisan, peer-to-peer network [of cities] . . . demonstrating climate leadership through meaningful actions in their communities." Internationally, there is the Global Covenant of Mayors for Climate and Energy, comprising more than 12,000 cities. A more ambitious but considerably smaller group of cities organizing to address global challenges is the Carbon Neutral Cities Alliance. It describes itself as "a collaboration of leading global cities working to achieve carbon neutrality in the next 10–20 years—the most aggressive [greenhouse gas] reduction targets undertaken anywhere by any city."

The group consists of around twenty leading cities that have stated the goal of becoming carbon-neutral, including Amsterdam, Copenhagen, Toronto, and Washington, DC.

Do such commitments make a difference, and does participating together with other cities make a discernible impact? One can be skeptical about true and lasting commitments. Signing up to do something is relatively easy, but taking the steps to become carbon-neutral or to just make meaningful reductions in a city's carbon emissions is harder work. Yet it does appear that many cities, especially now, are following through with their commitments and are taking a variety of often quite impressive steps to substantially reduce greenhouse gas emissions and deeply improve the quality of life for residents now and in the future.

Paradiplomacy is a new word that has emerged to describe the new ways cities are engaged at the global level. Cities such as Seoul are developing diplomacy plans and laying out their future global intentions. Many cities are participating in and collaborating with each other on aspirational global goals of various kinds. If cities, especially larger cities, have the chance to make significant global impacts—whether reducing greenhouse gas emissions and human impacts from sea level rise and heat, working for improved worker conditions (say, in Bangladeshi shirt factories), or taking steps to reduce world hunger—are they not duty bound to take these actions, consistent with Singer's example of saving a drowning child?

The Global Footprint of Cities

Cities, especially in the Global North, leave a remarkably large ecological footprint. An ecological footprint, as pioneered by William Rees and Mathis Wackernagel at the University of British Columbia, is a calculation of the land area needed to support and supply the many resources and goods, from food to energy and building materials, that a city requires.[5] A large modern city draws and extracts large amounts of materials, energy, and food from distant places to support an affluent lifestyle. Our urban lives and lifestyles in the Global North are responsible for much of the consumption of the planet's resources. In this way, there is a deeply inequitable global distribution of wealth and power that cities can and should seek to rectify.

Global cities of the North commonly leave ecological footprints that are many times larger than the surrounding regions or bioregions in which they are situated. A study some years ago found that London's ecological footprint was some 300 times the land area of the city itself. Cities thus are, as Rees says, "appropriating the carrying capacities" of other landscapes and nations, often from a distant and anonymous hinterland.

Calculating ecological footprints and setting tangible goals for their reduction is a good step, which the City of Vancouver undertook, intending to reduce the city's ecological footprint by one-third by 2020. Vancouver is one of the few cities that has explicitly included a target for reducing its ecological footprint (or even acknowledging the footprint) in official plans. This would be a good start for a city that sees itself as ethical.

A study in *Nature Communications* makes clear that much of the enjoyment of consumer goods in cities and countries of the Global North is built on a framework of externalizing the negative effects of their production. The researchers estimated that consumption by the G20 countries results in particulate pollutants in the Global South that lead to some 2 million premature deaths each year.[6] The authors called on the G20 to acknowledge its "consumer responsibility" and to exert leadership on this issue, though precisely what they could or should do is unclear.

What can cities do to address such moral problems and work to reduce their footprints? There are many steps they can take, large and small. Assuming greater accountability and responsibility for the impacts, direct and indirect, associated with the many consumer products we purchase and enjoy would be one important category of action. The production of inexpensive consumer products, such as electronics and shirts and other garments, often comes at a high price for those living and working in source cities and countries. For example, much of the economy of Bangladesh depends on garment production, often for large international brands, yet working conditions are dismal. The Rana Plaza building collapse in Dhaka in 2013, which led to more than 1,100 deaths, highlights the dangers of working conditions that would be unacceptable in the Global North.[7] While some improvements in safety and working conditions were introduced following the collapse, many were modest and short-lived. Cities can be a force for better and safer working conditions by employing more careful procurement (how and what they buy as a government) as well as using their considerable economic and political clout to push for stronger safeguards for workers.

Cities, especially larger cities, have the potential to steer their considerable spending in a more globally sustainable direction. Procurement is one significant category of city decision-making that can effect changes. New York City spends nearly $40 billion a year on a variety of goods and services, for example, and even smaller cities can make a difference by buying products that are better for the environment and reduce a city's ecological footprint.[8] Direct expenditures often grow, too; in New York City's case, they were 25 percent higher in fiscal year 2022 than the previous year.

Many cities have adopted some form of sustainable procurement process. Portland, Oregon, specifies that a number of its purchased goods must be made with sustainable materials and practices, such as furniture that minimizes toxic chemicals and protects indoor air quality or low-carbon concrete. When purchasing uniforms and other textiles, New York and Portland can directly influence the working conditions in cities like Dhaka. In fact, Portland stipulates that textiles can be purchased only from manufacturers following its Code of Conduct for Apparel Manufacturers, which requires an above-poverty wage, limits the number of regular work hours per week, and prohibits worker abuse and employment of children under the age of fifteen, among other standards, though says little to nothing about factory safety, which could address the issues raised by the Rana Plaza collapse.[9]

In recent years there has been much advocacy for cities with circular and regenerative metabolisms. Shifting or reforming a city's metabolism can happen in several key ways. One is by reducing the size of metabolic flows—for instance, requiring city buildings to be more energy efficient, reduce energy consumption, or even better, be at least net-zero, that is, produce at least as much energy (through rooftop photovoltaic panels, for example) as they need over the course of a year. Cities can also work to shorten their supply lines by producing and consuming more goods and materials locally. Reducing urban demand for faraway food and forest products, and fostering more local production in and around cities, can significantly reduce deforestation and biodiversity loss. There are now a number of wonderful stories about cities whose local mills cut and process significant amounts of timber for construction and flooring from salvage trees.

Urban metabolisms can also become more circular—that is, encourage more reuse and recycling of resources and materials. As green architect William McDonough was fond of pointing out with his memorable motto "waste equals food," there is nothing wasted in nature, so nothing should be wasted in the city. Wastewater can be reused and recycled; organic household waste and its useful biogas can be collected. There are countless ways in which resource flows in a city can be redesigned and reconfigured to move toward McDonough's vision.

There is a good argument to be made that we should move beyond small changes at the edges and take bolder steps that will create new and more sustainable and regenerative economies. As discussed earlier in this book, there is a global move afoot to shift in the direction of a regenerative and circular economy, and some cities such as Amsterdam have already committed to such a vision. This new type of economy benefits local workers and residents. There are many selfish reasons to support such a shift, but it is also an economic model that better protects the global environment and acknowledges the many ways that local production and consumption affect others hundreds of miles away.

Can Cities Be a Force for Global Conservation?

Cities can and must be global leaders for stewardship and conservation. Protection of biodiversity will increasingly depend on the actions of cities both directly in the way they invest in local habitat protection and restoration but also in the many ways they support more distant nature by modifying their consumption patterns, exerting global conservation leadership, and taking tangible steps to support conservation-supported enterprises and businesses around the world.

Committing to global goals and recognizing the need to affirmatively take responsibility for locally generated carbon emissions will sometimes pit one city against others. Bill Peduto, former mayor of Pittsburgh, encountered this conflict in western Pennsylvania when he sought to discourage the rise in "cracker plants"—manufacturing plants that produce plastics through a process that takes advantage of a glut of inexpensive natural gas and a result of a fracking boom.

Cities like Pittsburgh can do many things to directly reduce their ecological footprints and carbon emissions, from making it easier for citizens to walk and ride bikes to investing in more public transit. Such steps will at once help the city reach its climate goals and achieve other important collective benefits, such as enhancing the health of residents. From an ethical point of view, such steps (again) serve to protect the health and well-being of local constituents and residents but also acknowledge that local decisions (e.g., how car-dependent a city's transport system is, how extractive of fossil fuels, or how consumptive and wasteful overall) have serious impacts on faraway people. Flooding in very vulnerable, low-lying countries such as Bangladesh is in no small degree a result of opulent and careless lifestyles in cities like Pittsburgh and New York. There is, then, an ethical duty to acknowledge and rectify historic culpability for these impacts.

Pittsburgh is also one of the first US cities to have embraced the UN Sustainable Development Goals (SDGs) and to have begun to evaluate the extent to which the city's programs and actions address them. These goals—seventeen in total—have become our collective global aspirations for addressing poverty and environmental sustainability. In November 2020 Pittsburgh released its first-ever voluntary local review. As a press release states, "The report classifies city work, projects and initiatives, under each SDG outcome to produce an understanding of what work is contributing to what outcome."[10] It is a useful assessment tool but also a statement of commitment to shared global goals. "The City will use this periodic report to hold itself accountable to its work and operations supporting the SDGs and measure its progress towards achieving the SDGs."[11] Pittsburgh's plan to "hold itself accountable" to global goals and aspirations is itself a statement of the power and importance of global goals, a recognition that cities are part of a larger planetary community of life and that every city must work to do its part.

Cities are increasingly setting their own ambitious, yet globally inspired, goals. Copenhagen, for example, declared its intent to become the first carbon-neutral capital city in the world by 2025 and has a detailed plan for how to reach this goal. Already it is leading the transition to renewable energy. More than 60 percent of trips made in this city are by bicycle, and it would be hard to find a city that has done more to create a bicycle-friendly environment. This includes adding many miles of bike lanes and bike paths, using synchronized traffic lights that give riders a steady green, and building many new bicycle bridges, among other things. Paris has also made immense strides to shift mobility away from cars and to reduce its carbon emissions, committing to the vision of a fifteen-minute city and making it increasingly easy to move around by walking or cycling.

Many cities are investing in renewable energy and converting their extensive vehicle fleets to electric as part of larger climate change strategies. Metro Miami-Dade County, Florida, for instance, recently announced its intent to purchase more than forty new electric buses as part of its efforts to electrify its now mostly diesel-powered fleet.[12] These are zero-emission vehicles that will benefit the planet as well as the local neighborhoods through which they travel, and they will also be quiet. Similarly, the New York City sanitation department announced the purchase of electric garbage trucks. As a department that operates 6,000 vehicles, the transition to electric trucks is a very big deal indeed.[13] Similarly, the city established a goal of converting all 5,800 of its buses to electric by 2040 (and will purchase only electric buses beginning in 2028).

Rethinking and redesigning a city's building stock is also an essential step, one many cities have already taken. Achieving net-zero energy is an important goal for cities, and we are now seeing wonderful new building designs that incorporate nature and health as central design features but also radically minimize energy consumption and carbon emissions.

Given that global carbon levels have now well exceeded 400 parts per million, designing net-zero buildings (or anything we design and operate in cities) may actually not be enough. It can be argued that we increasingly need to design buildings and cities that achieve "negative emissions." Some of the technology to do so, notably direct air capture, is still young, but it's quite promising and will have many applications in cities. Could new urban buildings be designed to incorporate direct air capture and carbon sequestration? The global architectural firm SOM unveiled plans for such a building—what it calls the Urban Sequoia—which will sequester an estimated 1,000 tons of carbon per year (the equivalent of a nearly 50,000-tree forest).[14] The emergence of mass timber buildings in cities around the world is yet another approach to urban carbon sequestration that's gaining ground, and there will be many opportunities for cities to put these ideas into practice.

Cities can join together to set common goals for reducing especially damaging kinds of consumption. In 2019, for example, fourteen cities around the world teamed up to commit to reducing their meat consumption and to becoming Good Food Cities, an initiative organized by C40 Cities.[15] Meat consumption has been especially implicated in a host of global environmental problems, including greenhouse gas emission and especially deforestation and habitat loss connected with the expansion of ranchland and agriculture.[16] There are health implications as well, as meat consumption leads to higher rates of colorectal cancer.

Global meat consumption has been rising, both in absolute and per capita terms, and again, this represents a significant threat to human and planetary health. Cities have some degree of control and some levers for influencing meat consumption and can justify doing so for human and planetary health reasons. New York City, for example, instituted a "meatless Monday" initiative in all of its 1,800 public schools, and many other cities have taken similar steps. Such efforts are also not without controversy, of course. In 2020, newly elected mayor of Lyon, France, Grégory Doucet, a member of the Greens party, made the decision to take meat off the menu in all of Lyon's schools, despite the objection of the French government, which claimed it would be putting the health of children at risk.[17]

Good Food Cities include Los Angeles, Lima, and Seoul, which have committed to align "their food procurement to a 'planetary health diet'—rich in plant-based food with less food from animal sources—by 2030. This equates to a maximum average of 300 grams of meat per person per week."[18] Each city has identified a variety of impressive steps it plans to take to reduce its residents' meat consumption.

Could a city aspire to become a "meatless city," perhaps? It is a provocative question, but it was the main question of an online workshop held by the New York University School of Law in June 2021 titled "How Cities Can Help Lead the Transition to a Plant-Forward Food System."[19] In advance of the workshop, organizers published a series of background materials summarizing what cities are already doing to make this a reality: Berkeley and New York City have both set a procurement goal to reduce beef purchases by half; San Francisco has taken similar steps to reduce purchases of meat for its jails and hospitals. And a number of cities' schools have meatless Mondays.[20]

One example of cities working together globally around the issue of food is the Milan Urban Food Policy Pact, which was initiated by that city in 2015 and now has 200 signatories. The pact is essentially a global pledge and a detailed framework of recommended actions for participating cities.[21]

Global Leadership and the (Many) Duties beyond Borders

Do cities have an ethical obligation to work to protect and conserve nature beyond their borders or boundaries? My answer is yes—and in several key ways. Cities can and must think beyond their boundaries, and much of the history of regional planning certainly reflects this need for extralocal perspectives and coordinated plans and actions.

Less common are efforts on the part of cities to protect and restore the larger ecosystems in which they sit and the more distant hinterlands that help to support and sustain the cities. One well-known example is New York City's effort to protect the watersheds that supply the majority of the city's drinking water supply. This initiative, the New York City Watershed Protection Program, dates to the late 1990s, when the city sought an alternative approach to building new and very costly water filtration plants. Instead, the city took steps to protect the watersheds, including the Catskill/Delaware watersheds, where most of the city's unfiltered water comes from. These extralocal watersheds deliver to the city some 1 billion gallons of drinking water a day.[22] Over about two decades, the city purchased (mostly in fee simple) and protected about 154,000 acres of forest and farmland (in about 1,800 parcels) and spent about $500 million in the process. In combination with other steps, including funding agricultural best management practices, the city's efforts were mostly successful at protecting its water supply, as well as securing and setting aside a considerable amount of nature more than 100 miles beyond its city borders.

Every city in the world benefits from the watersheds and bioregions in which they sit and should be counted on to take steps to sustainably source from its immediate hinterlands the goods, materials, and resources it needs. Other examples include supporting wind farms and other renewable energy projects that may be equally far away and protecting and supporting the regional agriculture from which a city sources much of its food and vegetables. Regional- and even continental-scale conservation efforts would also benefit tremendously from actions that cities take beyond their borders, for example habitat restoration and land acquisition guided by larger visions (such as the Eastern Wildway or the Yellowstone to Yukon Conservation Initiative).

Sometimes a city's conservation actions can serve to advance important regional conservation initiatives and goals. Austin, Texas, for example, has been purchasing carbon credits (as part of achieving its goal to become a carbon-neutral city), which in turn generates funds to support tree-planting in riparian environments and floodplains in the larger region, outside the boundaries of the city. This is an example of urban offsets that help fund extralocal conservation. The Austin initiative is a partnership with the nonprofit TreeFolks and is facilitated by Seattle-based City Forest Credits, which calculates and certifies the amount of carbon sequestered by the trees planted over a twenty-five-year period.[23] TreeFolks has also started an initiative called Carbon Plus and, with the help of City Forest Credits, is calculating the additional environmental benefits (beyond carbon) generated by the tree-planting and floodplain restoration.

Carbon offsets, and green offsets more generally, are fraught with limitations, of course. Some recent high-visibility offsets have raised questions about their real impact and whether the resulting conservation would have occurred anyway. As part of their work to verify carbon credits, City Forest Credits also assesses what it calls "threat of loss" and must conclude in an existing forest that, without appropriate conservation action, trees would be lost (for instance to urban development).

Many cities perch on the edge of an ocean and have wonderful opportunities to engage in conservation leadership there. I have argued elsewhere for a vision of blue urbanism, or "ocean cities," that understands and nurtures the essential connections between cities and the marine habitats that sustain them. Coastal cities could work to expand marine protected areas near and far. Only about 7 percent of the earth's oceans are in a fully protected area. While cities may not have the jurisdiction or authority to establish and protect more distant marine areas, there are strong advocacy and leadership roles they could assume.

One specific example can be seen in the political drama that surrounded the Northeast Canyons and Seamounts Marine National Monument. This remarkable marine habitat lies just 130 miles off the New England coast as the seagull flies, not far from Boston. The Trump administration took away restrictions on commercial fishing, but the Biden administration restored them partly in response to the research and advocacy needs of several New England aquaria.[24] While it technically wasn't city governments that engaged in these conservation actions, the staff and leadership of the aquaria, which are located in cities, engaged in this meaningful and ultimately successful advocacy.[25]

There are many other, less obvious ways a city and its residents might work on behalf of global conservation. One is through the annual influx and outflux of tourism, a remarkably potent way in which a city directly impacts the ecology of many other parts of the world. Residents of global cities like New York are highly connected with, and easily and commonly travel to, many distant parts of the world. New York City has been declared the "most connected city" in the Western Hemisphere, with regular flights to some 147 destinations.[26] With the rise of so-called restorative tourism, there is the potential for millions of New York City residents to be challenged to visit and recreate in ways that reduce ecological impacts and in fact contribute to the protection and restoration of natural areas around the world. Perhaps that happens by choosing an ecotourism itinerary or option or by making a carbon offset payment, but the potential is there to challenge and guide the immense tourism market in ways that advance global conservation.

Equally true, larger cities will host thousands or even millions of visitors from other countries and cities, and they have a chance to educate, engage, and showcase tools, ideas, and projects that might be carried back home and applied there. Before the pandemic, New York City hosted some 67 million visitors a year, giving many tourists the opportunity to learn about and visit places such as Central Park or the High Line or the Javits Center to learn about the plight of migrating birds and the important role of investing in bird-friendly buildings and glass!

Half-Earth Cities

Cities can do many things on behalf of nature, and there are an increasing number of positive examples of cities understanding their larger global mandate. Increasingly, cities and metropolitan regions must see the ways their design, planning, and consumption affect others, perhaps hundreds or thousands of miles away, and must take steps to moderate those effects and positively improve lives and environments.

There is little doubt that, today, all global actors and entities, including cities, must act in much bolder ways. Global conservation needs and actions are just too great and too in need of quick action to accept modest, minimal actions; small steps and tinkering at the margins are ethically unacceptable given the challenges we face globally.

In June 2021 a report jointly issued by the UN Environment Programme and the Food and Agriculture Organization of the UN estimated that we need to globally rewild and restore a minimum of 1 billion hectares of land by 2030 if we are to effectively stanch the loss of biodiversity.[27] This is an area the size of China, and there are few precedents or past actions that suggest that such bold goals are possible to achieve. It is a bold goal, and one that cities must work together to achieve. Cities can and should be motivated by such larger global goals and visions, and city leaders and players on the global scene should work to achieve them.

Another compelling vision and bold goal that cities can embrace is E. O. Wilson's provocative challenge of setting half the earth aside for nature—what he calls Half Earth. Spearheaded by the Half-Earth Project (of the E. O. Wilson Biodiversity Foundation), the idea opens the real possibility of Half-Earth cities (a term first used by Australian designer Paul Downton).[28] In Wilson's words, "In a world gaining so swiftly in biotechnology and rational capability, it is entirely reasonable to envision a global network of inviolable reserves that cover half the surface of Earth."[29] It's the conservation moon shot that we need, and cities as engines of global consumption need to be in the control room guiding and steering the trajectory.

What can cities do to begin to realize the Half-Earth vision? And more generally, do they have ethical duties to do what they can, and to muster the considerable resources they have, to support conservation? Cities, especially in the Global North, as we have seen, import large amounts of energy, food, water, and building materials from far away. It is undeniable that urban life in the North consumes a disproportionate amount of the planet's resources.

Cities can aspire to achieve Half Earth locally, for instance by ensuring that 50 percent of a city's surface area is tree canopy, parks, and rooftop gardens. They can also achieve significant conservation goals regionally, as more and more cities seek to protect and restore forests and natural lands that protect larger watersheds. Cities can also commit to protecting more distant forests, for instance by sustainably procuring wood, especially from local and regional sources. More than a decade ago, New York City adopted a policy discouraging the purchase of tropical hardwoods from countries like Brazil, setting a positive example for other cities.

How cities might directly support the protection and conservation of larger ecosystems beyond their boundaries, perhaps hundreds or thousands of miles away, remains an open question. Partly it is a matter of actively participating in and supporting global conservation initiatives. It is also perhaps about providing financial and technical support for on-the-ground conservation efforts and organizations working to protect and steward land and sea, say, in the Amazon basin or the Canadian boreal forest.

Cities can certainly calculate their ecological footprints and establish specific, measurable targets to reduce them, as Vancouver has done in aiming to reduce its footprint by one-third. This target is embedded in the larger and quite ambitious Greenest City Action Plan, which identifies a comprehensive set of actions the city can take, from shifting to entirely renewable energy, to encouraging more trips by walking, bicycling, and public transit, to planting thousands of new trees in the city, all of which would reduce the city's impact on the larger planetary environment.[30] Cities can support global conservation through many projects and policies that shift resource flows from global to local (underscoring the importance of urban metabolism). Reducing urban demand for faraway agricultural products and fostering more local production in and around cities can help to reduce deforestation and biodiversity loss.

Another answer is to recognize the ethical shortsightedness of cities that work hard to advance a vision of biophilic urbanism locally, which I discussed in an earlier chapter. Cities understandably emphasize local nature—the trees and parks that sustain daily life—but many cities often ignore more distant nature. It is paradoxical and more than a little ethically inconsistent to protect local biodiversity and nature at the same time that a city and its residents (by virtue of their collective ecological footprints and consumption patterns) are directly or indirectly helping to diminish or destroy nature in more remote and faraway locales. It is inconsistent with enlightened self-interest, of course, as we increasingly recognize that wherever we live, we depend on healthy global ecosystems for survival. But it is also inconsistent with the full vision and spirit of biophilic cities, as described earlier. Cities that truly love nature must love (and work on behalf of) more distant nature as well.

We can and must rethink the basic assumptions and functions of local economies as well. In an earlier chapter, I discussed Kate Raworth's groundbreaking vision of Doughnut Economics.[31] Guided by the image and philosophy of the doughnut, Amsterdam is moving quickly to become perhaps the world's first truly circular city. It has set the goal of being fully circular—meaning that all of the goods and materials that make up the city and its economy will be reused and recycled endlessly—by the year 2050, and as an intermediate goal, it will be 50 percent circular by 2030. What does this mean in practice? As Raworth says, "Refurbishing, repurposing, reusing, recycling, never throwing away."[32] That's what we need every city (and every business in every city) to do, shifting away from a "linear degenerative economy."

Cities, especially larger cities, are economic engines and powerhouses that in theory can help propel many global conservation efforts. One powerful notion is that cities must find ways to share, send, or spend a portion of their GDP on global conservation efforts, which could make a huge difference. Larger cities can steer their investments in the direction of conservation and sustainable enterprises and commerce. New York City recently announced its intent, for instance, to invest 2 percent of its pension funds in companies working on renewable energy and climate solutions.

Some years ago, the company Patagonia helped create an initiative called 1% for the Planet, which called on companies to commit to donating at least 1 percent of their net profits to environmental conservation groups. Cities, especially larger cities such as London and New York, have huge budgets and the ability to make similar commitments—1 percent would seem a modest but good start.

A recent UN report concludes that as a planet we need to be investing around 0.1 percent of global GDP every year to protect and restore the global ecosystem services that nature provides us.[33] A tenth of a percent of GDP does not seem like a lot to ask and might be a good target for cities. As of 2021, the New York metro area's regional GDP was a quite large $1.7 trillion; that could yield a remarkable level of resources that could be used to support nature beyond the city's boundaries and perhaps hundreds or thousands of miles away.[34]

Conclusions

Cities are major global actors, increasingly participating in global networks and signing on to global environmental and social goals. The wealthier cities of the Global North, in particular, have the political and economic clout to globally promote and advance human well-being and nature conservation, and their resources and abilities create an ethical duty to do good work on the global scale. Moreover, residents of cities today exert a large ecological footprint, and their consumption patterns impact distant parts of the planet. While it is an open question what specifically the duties are that a city has beyond its borders, many tangible actions can be taken. These include efforts to reduce excessive local consumption and its global impacts (including greenhouse gas emissions) and to take actions to shift a city's economy to be more circular, where materials are endlessly reused and recycled. Cities can also exhibit global leadership on conservation and can support, financially and otherwise, the protection and restoration of the planet's ecosystems. Embracing the goal and vision of Half Earth would be one ambitious step.

Discussion Questions

Do cities have a duty to think about and mitigate the impacts of their consumption in distant locales?

What can cities do and what specific steps can they take to address global challenges such as hunger, famine, deforestation, and biodiversity loss?

Should cities work on behalf of global goals and visions such as Half Earth? Do cities of the Global North have a special responsibility to correct or compensate for the impacts of their earlier development decisions (e.g., the impacts of climate change, especially as experienced in countries such as Bangladesh and India)?

14

Working toward the Ethical City

Cities are one of the most impressive inventions of modern human history. They are engines for economic growth and essential opportunities for face-to-face collaboration and commerce. They have provided unparalleled opportunities for social evolution, culture, art, and creative endeavors of all sorts. Few realms of human existence involve more potential for creating good (or bad) outcomes, improving the lot of people, fostering care, and protecting and restoring global nature than cities.

Every city is a venue for countless decisions and ethical judgments made both by those with official roles (e.g., mayors, city councillors, and planning directors) and by many other individuals and groups. The ecological footprints of cities are large. It is hard to overstate the extent to which a city represents a set of complex, nested ethical choices and dilemmas.

The size of urban budgets is often quite large, suggesting that cities have the potential to make a difference in many ways. New York City's fiscal year 2023 budget, for example, was a whopping $101 billion; even a modest shift in that city's procurement policy or in how it invests its huge retirement funds (e.g., away from fossil fuels) would have significant impacts. Smaller cities have less economic and political leverage but still have many decisions to make, small and large.

The Most Good a City Can Do
The design, planning, and management of cities hold remarkable potential for igniting change and doing good. Here I find myself wanting to invoke the admonitory title of Peter Singer's important book *The Most Good You Can Do* . . . in cities! From guiding the physical shape and form of cities to providing affordable housing, transport, and essential connections and contact with

the natural world, cities have the chance to profoundly affect the quality of human and nonhuman lives.

A key message of this book has been that there are many ethical decisions and dilemmas in daily governance in cities. From land use decisions and judgments about changes in allowable use and density to the policies that guide the use of deadly force by police and the ethical choices we make about how we equitably raise funds and allocate annual city budgets, it is hard to identify a realm of city governance or an aspect of city life that does not involve significant questions of ethics. And there are many urban actors, from police officers and bus drivers to technology administrators and urban planners, who should be thinking about ethics and who should be enlisted in the mission of making their cities more ethical and just.

My hope is that cities will look to undertake a kind of cascading ethical practice, where one choice can productively dovetail with others. For instance, finding ways to break the incarceration pathway involves rethinking how we understand prisons and jails, hopefully increasingly understanding them less as dead-end vehicles for excessively punitive societal action and more as opportunities to restart and reboot one's life and to contribute to society. An agenda of second chances for formerly incarcerated people might include providing jobs and career paths in urban forestry and green roof installation, which would at once provide meaningful work and income and also make the city greener and more biophilic. The dignity, pride, and rehabilitative power of work go hand in hand with efforts to rewild a city. Mandating bird-safe glass in cities will reduce the pain and suffering of millions of birds and is the right things for a city to do, but it is also an opportunity to expand the health-enhancing benefits of seeing and hearing birds. And such a step will also provide the chance to correct long-standing inequalities in which people and neighborhoods get to enjoy these deeply restorative nature benefits.[1] Addressing the health risks connected with urban heat, a huge and growing challenge in every American city and in most cities around the world, is also a chance to right past (and current) inequalities and inequities.

The design of a city, I have argued throughout the book, is both a reflection of a city's values and ethics and a powerful determinant and influence on them. There is truth in Winston Churchill's famous saying "We shape our buildings and afterwards our buildings shape us." We design and shape our cities, and then the spaces and interactions we allow or facilitate in turn help to (hopefully) make for a better, more ethical city. This happens in obvious ways but also in many less obvious ways. There is considerable evidence that in the presence of greater nature, we are more likely to be generous, more likely to be cooperative, and more likely to think longer-term. It seems, then, not surprising, given the overall power of nature and the essential truth behind the idea of biophilia, that we would be better human beings when living closer to our ancestral ecological home.

What does that vision include? What are some of the primary elements that would make up an ethical city?

It is a place that works every day to treat people fairly and with dignity and kindness and shows compassion and understanding for the many people and other forms of life that inhabit the city.

It is a place that strives for social justice and inclusivity; a city that recognizes the many forms of inequality and inequity that exist and works to eliminate them, at the same time taking responsibility for past injustices.

It is a place that elevates the larger public interest over narrow individual interests but also acknowledges and actively protects essential rights such as political participation, minimum levels of health, safety, housing, environment, and contact with nature, among others.

It is a place that strives to create the conditions for its citizens to flourish and to take appropriate steps to protect their health, safety, and well-being.

It is a place that seeks to expand opportunity and to accommodate and tolerate a variety of different lifestyles and life plans but also recognizes that there are necessary constraints and limits placed on personal freedoms.

It is a place where officials emphasize transparency, openness, honesty, and fairness in how decisions are made and in how people are treated.

While I have attempted to sketch out (here and in the preceding pages) the broad contours of what an ethical city might look like, there are many unresolved questions and obviously much more discussion and debate to be had. I imagine that many readers will disagree with various arguments and admonitions I've made along the way, and that is to be expected and celebrated. In the end, there may not be *one* version of a city that is ethical but in fact many, depending perhaps on the priorities and unique backgrounds, values, and cultures that characterize any particular city.

Metrics for an Ethical City

An important question is how we will know when a city is ethical and by what metrics we will judge this success or progress. How will we know when a city is ethical? Earlier, I discussed the growing sense among many that current economic measures and indicators, especially GDP, are inadequate, at best, and leading cities in the wrong direction, at worst. What are

> **Sidebar 14-1 Alternative Metrics for an Ethical City**
> Gross ecosystem product
> Real progress indicator
> Audible sounds of laughter throughout a city
> Extent of native birdsong heard
> Extent of biodiversity in the city; number of species we are coexisting with
> Living within our planetary boundaries
> Extent of tree canopy and number of native trees residents can identify
> Circular urban metabolism
> Number of residents spending time outside
> Number of people picnicking (when the weather permits)
> Youth suicide rate
> Poverty rate and number of homeless
> Moments of awe per capita
> Extent of intergenerational mixing
> Number of hours of volunteer work per capita

the alternatives? Some possibilities have been hinted at here, and sidebar 14-1 lists some of them. Those who support the idea of natural capitalism, such as Stanford University's Gretchen Daily, argue for a "gross ecosystem product," which would judge success by the integrity and health of a city's ecosystems. This seems like a good alternative. Or maybe an indicator that measures collective joy, delight, or awe? Ethicist Peter Singer has suggested a smile index as one good measure (though the admonition to smile has a patriarchal dimension for many women).

I often offer my own candidate metrics, ones that emphasize connections with nature, and immersion in nature especially, such as the goal of every resident (throughout all generations) being able to hear native birdsong. Perhaps there is no single metric or indicator but a suite of indicators that makes more sense, with combinations that will suit or match the specific values of a particular city.

Anticipating Future Ethical Questions

Cities must also anticipate the ethical challenges and dilemmas they will face in the future. Cities today are the vanguards of new technology, new ways of living, new products and services, and the place where these are unveiled and tested with many uncertain outcomes and potential repercussions. Autonomous vehicles have the potential to reshape cities and relationships in cities in ways we don't fully appreciate yet. Will this free up some space committed to cars (e.g., parking that is no longer needed)? This would raise questions about how to repurpose such spaces (perhaps for more nature). On the other hand, some believe driverless cars will just further strengthen our reliance on automobility, and perhaps we become even more isolated from each other, sitting for longer periods of time while being driven around.

What will be the impact and implications of robots and robotics in cities and the advancement of artificial intelligence, and what ethical quandaries arise? There are the classic (Hollywood) questions about the moral status of robots but also many more ethical questions we have not seriously debated (such as the rapid increase in police use of drones) or even thought of. And the broader vision of smart cities—cities that are heavily sensored and have invested heavily in digital technologies—raises its own sets of questions. All this is to say that the ethical landscape of cities is dynamic and will likely change a lot in the coming years, suggesting that we need a versatile and nimble set of ethical concepts and ideas to guide us in the future.

New Ways to Infuse Ethics

One important and largely unexplored question is how cities can more intentionally strengthen their ethical considerations during deliberations. More nature, as I have said, and more truly inclusive public spaces would help. And perhaps there are ways, likely many ways, to set out or embed various reminders or cues to ethics. I can remember growing up and attending city council meetings in my home city of Alexandria and watching discussions take place against the backdrop of a beautiful, historical, bird's-eye-view painting of this waterfront city, a visual reminder of the history of this place and perhaps of the need to take the longer view when making especially impactful decisions.

Ethical "cues" can be made to be even more clear and direct, of course. Years ago, I had the chance to take a tour of Oslo's wonderful city hall. One of the elements I remember as most unique was a wall tapestry designed by artist Else Poulsson. It presents the seven virtues, and it was reportedly her intent to keep ethics and civic values top of mind for the city councillors deliberating in this space.

Cities should look for ways to institutionalize an ethical frame or ethical analysis. I like the bold effort in Wales of creating the position of future generations commissioner: here is a specific person, with a specific charge to think about future generations and their well-being. A city future generations commissioner (or perhaps a city councilman with that portfolio) would be an interesting idea.

Alexandria has experimented with hiring an ethicist to help the city's departments work through their resources and hiring decisions, an extension of the work ethicists do in hospital settings.[2] This is already quite common, as ethicists and bioethicists have historically worked to assist hospitals and medical professionals in dealing with very difficult health and medical decisions, such as who should be given priority in organ transplants or how and by what criteria a hospital ought to allocate scarce medical resources and equipment.

Should every city seek to create the position of chief ethicist, in the same vein that they now commonly hire chief resilience officers or sustainability directors? Or perhaps they could create the position of city ethicist as a kind of counterpart to the typical position of city attorney—someone who would advise and work to keep ethics and values top of mind in council deliberations.

Ethics training for key municipal staff, including the city manager, parks director, and planning director, would also make good sense. I feel as though urban planners, my own particular professional background, are in an especially good position to serve in an ethical analyst role, and more of what they usually do (review land use and development proposals, prepare and update local comprehensive plans) could be imbued with an ethical focus.

Many cities already have in place some form of ethics commission or board, usually charged with implementing policies and advising about such things as conflicts of interest or giving and receiving gifts. These are important functions, to be sure, but local ethics codes and standards often need significant strengthening. And perhaps such bodies could play an even larger role in guiding a city's policies and programs and in helping officials and citizens alike better understand the full set of ethical quandaries and choices faced by a city.

A key challenge explored in this book, and a primary way to think about an ethical city, is to consider how the many voices and interests—from those who have traditionally been discriminated against to those who will live in the city in the future and the many nonhuman lives that exist in cities but are generally not valued—can be better and more fairly taken into account.

New Ways of Making Decisions

It is clear as well that a city sets the structure and lays out the conditions for ethical and political discourse. This happens through efforts to make decisions in more collaborative ways, designing community parks, for example, from the community up, or making it easier to participate in local politics. The fairer these conditions and structures of participation and engagement are, the more likely a city's decisions are to reflect the will and wishes of citizens. This remains one of the key tasks facing ethical cities.

As this book has hopefully shown, there are many process reforms and strategies that can help and lead to better, fairer, more ethical outcomes. Many of these are relatively new (e.g., participatory budgeting or co-design processes) but some are ancient (e.g., the Iroquois seventh generation principle). One of my favorite ideas comes from the future design movement in Japan. Experiments there show convincingly that it is possible to design processes for local planning and decision-making that explicitly include the interests and perspectives of future residents.

Technology may provide more effective ways of engaging a city's residents and effectively collecting and listening to its many voices. Some technologies at our disposal are ubiquitous, such as laptops and cell phones, but others that are a bit newer, such as distributed sensor networks and handheld air-quality- and heat-monitoring devices, have the potential to shift power in more egalitarian ways in the direction of residents, neighborhoods, and nonprofits and will be healthy and helpful in moving toward the concept of an ethical city.

It's also as much about establishing new institutions as it is about making any specific decision. New York City's establishment of the Office of Animal Welfare is a positive example and a way in which the interests of animals become (somewhat, at least) more visible and important. This office has come under some criticism for lack of staffing and slow action, but the idea of elevating and giving official attention and voice to animals in cities is a very good idea.[3]

A number of cities have now created civilian police review boards—another example, from quite a different city sector, of how a city institutionalizes certain necessary and inclusive ethical perspectives. The City of Chicago, with a troubled past when it comes to police violence and brutality, created an interesting model in its new Community Commission for Public Safety and Accountability in 2023. Composed of seven elected community members with oversight of the city's police superintendent, it has real potential to provide transparency and accountability in that city.

Ethical Anchors and Institutions

It is an interesting question where key supporters of ethical cities might be seen. Where are the key ethical and moral anchors in a city, and how can they be more effectively consulted and used on the way to creating a more ethical city? Churches and religious communities are another obvious pillar of support for ethics; religious belief systems such as Christianity, Islam, and Buddhism have support for the values of compassion, love, and respect embedded in them.

There is a long tradition in many churches of actively working on behalf of those in need, whether that's providing shelter for the homeless or food for soup kitchens, and producing an ethic of compassion. In some cities, churches also appear to be actively supporting (and potentially donating to) reparation funds.

In his book *The Creation*, E. O. Wilson pens an eloquent plea to pastors and religious leaders in support of joining forces to conserve and protect the world's biodiversity.[4] Wilson, who is himself a secular humanist, develops an argument that even though we may disagree about the existence of God, protecting the world's biodiversity is a shared value, and there is a common or potentially shared meaning of the word *creation* (i.e., no matter whether you believe it was God's hand or the processes of evolution that brought about the remarkable variety, abundance, and beauty of the natural world).

What other ethical pillars or key institutions or groups might exist to support the emergence of ethical cities? Especially when it comes to animals, domestic and wild, the Society for the Prevention of Cruelty to Animals and other animal support organizations are another important voice on behalf of compassion and expand the moral community that ought to be taken into account when making decisions. Local conservation groups can also be a positive force. Consider the Audubon groups that exist in many cities around the country and that have had such a positive impact in shaping and planning environmental policy, especially around birds.

Local institutions such as natural history museums and zoological parks can also help with the agenda and can be especially important in educating and raising awareness about the biodiversity all around us and the many ways that a biophilic city could support and make room for other forms of life. A good example is the Phipps Conservatory in Pittsburgh, at once a major destination for residents and tourists alike and a catalyst for positive change in the community around environment and sustainability. The conservatory has spearheaded efforts to think of the city as an ecosystem and to design and build in ways that reduce ecological impacts and foster connections to nature.

Urban school systems can and should teach more about ethics, and there is a need for a renewed and expanded focus on civics classes. Colleges and universities that train the next generations of urban planners, architects, and city administrators (as well as future elected officials) would be wise to include more coursework on the ethics of cities, providing future urban professionals the chance to grapple with and work through many ethical dilemmas ahead of time and to clarify their own ethical positions and guideposts.

Who is ultimately responsible for safeguarding the ethics of a city? Citizens, of course, are important, likely more than professionals, and certainly more important when they are able to organize and exercise some political muscle and clout. There are even candidates campaigning for local city councils on the vision of a nature-rich city, which is promising for the biophilic cities movement.

Taking full advantage of public opinion may also be an important step. Polling numbers are no substitute for votes and elected officials, but they can help sway them. And polling often seems to go in the direction of more ethical, just, and inclusive cities. Popular support for more just and equitable cities is greater than we think. A 2020 Pew study on economic inequality, for example, found that a majority of respondents (61 percent) believe there is too much inequality (though other issues, such as affordable health care and drug addiction, are viewed as more important, though these issues are connected to social justice, to be sure).[5]

Many of the professionals primarily engaged in building, designing, and rebuilding cities are subject to explicit ethical statements and codes of ethics. While many specific versions of their professional codes have to do more with ethical professional conduct, they do represent a point of ethical leverage as well. There is a laudable history of activism and social engagement in architecture, as well as support for sustainable and ecological design (for instance through the work of the American Institute of Architects' Committee on the Environment). Architects are often strong voices for public values in cities and for the importance of good design, as are urban planners. And there are a variety of other professions, in fields from engineering to education and public health, that might also be enlisted in support of the vision of an ethical city.

Cities will face obstacles to taking bolder positions and stands and to working to maximize the good they bring about. Conservative state legislatures have in recent years enacted preemption laws preventing cities and local governments from enacting a variety of progressive (and ethical) programs and regulations, notably stronger gun safety and gun control measures but also important efforts to strengthen environmental protections (including for trees). These state preemption laws fly in the face of democracy, undermining cities that are undoubtedly closer to understanding the true democratic desires and will of constituents.

Nonetheless, the many strands of action and policy that cities undertake, underpinned by strongly held values and ethical principles, give me hope for the future and the future role of cities. I look forward to future cities flexing their ethical muscles and applying thoughtful and expansive ethical lenses to the many decisions they face, large and small.

Acknowledgments

There are many people to thank who helped me on the journey of writing this book. Many colleagues helped clarify the arguments and suggested literature and ideas that should be included. It is fitting that this book should be published by UNC Press, as it was in Chapel Hill in the 1980s, as a young PhD student, that I became interested in studying the ethics of cities and built environments. A number of UNC faculty encouraged this work and saw its potential, including Dave Godschalk, Dave Brower, and Ed Kaiser in city and regional planning and Bill Keech in political science. Fast-forward thirty years, and the current book, which expands in important ways my earlier topics and coverage, found a great home at UNC Press. I'd like to thank the UNC Press staff for their great assistance along the way and especially Lucas Church for his excellent guidance and strong support for the project.

This book builds on the foundation of a much earlier book, *Ethical Land Use*, that I published with Johns Hopkins Press. That earlier work would not have seen the light of day without the strong support and guidance of Fritz Steiner and George Thompson. Growing up in a political household, where discussion of policy and the ethical dimensions of cities (though perhaps rarely referred to in that way) was regular dinner table fare, also had a strong influence on this interest of mine, and it is hard to overemphasize the important role my parents played in making this work possible. Finally, my family today, my wife Anneke and kids Caro and Jadie, are a continual source of inspiration and encouragement, without which it would be difficult to write anything. And as always, I take full responsibility for the content and opinions expressed herein and hope that at the least it will provoke some new discussion about the important, though often overlooked, ethical dimensions of urban problems.

Notes

Introduction

1. "San Francisco to Repeal Boycott of Anti-LGBTQ+ states," Associated Press, August 27, 2023, https://apnews.com/article/san-francisco-travel-ban-repeal-lgbtq-51bdf8bdb70ab4afbb26fd4f7f15b337.

2. Charles Malinchak, "Bethlehem Names Chimney Swift as City's Official Bird," *Morning Call* (Allentown, PA), February 3, 2021.

3. Leslie Kern, *Feminist City* (Brooklyn, NY: Verso Books, 2020), 14.

4. Simon Sinek, *The Infinite Game* (New York: Penguin, 2019).

5. Douglas Hanks, "Daring Florida to Oust Them, City Commissioners Pursue Their Own Ban on Assault Rifles," *Miami Herald*, February 18, 2018.

6. See Kristi Coale, "As Cancer Concerns Lead Cities to Ban Herbicide, S.F. Scales Back Use of Roundup," *San Francisco Public Press*, November 18, 2020.

7. City of Portland, "Texas Withdraws Abortion Rights, Portland City Council Withdraws Business," press release, September 3, 2021, www.portland.gov/wheeler/news/2021/9/3/texas-withdraws-abortion-rights-portland-city-council-withdraws-business.

8. E.g., see "Property Tax Burdens Fall on Nation's Lowest-Income Homeowners, Study Finds," University of Chicago News, March 9, 2021, https://news.uchicago.edu/story/property-tax-burdens-fall-nations-lowest-income-homeowners-study-finds.

9. Lauren Gambino, "Pittsburgh Fires Back at Trump: We Stand with Paris Not You," *Guardian*, June 1, 2017.

10. E.g., see Joshua Bote, "Cities Are Doing More Than States, Federal Government to Protect LGBTQ Rights, Human Rights Campaign Report Finds," *USA Today*, December 3, 2020.

11. "Memories of Life, Love and Activism at the Lyon-Martin House," *San Francisco Bay Times*, June 10, 2021.

12. E.g., see Brentin Mock, "What It Actually Means to Pass Local 'Reparations,'" *Bloomberg CityLab*, April 15, 2021, www.bloomberg.com/news/articles/2021-04-15/what-reparations-look-like-in-evanston-and-asheville.

13. Andrea Lopez-Villafana, "San Diego Proposes 'Freeway Lids' to Create Open Space, Reconnect Neighborhoods," *Los Angeles Times*, June 27, 2021.

14. Andrew Simms, "Ecological Debt—Balancing the Environmental Budget and Compensating Developing Countries," International Institute for Environment and Development, opinion paper, September 2001, https://pubs.iied.org/11011iied.

15. See David J. Velinsky, Gerhardt F. Riedel, Jeffrey T. F. Ashley, and Jeffrey C. Cornwell, "Historical Contamination of the Anacostia River, Washington, DC," *Environmental Monitoring and Assessment* 183 (March 2011): 307–28.

16. "For a Cleaner Anacostia River," DC Department of Energy and Environment, September 20, 2021, https://doee.dc.gov/publication/cleaner-anacostia-river-anacostia-river-sediment-project.

Chapter 1

1. Julia Wolfson, Stephen P. Teret, Deborah Azrael, and Matthew Miller, "US Public Opinion on Carrying Firearms in Public Spaces," *American Journal of Public Health* 107, no. 6 (June 2017): 929–37.

2. Laura D'Olimpio, "The Trolley Dilemma: Would You Kill One Person to Save Five?" *Conversation*, June 2, 2016, https://theconversation.com/the-trolley-dilemma-would-you-kill-one-person-to-save-five-57111.

3. Charles Montgomery, *Happy City: Transforming Our Lives through Urban Design* (New York: Farrar, Straus and Giroux, 2014).

4. Or what Etzioni refers to as "affirmation," or acts "affirming" our moral commitments. See Amitai Etzioni, *Happiness Is the Wrong Metric: A Liberal Communitarian Response to Populism* (New York: Springer, 2018).

5. For more about market failure, see Timothy Beatley, *Ethical Land Use: Principles of Policy and Planning* (Baltimore: Johns Hopkins University Press, 1994). See also Terry Moore, "Why Allow Planners to Do What Planners Do?," *Journal of the American Planning Association*, October 1978.

6. *Cambridge Dictionary*, s.v. "kind," accessed June 28, 2023, https://dictionary.cambridge.org/dictionary/english/kind.

7. I'd like to acknowledge Bill Tammens's 1990 article in the *Baltimore Sun* for reminding me of the precise language. He also cleverly points out the irony of applying the word *gentle* to the state of Maryland, given its history of slavery and Civil War battles. Bill Tammens, "Gentle Maryland," *Baltimore Sun*, November 2, 1990.

8. See Lee Rowland, "A Range of Kindness Activities Boost Happiness," *Journal of Social Psychology* 159, no. 3 (April 2018).

9. Stanford Encyclopedia of Philosophy, s.v. "Autonomy in Moral and Political Philosophy," updated June 29, 2020, https://plato.stanford.edu/entries/autonomy-moral.

10. David Bromwich, *Moral Imagination* (Princeton, NJ: Princeton University Press, 2014), 26.

11. See "Advancing Racial Equity for Black Louisville," City of Louisville, accessed June 28, 2023, https://louisvilleky.gov/mayor-greg-fischer/document/advancing-racial-equity-black-louisville.

12. See esp. Suzanne Simard, *In Search of the Mother Tree: Discovering the Wisdom of the Forest* (New York: Knopf, 2021).

Chapter 2

1. Chelsea Johnson (founder, Tree Something, Say Something), phone interview with author, February 20, 2019.

2. For more about her story, see her book: Mona Hanna-Attisha, *What the Eyes Don't See: A Story of Crisis, Resistance, and Hope in an American City* (New York: Random House, 2018).

3. Edwin Rios, "Meet 5 Everyday Heroes of Flint's Water Crisis," *Mother Jones*, January 27, 2016, www.motherjones.com/politics/2016/01/flint-water-crisis-lead-heroes.

4. Ronald L. Sandler, *Character and Environment: A Virtue-Oriented Approach to Environmental Ethics* (New York: Columbia University Press, 2008).

5. Julia Driver, *Uneasy Virtue* (Cambridge, UK: Cambridge University Press, 2001).

6. Amitai Etzioni, *Happiness Is the Wrong Metric: A Liberal Communitarian Response to Populism* (New York: Springer, 2018), 15.

7. David Orr, *Earth in Mind: On Education, Environment, and the Human Prospect* (Washington, DC: Island, 2004), 32.

8. Laura Smith-Spark, "Sarah Everard Case Prompts Outpouring from Women Sharing Stories of Abuse and Harassment on UK Streets," CNN, March 11, 2021, https://www.cnn.com/2021/03/11/uk/sarah-everard-women-harassment-streets-gbr-intl/index.html.

9. Sara Miller Llana, "Reading, Writing and Empathy: How Denmark Is a Leader in Teaching Social Skills," *Christian Science Monitor*, September 15, 2017, https://www.csmonitor.com/World/Europe/2017/0915/Reading-writing-and-empathy-How-Denmark-is-a-leader-in-teaching-social-skills.

10. Niles Anderegg, "How Citizen Academies Help Promote Public Engagement and Civic Education," International City/County Management Association Blog, September 27, 2018, https://icma.org/blog-posts/how-citizen-academies-help-promote-public-engagement-and-civic-education.

11. Penelope Muse Abernathy, *News Deserts and Ghosts Newspapers: Will Local News Survive?* (Chapel Hill: University of North Carolina Press, 2020), 91.

12. Sarah Barlett and Julie Sandorf, "How New York City Is Saving Its Local News Outlets," *New York Times*, May 20, 2021.

13. City of New York, "Mayor de Blasio Signs Executive Order to Ensure Information about City Services Reaches All New Yorkers," press release, May 22, 2019, www1.nyc.gov/office-of-the-mayor/news/260-19/mayor-de-blasio-signs-executive-order-ensure-information-city-services-reaches-all-new.

14. Abraham Lincoln, first inaugural address, Washington, DC, March 4, 1861.

Chapter 3

1. John Rawls, *A Theory of Justice* (Cambridge, MA: Belknap Press of Harvard University Press, 1972).

2. For an especially good discussion of this history, see Richard Rothstein, *The Color of Law: A Forgotten History of How Our Government Segregated America* (New York: Liveright, 2018).

3. Julia Menasce Horowitz, Ruth Igielnik, and Rakesh Kochhar, *Most Americans Say There Is Too Much Economic Inequality in the U.S., but Fewer Than Half Call It a Priority*, (Washington, DC: Pew Research Center, 2020), www.pewresearch.org/social-trends/wp-content/uploads/sites/3/2020/01/PSDT_01.09.20_economic-inequailty_FULL.pdf.

4. Richard Wilkinson and Kate Pickett, *The Inner Level: How More Equal Societies Reduce Stress, Restore Sanity and Improve Everyone's Well-Being* (New York: Penguin, 2019).

5. Wilkinson and Pickett, *Inner Level*, 237.

6. John Rawls, *A Theory of Justice* (Cambridge, MA: Harvard University Press, 1970). See especially pp. 136–42.

7. Robert D. Bullard, *Dumping in Dixie: Race, Class, and Environmental Quality* (Boulder, CO: Westview, 1990), 35.

8. See Julian Agyeman, Robert D. Bullard, and Bob Evans, eds., *Just Sustainabilities: Development in an Unequal World* (Cambridge, MA: MIT Press, 2003).

9. See Pittsburgh Shade Tree Commission, *Equitable Street Tree Investment Strategy* (Pittsburgh, PA: Pittsburgh Shade Tree Commission, 2021), https://apps.pittsburghpa.gov/redtail/images/13230_final_Equitable_Street_Tree_Investment_Strategy_-_2_24_21_-_apc.pdf.

10. "Cully Park," City of Portland (website), accessed October 31, 2023, https://www.portland.gov/parks/cully-park.

11. "Cully Park," City of Portland.

12. "Oakland Goes Outside," San Francisco Foundation, accessed November 6, 2023, https://sff.org/what-we-do/collaboratives/oakland-goes-outdoors/.

13. Kriston McIntosh, Emily Moss, Ryan Nunn, and Jay Shambaugh, "Examining the Black-White Wealth Gap," Brookings Institution, February 27, 2020, www.brookings.edu/articles/examining-the-black-white-wealth-gap.

14. See "Racial Equity Impact Assessments," Council Office of Racial Equality, accessed June 28, 2023, www.dcracialequity.org/racial-equity-impact-assessments.

15. Jose Martinez, "MTA Could Make Many More Subway Stations Accessible, Study Finds," *City*, February 20, 2020, www.thecity.nyc/transportation/2020/2/20/21210518/mta-could-make-many-more-subway-stations-accessible-study-finds.

16. Steve Wright, "Why Planning Education Should Embrace Universal Design," *Planning Magazine*, May 2021.

17. Anna Zivarts, "The '15-Minute City' Isn't Made for Disabled Bodies," *Bloomberg CityLab*, April 22, 2021, www.bloomberg.com/news/articles/2021-04-22/the-people-that-the-15-minute-city-leave-behind.

18. Louise Aronson, *Elderhood: Redefining Aging, Transforming Medicine, Reimagining Life* (New York: Bloomsbury, 2019).

19. Lynda Gratton and Andrew Scott, *The 100-Year Life: Living and Working in an Age of Longevity* (London: Bloomsbury, 2016).

20. For more about the insights I learned from our time in the Netherlands, see Timothy Beatley, *Green Urbanism: Learning from European Cities* (Washington, DC: Island Press, 2000).

21. Rina Mae Acosta and Michelle Hutchinson, *The Happiest Kids in the World* (New York: Experiment Publishers, 2017).

22. Allison Arieff, "Where Are All the Female Architects?," *New York Times*, December 15, 2018.

23. Patrick Sisson, "City Councils across U.S. Fall Short on Equal Gender Representation," *Curbed*, August 24, 2017, https://archive.curbed.com/2017/8/24/16196332/women-in-politics-government-new-york-city.

24. Danielle Kurtzelen, "FEC Says That Candidates Can Use Campaign Funds for Child Care," NPR, May 10, 2018, www.npr.org/2018/05/10/610099506/fec-says-that-candidates-can-use-campaign-funds-for-child-care.

25. Mary Anne Case, "Why Not Abolish the Laws of Urinary Segregation?," in *Toilet: Public Restrooms and the Politics of Sharing*, ed. Harvey Molotch and Laura Norén, 211–25 (New York: New York University Press, 2010).

26. Boris Kingma and Wouter van Marken Lichtenbelt, "Energy Consumption in Buildings and Female Thermal Demand," *Nature Climate Change* 5 (December 2015).

27. Greg Lindsey, "Bicycles, Gender, and Risk: Driver Behaviors When Passing Cyclists," Gender Policy Report, July 15, 2019, https://genderpolicyreport.umn.edu/bicycles-gender-and-risk.

28. Caroline Criado Perez, *Invisible Women: Exposing Data Bias in a World Designed for Men* (New York: Abrams, 2021).

29. See "ATLGBTQ: Mayor's Division of LGBTQ Affairs," City of Atlanta (website), accessed June 28, 2023, www.atlantaga.gov/government/mayor-s-office/executive-offices/office-of-equity-diversity-and-inclusion/lgbtq.

30. "Seattle LGBTQ Commission," City of Seattle (website), accessed June 28, 2023, www.seattle.gov/lgbtq.

31. Human Rights Campaign Foundation and Equality Federation Institute, *Municipal Equality Index 2020: A Nationwide Evaluation of Municipal Law* (Washington, DC: Human Rights Campaign Foundation, 2020), https://hrc-prod-requests.s3-us-west-2.amazonaws.com/MEI-2020-Final-2020.pdf.

32. Katie Wilson, "What Seattle Mayoral Candidates Think about Guaranteed Income," *Crosscut*, May 12, 2021, https://crosscut.com/opinion/2021/05/what-seattle-mayoral-candidates-think-about-guaranteed-income.

33. For a fuller description of Evanston's efforts and approach to reparations, see Brentin Mock, "What It Actually Means to Pass Local 'Reparations,'" *Bloomberg CityLab*, April 15, 2021, www.bloomberg.com/news/articles/2021-04-15/what-reparations-look-like-in-evanston-and-asheville.

34. Quoted in Julie Bosman, "Chicago Suburb Shapes Reparations for Black Residents: 'It's a Start,'" *New York Times*, March 22, 2021.

35. Caitlin Dewey, "From Urban Renewal to Highway Removal," *Planning Magazine*, December 2020.

36. "Guaranteed Income: A Community's Vision for Freedom," Compton Pledge, accessed October 30, 2023, https://comptonpledge.org/about/.

37. "Pittsburgh Equity Indicators," City of Pittsburgh (website), accessed June 28, 2023, https://pittsburghpa.gov/equityindicators.

38. City of Portland, Oregon, *The Portland Plan*, April 2012, p. 18, https://www.portland.gov/bps/planning/documents/portland-plan/download.

Chapter 4

1. UN Universal Declaration of Human Rights, 1948, accessed June 28, 2023, www.un.org/en/about-us/universal-declaration-of-human-rights.

2. "What Is the Human Right to Housing?," National Economic and Social Rights Initiative flyer, accessed June 28, 2023, https://dignityandrights.org/wp-content/uploads/2019/11/Foundation-of-a-Human-Right-to-Housing.pdf.

3. Editorial, "Will Kansas City Become the First Major City with Free Bus Service?," *Kansas City (MO) Star*, November 12, 2019.

4. Laura Bliss, "Why Kansas City's Free Transit Experiment Matters," *Bloomberg CityLab*, December 13, 2019, www.bloomberg.com/news/articles/2019-12-13/is-free-transit-the-equity-fix-kansas-city-needs.

5. Kevin Collison, "New KC Streetcar Rolls into Town, Ridership Breaks 6 Million," May 14, 2019, https://cityscenekc.com/new-kc-streetcar-rolls-into-town.

6. Deena Winter, "Scooter Company Bird Avoided Low-Income Neighborhoods; City Re-upped License Anyway," *Minnesota Reformer*, May 6, 2021, https://minnesotareformer.com/2021/05/06/scooter-company-bird-avoided-low-income-neighborhoods-city-reupped-license-anyway/.

7. Bruce Appleyard and William Riggs, "Human Rights to the Street: Ethical Frameworks to Guide Planning, Design, and Engineering Decisions toward Livability, Equity and Justice," *Journal of Transport and Land Use* 14, no. 1 (2021): 911–31.

8. Quoted in Chendan Yan, "Who Owns the 'Right to the City'? Moving towards Urban Inclusivity," Yale School of the Environment Blog, June 6, 2016, https://resources.environment.yale.edu/blog/2016/06/who-owns-the-right-to-the-city-moving-towards-urban-inclusivity.

9. "Understanding the Health Care Security Ordinance," City of San Francisco (website), accessed June 28, 2023, https://sfgov.org/olse/health-care-security-ordinance-hcso.

10. "Equitable Internet Initiative," Detroit Community Technology Project, accessed June 28, 2023, https://detroitcommunitytech.org/eii.

11. A shorter version of this section appeared as Timothy Beatley, "A Constitutional Right to a Green City," *Planning Magazine*, October 2018.

12. Penn. Const. art. I, § 27.

13. See Maya van Rossum, *The Green Amendment: The People's Fight for a Clean, Safe, and Healthy Environment* (New York: Disruption Books, 2022).

14. See NYC Nature Goals 2050, accessed June 28, 2023, https://naturegoals.nyc/.

15. Amitai Etzioni, "We Must Not Be Enemies," *American Scholar*, Winter 2017.

Chapter 5

1. Justin Jouvenal, "A Mystery 32 Stories Up: Is a Grandfather, 68, Leaping off the D.C. Area's Tallest Buildings?," *Washington Post*, October 2, 2019.

2. James Carmody and Nicolas Perpitch, "BASE Jumpers Leap off Perth CBD Exchange Tower Skyscraper in Front of Stunned Onlookers," ABC News, September 10, 2019, www.abc.net.au/news/2019-09-10/base-jumpers-leap-off-perth-cbd-skyscraper-exchange-tower/11495862.

3. Ed Grabianowski, "How BASE Jumping Works," Map Quest Travel, accessed June 28, 2023, www.mapquest.com/travel/outdoor-activities/urban-sports/base-jumping.htm.

4. Grabianowski, "How BASE Jumping Works."

5. Mark Follman, Julia Lurie, Jaeah Lee, and James West, "The True Cost of Gun Violence in America," *Mother Jones*, April 15, 2015, www.motherjones.com/politics/2015/04/true-cost-of-gun-violence-in-america.

6. See Timothy Beatley, *The Bird-Friendly City: Creating Safe Urban Habitats* (Washington, DC: Island, 2020).

7. John Stuart Mill, *On Liberty*, ed. Elizabeth Rapaport (1859; repr., Indianapolis: Hackett, 1978), 9.

8. Milton Friedman, "Milton Friedman—Helmet and Seat Belt Laws," YouTube video, 3:50, posted by LibertyPen on November 19, 2010, https://www.youtube.com/watch?v=Yki8I5VY6So.

9. Steve Lopez, "She Is Naked, Sick, Dirty, Crawling across Sunset Boulevard—How Can This Happen in L.A.?," *LA Times*, October 10, 2020, https://www.latimes.com/california/story/2020-10-10/homeless-woman-silver-lake-mental-illness.

10. Mill, *On Liberty*, 9.

11. Mill, *On Liberty*, 12.

12. Mill, *On Liberty*, 10–11.

13. Elizabeth Weil and Mollie Simon, "California Will Keep Burning. But Housing Policy Is Making It Worse," *ProPublica*, October 2, 2020, www.propublica.org/article/california-will-keep-burning-but-housing-policy-is-making-it-worse.

Chapter 6

1. Deanna Paul, "'Police Must First Do No Harm': How One of the Nation's Roughest Cities Is Reshaping Use-of-Force Tactics," *Washington Post*, August 21, 2019.

2. Jonathan Mummolo, "Militarization Fails to Advance Police Safety or Reduce Crime but May Harm Police Reputation," *Proceedings of the National Academy of Sciences* 115, no. 37 (2018): 9181–89.

3. ACLU of New York, "NYCLU Releases Report Analyzing NYPD Stop-and-Frisk Data," press release, March 14, 2019, www.nyclu.org/en/press-releases/nyclu-releases-report-analyzing-nypd-stop-and-frisk-data.

4. Katie Mettler and Deanna Paul, "Phoenix Fires Officer Who Pulled Gun on Parents after Their 4-Year-Old Took Doll from Dollar Store," *Washington Post*, June 16, 2019.

5. Mettler and Paul, "Phoenix Fires Officer."

6. See Shirley Li, "The Evolution of Police Militarization in Ferguson and Beyond," *Atlantic*, August 15, 2014, www.theatlantic.com/national/archive/2014/08/the-evolution-of-police-militarization-in-ferguson-and-beyond/376107.

7. See Griff White, "In New Mexico a Bold Experiment Aims to Take Police out of the Equation for Mental Health Calls," *Washington Post*, October 9, 2021.

8. These types of stops are estimated to account for 84 percent of police points of interaction with the public. See Brett Simpson, "Why Cars Don't Deserve the Right of Way," *Atlantic*, October 15, 2021, www.theatlantic.com/ideas/archive/2021/10/end-police-violence-get-rid-traffic-cop/620378.

9. Editorial, "Louisville Must Restrict Police Chases before People Are Hurt, Killed," *Courier-Journal* (Louisville, KY), November 22, 2019.

10. Cory Shaffer, "Cleveland Police Policy Allows High-Speed Chase for Violent Crimes: Here's What They Must Consider," *Cleveland*, December 20, 2019, www.cleveland.com/court-justice/2019/12/cleveland-police-policy-allows-high-speed-chase-for-violent-crimes-heres-what-they-must-consider.html.

11. "Vehicle Pursuits," section 3.2.02 in "Policies and Procedures," City of Cleveland, Division of Police, accessed October 31, 2023, https://www.clevelandohio.gov/sites/clevelandohio/files/policies-procedures/3.2.02%20Vehicle%20Pursuits.pdf.

12. Manuel Bojorquez, "Police Tactics Questioned after UPS Truck Police Chase Ends in Deadly Shootout," CBS News, December 7, 2019, www.cbsnews.com/news/ups-truck-police-chase-ends-in-deadly-shootout-police-tactics-questioned-2019-12-06.

13. Quoted in Adam Ferrise, "Cleveland Police Pursuit Policy Called into Question after Officers Take Gunfire Twice in One Week," *Cleveland*, April 17, 2018, www.cleveland.com/metro/2018/04/cleveland_chase_policy_questio.html.

14. Leif Reigstad, "A No-Knock Raid in Houston Led to Deaths and Police Injuries. Should Police Rethink the Practice?," *Texas Monthly*, February 1, 2019, www.texasmonthly.com/news-politics/a-no-knock-raid-in-houston-led-to-deaths-and-police-injuries-should-police-rethink-the-practice.

15. Kevin Rector, "Most LAPD Officers Who Break Deadly Force Policy in Shootings Avoid Serious Discipline," *Los Angeles Times*, March 12, 2022.

16. Emily Gallagher, "Rikers Island Is a Human Rights Atrocity. New York Must Close It Immediately," *Jacobin*, September 24, 2021, https://jacobin.com/2021/09/rikers-island-shut-down-covid-19-deaths-emily-gallagher.

17. "School-to-Prison Pipeline," ACLU, accessed June 28, 2023, www.aclu.org/issues/juvenile-justice/school-prison-pipeline.

18. E.g., see Erica Rucker, "Erika Shields Is Promoting the School to Prison Pipeline by Pushing for Officers in Schools," *Leo Weekly* (Louisville, KY), September 29, 2021.

19. Betsy Pearl and Lea Hunter, "Second Chance Cities: Local Efforts to Promote Re-entry Success," Center for American Progress, April 19, 2018, www.americanprogress.org/article/second-chance-cities-local-efforts-promote-re-entry-success.

20. Pearl and Hunter, "Second Chance Cities."

21. "UpClose with Dan Meyer," Council on Criminal Justice, accessed June 28, 2023, https://counciloncj.org/upclose-with-dan-meyer.

Chapter 7

1. "What Does Privacy Mean?," International Association of Privacy Professionals, accessed June 28, 2023, https://iapp.org/about/what-is-privacy.

2. Bruce Schneier, "Surveillance Kills Freedom by Killing Experimentation," *Wired*, November 16, 2018, www.wired.com/story/mcsweeneys-excerpt-the-right-to-experiment.

3. As quoted in Zoe Alker, "Imprisonment," *Digital Panopticon*, accessed June 28, 2023, www.digitalpanopticon.org/Imprisonment.

4. Neal Ungerleider, "NYPD, Microsoft Launch All-Seeing 'Domain Awareness System' with Real-Time CCTV, License Plate Monitoring," *Fast Company*, August 8, 2012, www.fastcompany.com/3000272/nypd-microsoft-launch-all-seeing-domain-awareness-system-real-time-cctv-license-plate-monito.

5. Bryan McKenzie, "Rutherford Balks at Public Cameras," *Daily Progress* (Charlottesville, VA), April 27, 2010.

6. Hawes Spencer, "Longo's Legacy: Cameras Coming to a Mall and a Cop Near You," *C-Ville Weekly* (Charlottesville, VA), March 10, 2016.

7. This was Elliott Harding, candidate for the Twenty-Fifth District, Virginia Senate.

8. "Harding Apologizes for Taking Deeds Campaign Literature," *Daily Progress*, October 29, 2019.

9. Jim Dwyer, "Caught on Camera, a Senator Who'd Like to Shut Them Down," *New York Times*, June 26, 2018.

10. "Red Light Running," Insurance Institute for Highway Safety, accessed June 28, 2023, www.iihs.org/topics/red-light-running.

11. "Red Light Running."

12. Kate Conger, Richard Fausset, and Serge F. Koveleski, "San Francisco Bans Facial Recognition Technology," *New York Times*, May 14, 2019.

13. Veena Dubal, "San Francisco Was Right to Ban Facial Recognition. Surveillance Is a Real Danger," *Guardian*, May 30, 2019.

14. See, e.g., Bernard Marr, "Smartphone Tracking Data and Artificial Intelligence Turn People's Movements into Detailed Insights and Profits," *Forbes*, October 7, 2020. https://www.forbes.com/sites/bernardmarr/2020/10/07/smartphone-tracking-data-and-artificial-intelligence-turn-peoples-movements-into-detailed-insights-and-profits.

15. This is a new product offered by a company Omnilert. See "School District Shares Lessons Learned from AI Visual Gun Detection," Omnilert, accessed October 31, 2023, https://www.omnilert.com/blog/lessons-learned-ai-gun-detection.

16. See NYC Office of the Mayor, "Mayor Adams Releases First-of-Its-Kind Plan for Responsible Artificial Intelligence Use in NYC Government," press release, October 16, 2023, https://www.nyc.gov/office-of-the-mayor/news/777-23/mayor-adams-releases-first-of-its-kind-plan-responsible-artificial-intelligence-use-nyc.

17. See Jay Stanley, "Police Drones Could Turn America into a Surveillance State," *Wall Street Journal*, July 28, 2023, https://www.wsj.com/articles/police-drones-could-turn-america-into-a-surveillance-state-faa-exemptions-667a53c6.

Chapter 8

1. See Samuel Scheffler, *Death and the Afterlife* (Oxford, UK: Oxford University Press, 2016).

2. JoAnna Wendel, "When Will the Sun Die?," *Space*, August 7, 2019, www.space.com/14732-sun-burns-star-death.html.

3. Marcia Bjornerud, *Timefulness: How Thinking Like a Geologist Can Help Save the World* (Princeton, NJ: Princeton University Press, 2018).

4. Bjornerud, *Timefulness*, 7.

5. Roman Krznaric, *The Good Ancestor: A Radical Prescription for Long-Term Thinking* (New York: Experiment, 2020).

6. Krznaric, *Good Ancestor*, 7.

7. Krznaric, *Good Ancestor*, 7.

8. Bjornerud, *Timefulness*, 18.

9. Bjornerud, *Timefulness*, 162.

10. Daniel Pauly, "The Ocean's Shifting Baseline," TED Talk, April 2010, https://www.ted.com/talks/daniel_pauly_the_ocean_s_shifting_baseline.

11. Alexander Rose, interview with author, September 2017.

12. "Our Purpose," Zealandia Sanctuary, accessed October 31, 2023, https://www.visitzealandia.com/About/Our-Purpose.

13. John Rawls refers to this idea as the just savings principle.

14. India Block, "Renzo Piano Unveils Design for New Genoa Bridge Following Disaster," *Dezeen*, December 19, 2018, https://www.dezeen.com/2018/12/19/Renzo-piano-new-genoa-bridge-design/.

15. City of Norfolk, *Vision 2100*, November 22, 2016, https://www.norfolk.gov/DocumentCenter/View/27768/Vision-2100---FINAL.

16. "FAQ," San Francisco Bay Restoration Authority, accessed June 28, 2023, www.sfbayrestore.org/faq.

17. James Canton, *The Oak Papers* (Edinburgh, UK: Canongate, 2020), 5

18. Future Generations Commisioner for Wales, *Transport Fit for Future Generations*, September 2018, https://www.futuregenerations.wales/wp-content/uploads/2018/11/20180912-Transport-Fit-for-Future-Generations-C-1.pdf.

19. See Keishiro Hara, Ritsuji Yoshioka, Masahi Kuroda, Shuji Kurimoto, and Tatsuyoshi Saijo, "Reconciling Intergenerational Conflicts with Imaginary Future Generations," *Sustainability Science* 22, no. 14 (2019): 1605–19.

Chapter 9

1. Quoted in Justin McGuirk, "Can Cities Make Us Better Citizens?," *New Yorker*, August 26, 2018, https://www.newyorker.com/books/page-turner/can-cities-make-us-better-citizens.

2. International City/County Management Association, *2018 Municipal Form of Government Survey: Summary of Survey Results* (Washington, DC: ICMA, 2019).

3. Center for Popular Democracy, *Expanding Voter Registration in High Schools: A Toolkit for Local Leaders* (Brooklyn, NY: Center for Popular Democracy, 2019).

4. Editorial, "Los Angeles Needs a Bigger City Council. Here Are Three Ways to Get It," *Los Angeles Times*, July 16, 2023, https://www.latimes.com/opinion/story/2023-07-16/editorial-los-angeles-needs-a-bigger-city-council-here-are-three-ways-to-get-it.

5. Jennifer Peltz, "Judge Says New York City Can't Let Noncitizens Vote in City Elections," Associated Press, *PBS NewsHour*, PBS, June 27, 2022, https://www.pbs.org/newshour/politics/judge-says-new-york-city-cant-let-noncitizens-vote-in-city-elections.

6. Chip Yost, Vivian Chow, and Carlos Saucedo, "California City Considers Granting Illegal Immigrants the Right to Vote," KTLA, September 19, 2023, https://ktla.com/news/local-news/california-city-considers-granting-illegal-immigrants-the-right-to-vote/.

7. Editorial, "Take the Pay-to-Play out of L.A.'s Development Process," *Los Angeles Times*, August 5, 2017.

8. See David Sachs, "Measure 2E Supporters Say Their Victory Is Chipping Away at Citizens United and the Power of Money in Politics," *Denverite*, November 6, 2018, https://denverite.com/2018/11/06/denver-election-results-2e-campaign-finance.

9. Editorial, "Another Day, Another Pay-to-Play Allegation in City Hall," *Los Angeles Times*, December 6, 2018.

10. E.g., see Mike Lydon and Anthony Garcia, *Tactical Urbanism: Short-Term Action for Long-Term Change* (Washington, DC: Island, 2015).

11. "About Ioby," IOBY, accessed June 28, 2023, https://ioby.org/about.

12. "About the Green Benefit District," Green Benefit District, accessed June 28, 2023, www.greenbenefit.org/about-gbd.

13. Robyn Purchia, "Dogpatch, Potrero Hill Lead by Example," *San Francisco Examiner*, July 6, 2016.

14. "What Is PB?," Participatory Budgeting Project, accessed June 28, 2023, www.participatorybudgeting.org/what-is-pb.

15. See New York City Civic Engagement Commission, accessed June 28, 2023, www.nyc.gov/site/civicengagement/index.page.

16. "Participatory Budgeting," New York City Council, accessed June 28, 2023, https://council.nyc.gov/pb.

17. Gabriel Sandoval, "City Council Members Bringing Back Participatory Budgeting for Some, Not All," *City*, March 22, 2021, www.thecity.nyc/2021/3/22/22343716/nyc-participatory-budgeting-city-council-covid.

18. "It's Our Money," New York Civic Engagement Commission, accessed September 12, 2023, www.participate.nyc.gov/processes/itsourmoney.

19. Belen Dumont, "Tree, Sidewalk Projects Receive City Funds as Winners of 2021 Hartford Decided," *Hartford (CT) Courant*, July 13, 2021.

20. Michael Kransz, "How Should Grand Rapids Spend $2M? Residents Still Will Decide, but Process Delayed," MLive.com, July 22, 2021, www.mlive.com/news/grand-rapids/2021/07/how-should-grand-rapids-spend-2m-residents-still-will-decide-but-process-delayed.html.

21. New York University, "New Research on Participatory Budgeting Highlights Community Priorities in Public Spending," press release, July 22, 2020, www.nyu.edu/about/news-publications/news/2020/july/new-research-on-participatory-budgeting-highlights-community-pri.html.

22. Kiran Misra, "What Difference Would That Make?," *Chicago Reader*, April 30, 2021, https://chicagoreader.com/news-politics/what-difference-would-that-make.

23. Participedia, s.v. "Bristol Citizens' Assembly," accessed June 28, 2023, https://participedia.net/case/7218.

24. James Fishkin, Alice Siu, Larry Diamond, and Norman Bradburn "Is Deliberation an Antidote to Extreme Partisan Polarization? Reflections on 'America in One Room,'" *American Political Science Review*, July 27, 2021.

25. Bailey Flanigan, Paul Gölz, Anupam Gupta, Brett Hennig, and Ariel D. Procaccia, "Fair Algorithms for Selecting Citizens' Assemblies," *Nature*, August 2021.

26. See Philip Preville, "How Barcelona Is Leading a New Era of Digital Democracy," Sidewalk Talk, Medium, November 3, 2019, https://medium.com/sidewalk-talk/how-barcelona-is-leading-a-new-era-of-digital-democracy-4a033a98cf32.

27. Preville, "How Barcelona Is Leading."

28. Francesca Bria, "The EU Must Be Bold and Defend Its Digital Sovereignty," *Financial Times*, April 27, 2021.

29. Quoted in Thomas Graham, "Barcelona Is Leading the Fightback against Smart City Surveillance," *Wired*, May 18, 2018, https://www.wired.co.uk/article/barcelona-decidim-ada-colau-francesca-bria-decode.

30. E.g., see Tiffany Hsu and Steven Lee Myers, "A.I.'s Use in Elections Sets Off a Scramble for Guardrails," *New York Times*, June 25, 2023.

Chapter 10

1. See Justin McGuirk, "Can Cities Make Us Better Citizens?," *New Yorker*, April 26, 2018.

2. McGuirk, "Can Cities Make Us Better Citizens?""

3. McGuirk, "Can Cities Make Us Better Citizens?"

4. Richard Sennett, "The Open City," unpublished paper in author's possession.

5. Sennett, "Open City," 7.

6. Bentway, accessed June 28, 2023, https://thebentway.ca.

7. John Borgmeyer, "Judge Dismisses Collins Suit," *C-Ville Weekly* (Charlottesville, VA), July, 10, 2006, https://www.c-ville.com/Judge_dismisses_Collins_suit.

8. Jesse Singal, "The Contact Hypothesis Offers Hope for the World," *Cut*, February 10, 2017, www.thecut.com/2017/02/the-contact-hypothesis-offers-hope-for-the-world.html.

9. Alexander Garvin, *What Makes a Great City* (Washington, DC: Island, 2016), 18.

10. Garvin, *What Makes a Great City*, 198.

11. John R. Parkinson, *Democracy and Public Space: The Physical Sites of Democratic Performance* (Oxford, UK: Oxford University Press, 2012).

12. Parkinson, *Democracy and Public Space*, 2.

13. Parkinson, *Democracy and Public Space*, 204.

14. Parkinson, *Democracy and Public Space*, 215.

15. Jane Jacobs, *The Death and Life of Great American Cities* (New York: Vintage Books, 1961), 37.

16. Jacobs, *Death and Life*, 37.

17. Nightingale Housing, accessed June 28, 2023, www.nightingalehousing.org.

18. Quoted in Linda Poon, "A Lesson from Social Distancing: Build Better Balconies," *Bloomberg CityLab*, April 20, 2020, www.bloomberg.com/news/articles/2020-04-20/lesson-from-coronavirus-build-better-balconies.

19. William Drayton, "Secret Gardens: How to Turn Patchwork Urban Backyards into Neighborly Communal Parks," *Atlantic*, June 2000.

20. Dana R. Fisher, Erica S. Svendsen, and James Connelly, *Urban Environmental Stewardship and Civic Engagement: How Planting Trees Strengthens the Roots of Democracy* (Abingdon-on-Thames, UK: Routledge, 2015).

21. Fisher, Svendsen, and Connelly, *Urban Environmental Stewardship*, 111.

22. E.g., see Netta Weinstein, Andrew K. Przybylski, and Richard M. Ryan, "Can Nature Make Us More Caring? Effects of Immersion in Nature on Intrinsic Aspirations and Generosity," *Personality and Social Psychology Bulletin* 35, no. 10 (2009): 1315–29.

23. See Nellie Bowles, "A 17-Mile Hike to Unite San Francisco," *New York Times*, November 18, 2019.

24. Katie Jo Black and Mallory Richards, "Eco-gentrification and Who Benefits from Urban Green Amenities: NYC's High Line," *Landscape and Urban Planning* 204 (December 2020), https://doi.org/10.1016/j.landurbplan.2020.103900.

25. Winifred Curran and Trina Hamilton, "Just Green Enough: Contesting Environmental Gentrification in Greenpoint, Brooklyn," *Local Environment* 17, no. 9 (2012): 1027–42.

26. *Building Bridges across the River, 11th Street Bridge Park Equitable Development Plan* (Washington, DC: Building Bridges across the River, n.d.), accessed June 28, 2023, https://bbardc.org/wp-content/uploads/2018/10/Equitable-Development-Plan_09.04.18.pdf.

27. Levi Pulkkinen and Katie Hayes, "Washington State Poised to Ban Guns at Protests, Capitol Grounds," *Crosscut*, April 9, 2021, https://crosscut.com/politics/2021/04/washington-state-poised-ban-guns-protests-capitol-grounds.

28. "Memories of Life, Love, and Activism at the Lyon-Martin House," *San Francisco Bay Times*, June 10, 2021.

29. Pat Finn, "The World's Tallest Tower Should Never Have Been Built. Change My Mind," *Architizer*, accessed September 12, 2023, https://architizer.com/blog/inspiration/stories/change-my-mind-worlds-tallest-building.

30. See, e.g., Azim F. Shariff, Aiyana K. Willard, and Ara Norenzayan, "Religious Priming: A Meta-Analysis with a Focus on Prosociality," *Personality and Social Psychology Review* 20, no. 1 (2015): 27–48, https://journals.sagepub.com/doi/10.1177/1088868314568811.

31. Nicholas Fandos, Russell Goldman and Jess Bidgood, "Baltimore Mayor Had Statues Removed in 'Best Interest of My City,'" *New York Times*, August 16, 2017.

32. Quoted in Jackson Cote and Steph Solis, "Boston's Dudley Square Renamed Nubian Square after Years of Protests over District's Namesake: A 1600s Colonial Governor Who Benefited from Slavery," MassLive, December 20, 2019, www.masslive.com/boston/2019/12/bostons-dudley-square-renamed-nubian-square-after-years-of-protests-over-districts-namesake-a-1600s-colonial-governor-who-benefited-from-slavery.html.

33. Kevin Peterson, "Iconic Faneuil Hall as Inspiration for Race Dialogue and Reconciliation in Boston," Houston Institute, Medium, December 17, 2018, https://medium.com/houstonmarshall/iconic-faneuil-hall-an-inspiration-for-racial-dialogue-in-boston-142c914756c4.

34. Peterson, "Iconic Faneuil Hall."

35. See Teo Armus, "Door by Door, a Push to Rename Confederate Streets for George Floyd and Breonna Taylor," *Washington Post*, October 17, 2021.

36. Elizabeth Moscoso, "Should Van Dorn Street Be Renamed to Keckley Street?," *Zebra* (Alexandria, VA), September 5, 2019.

Chapter 11

1. See Corey Keyes, "Promoting and Protecting Mental Health as Flourishing: A Complementary Strategy for Improving National Mental Health," *American Psychologist*, February 2007.

2. Peter Holley, "Scooter Use Is Rising in Major Cities. So Are Trips to the Emergency Room," *Washington Post*, September 6, 2018.

3. "Precautionary Principle Policy Statement," in *San Francisco Environment Code* (Cincinnati, OH: American Legal Publishing, updated 2023), chap. 1, accessed June 28, 2023, https://codelibrary.amlegal.com/codes/san_francisco/latest/sf_environment/0-0-0-12.

4. Kristi Coale, "As Cancer Concerns Lead Cities to Ban Herbicide, SF Scales Back Use of Roundup," *San Francisco Public Press*, November 18, 2020.

5. Quoted in David Graham, "Why Do Some People Decide to Ride Out Hurricanes?," *Atlantic*, August 2017.

6. George Will, "Banking on Banks," *Washington Post*, May 23, 1985.

7. See Ann Brower, "Parapets, Politics, and Making a Difference: Lessons from Christchurch," *Earthquake Spectra* 33, no. 4 (November 2017): 1241–55.

8. "Ann Brower, "Earthquake Risk? Fix the Parapets First," Herald Online, *New Zealand Herald*, August 10, 2015. https://www.nzherald.co.nz/nz/ann-brower-earthquake-risk-fix-the-parapets-first/6MND2B4B62N7UIVGGZPX6EFE3Q/.

9. "Drug Overdose Deaths," Centers for Disease Control and Prevention, last reviewed August 22, 2023, https://www.cdc.gov/drugoverdose/deaths/index.html.

10. Jennifer Peltz, "A Look inside the First Official Safe Injection Sites in the US," Associated Press, *PBS NewsHour*, PBS, March 9, 2022, https://www.pbs.org/newshour/health/a-look-inside-the-1st-official-safe-injection-sites-in-u-s.

11. A recent op-ed in the *New York Post* makes this point well: "Without these interventions [for treatment and detox] harm-reduction sites are merely facilitating addiction while simultaneously destigmatizing antisocial behavior." Jared Klickstein, "Why 'Harm Reduction' Policies Are Causing More Harm Than Good," *New York Post*, April 20, 2023, https://nypost.com/2023/05/20/harm-reduction-policies-are-causing-more-harm-than-good/.

12. The New York law limited the amount of trans fats to no more than 0.5 grams per serving, effective July 2008. See Jessica Fu, "New York City Banned Trans Fats a Decade before the Rest of the Country. A New Study Finds Eaters Are Healthier for It," *Counter*, February 21, 2019, https://thecounter.org/trans-fat-restaurant-ban-new-york-city.

13. Melecia Wright, Wendy McKelvey, Christine Johnson Curtis, Lorna E. Thorpe, Hubert W. Vesper, Heather C. Kuiper, and Sonia Y. Angell, "Impact of a Municipal Policy Restricting Trans Fatty Acid Use in New York City Restaurants on Serum Trans Fatty Acid Levels in Adults," *American Journal of Public Health* 109, no. 4 (April 2019): 634–36.

14. Jonathan Lemire, "Smoking Rates on the Rise in New York City," Associated Press, September 15, 2014.

15. Allison Aubrey and Maria Godoy, "High-Sodium Warnings Hit New York City Menus," NPR, December 1, 2015, www.npr.org/sections/thesalt/2015/12/01/458031755/in-new-york-city-that-salty-combo-meal-now-comes-with-a-warning.

16. "How Many US Mass Shootings Have There Been in 2023?," BBC News, August 27, 2023, https://www.bbc.com/news/world-us-canada-41488081.

17. Anita Knopov, Rebecca J. Sherman, Julia R. Raifman, Elysia Larson, and Michael B. Siegel, "Household Gun Ownership and Youth Suicide Rates at the State Level, 2005–2015," *American Journal of Preventative Medicine* 56, no. 3 (2019): 335–42.

18. Deborah Azrael, Joanne Cohen, Cornel Salhi, and Matthew Miller, "Firearm Storage in Gun-Owning Households with Children: Results of a 2015 Survey," *Journal of Urban Health* 95, no. 3 (2018): 295–304, https://link.springer.com/article/10.1007/s11524-018-0261-7.

19. Azrael et al., "Firearm Storage," 1.

20. "Oakland Gun Storage Laws," City of Oakland (website), accessed June 28, 2023, www.oaklandca.gov/topics/oakland-gun-storage-laws.

21. Trevor Bach, "Cities Grow Bolder on Gun Control Laws," *US News and World Report*, January 10, 2020.

22. "Location Restrictions," Giffords Law Center, accessed June 28, 2023, https://giffords.org/lawcenter/gun-laws/policy-areas/guns-in-public/location-restrictions.

23. See Tye Farrow, "The Ultimate Test for Design: Does It Cause Health?," in *Healthy Environments, Healing Spaces: Practices and Directions in Health, Planning, and Design*, ed. Timothy Beatley, Carla Jones, and Rueben Rainey (Charlottesville: University of Virginia Press, 2018), 143–63.

24. "Active Design," New York City Department of Design and Construction, accessed June 28, 2023, www1.nyc.gov/site/ddc/about/active-design.page.

25. Katherine Harmon, "Social Ties Boost Survival by 50 Percent," *Scientific American*, July 28, 2010, www.scientificamerican.com/article/relationships-boost-survival.

26. Eric Klinenberg, *Palaces for the People: How Social Infrastructure Can Help Fight Inequality, Polarization and the Decline of Civic Life* (New York: Crown, 2018), 5.

27. E.g., see Kent Bloomer, *The Nature of Ornament: Rhythm and Metamorphosis in Architecture* (New York: W. W. Norton, 2000).

Chapter 12

1. Quoted in Caroline Spivak, "Bird-Friendly Buildings Bill Takes Flight in City Council," *Curbed*, December 10, 2019, https://ny.curbed.com/2019/12/10/21005140/bird-friendly-buildings-bill-passes-city-council.

2. Thomas Astell-Burt, Terry Hartig, Simon Eckermann, Mark Nieuwenhuijsen, Anne McMunn, Howard Frumkin, and Xiaoqi Feng, "More Green, Less Lonely? A Longitudinal Cohort Study," *International Journal of Epidemiology* 51, no. 1 (February 2022): 99–110.

3. Cecil Konijnendijk van den Bosch, "Promoting Health and Wellbeing through Urban Forests—Introducing the 3-30-300 Rule," IUCN Urban Alliance, February 19, 2021, https://iucnurbanalliance.org/promoting-health-and-wellbeing-through-urban-forests-introducing-the-3-30-300-rule.

4. Quoted in Monica Gagliano, *Thus Spoke the Plant* (Berkeley, CA: North Atlantic Books, 2018), 35.

5. Gagliano, *Thus Spoke the Plant*, 94.

6. Stefano Mancuso, *The Nation of Plants* (New York: Other Press, 2019), 106–7.

7. Stephen Kellert, *Birthright: People and Nature in the Modern World* (New Haven, CT: Yale University Press, 2012).

8. To learn more about the Perth Urban Wetlands, see the short film *Urban Wetland, Perth, Western Australia*, directed by Linda Bragg, https://www.biophiliccities.org/perth-urban-wetland-film.

9. See Timothy Beatley, "Why We Should Live in Cities with Otters," *Biophilic Cities Journal*, March 2019.

10. James E. McWilliams, "The Butcher Next Door: Why the Rise of DIY Urban Animal Slaughter Is Bad for People and Animals," *Slate*, June 6, 2012, www.slate.com/articles/life/food/2012/06/diy_animal_slaughter_urban_hipsters_think_it_s_a_good_idea_it_isn_t_.html.

11. Natasha Daly, "The Bitter Controversy Surrounding NYC's Carriage Horse Industry," *National Geographic*, March 26, 2020, www.nationalgeographic.com/animals/article/new-york-city-carriage-horse-industry-controversy.

12. William Neuman, "In His 5th Year as Mayor, de Blasio Finally Acts on Horse-Carriage Pledge," *New York Times*, August 30, 2018.

13. Matt Bershadker, "Help the Horses: Ban New York Carriage Rides," CNN, January 23, 2014, www.cnn.com/2014/01/23/opinion/bershadker-ban-horse-drawn-carriages/index.html.

14. Emily Court, "Barcelona Bans 'Horror' Horse Drawn Carriage Rides," *Plant Based News*, December 4, 2017, https://plantbasednews.org/opinion/barcelona-bans-horse-drawn-carriage-rides.

15. Emily Alpert Reyes, "L.A. Will Become Biggest City in the U.S. to Ban Fur Sales," *Los Angeles Times*, February 12, 2019.

16. See Wildlife Protection Act of 2010, Council of the District of Columbia, accessed June 28, 2023, https://doee.dc.gov/sites/default/files/dc/sites/ddoe/service_content/attachments/Wildlife%20Protection%20Act.pdf.

17. Emma Marris, "Modern Zoos Are Not Worth the Moral Cost," *New York Times*, June 11, 2021, https://www.nytimes.com/2021/06/11/opinion/zoos-animal-cruelty.html.

18. Peter Singer, interview with author, April 4, 2017. The next several paragraphs are drawn from Timothy Beatley, "Altruism, Ethics and Planning," *Planning Magazine*, June 2017.

19. Jeffrey C. Mays and Amelia Nierenberg, "Foie Gras, Served in 1,000 Restaurants in New York City, Is Banned," *New York Times*, October 30, 2019.

20. Mays and Nierenberg, "Foie Gras."

21. More about community-supported fisheries can be found in Timothy Beatley, *Blue Urbanism: Connecting Cities and Oceans* (Washington, DC: Island Press, 2014).

22. Singer interview.

23. Christopher D. Stone, *Should Trees Have Standing? Toward Legal Rights for Natural Objects* (Los Altos, CA: William Kaufman, 1974).

24. Lake Erie Bill of Rights, City of Toledo, 2, accessed June 28, 2023, www.beyondpesticides.org/assets/media/documents/LakeErieBillofRights.pdf.

Chapter 13

1. Watch a video of the Jackson Browne song on YouTube: "Jackson Browne—It Is One," YouTube video, 4:32, posted by grobanite1012, accessed June 28, 2023, www.youtube.com/watch?v=sxZJ3Rbq87E.

2. Peter Singer, "Famine, Affluence, and Morality," *Philosophy and Public Affairs* 1, no. 1 (Spring 1972): 229–43.

3. Singer, "Famine, Affluence, and Morality," 231.

4. Michele Acuto and Benjamin Leffel, "Understanding the Global Ecosystem of City Networks," *Urban Affairs* 58, no. 9 (2021).

5. William Rees and Mathis Wackernagel, *The Ecological Footprint* (Gabriola Island, BC: New Society, 1996).

6. Keisuke Nansai et al., "Consumption in the G20 Nations Causes Particulate Air Pollution Resulting in Two Million Premature Deaths Annually," *Nature Communications* 12, article 6286 (November 2021), https://www.nature.com/articles/s41467-021-26348-y.epdf.

7. Dana Thomas, "Why Won't We Learn from the Survivors of the Rana Plaza Disaster?," *New York Times*, April 24, 2018.

8. New York City Mayor's Office of Contract Services, *Citywide Procurement Indicators: Fiscal Year 2022* (New York: Mayor's Office of Contract Services, 2022), www.nyc.gov/assets/mocs/downloads/Resources/citywide-indicator-reports/Indicators_Report_FY_2022.pdf.

9. "City of Portland Sustainable Procurement Policy," City of Portland (website), accessed June 28, 2023, www.portlandoregon.gov/brfs/article/695574.

10. City of Pittsburgh, "City of Pittsburgh Releases First Voluntary Local Review of the United Nations Sustainable Development Goals," press release, November 24, 2020.

11. City of Pittsburgh, "City of Pittsburgh Releases," 1.

12. Miami-Dade County, "Miami-Dade County Moves Forward in Acquiring More Electric Buses," press release, June 22, 2021.

13. Sami Grover, "New York City to Welcome 7 New Electric Garbage Trucks," Treehugger, July 6, 2021, https://www.treehugger.com/new-york-city-7-new-electric-garbage-trucks-5191442.

14. Skidmore, Owings & Merrill, "At COP26, SOM Unveils Urban Sequoia, a Proposal to Transform the Built Environment into a Network for Absorbing Carbon," press release, November 11, 2021, www.som.com/news/at-cop26-som-unveils-urban-sequoia-a-proposal-to-transform-the-built-environment-into-a-network-for-absorbing-carbon.

15. C40 Cities, "14 Cities Commit to Sustainable Food Policies That Will Address the Global Climate Emergency," press release, October 10, 2019, www.c40.org/other/good-food-cities.

16. E.g., see H. Charles J. Godfray, Paul Aveyard, Tara Garnett, Jim W. Hall, Timothy J. Key, Jamie Lorimer, Ray T. Pierrehumbert, Peter Scarborough, Marco Springmann, and Susan A. Jebb, "Meat Consumption, Health and the Environment," *Science* 361, no. 6399 (July 2018), https://www.science.org/doi/10.1126/science.aam5324.

17. "France Row as Lyon Mayor Keeps Meat off School Menus," BBC News, February 21, 2021, https://www.bbc.com/news/world-europe-56144913.

18. Greenpeace, "Mayors from 14 Major Cities Commit to Cut Meat Consumption—Greenpeace Response," press release, October 10, 2019, www.greenpeace.org/international/press-release/24789/mayors-from-14-major-cities-commit-to-cut-meat-consumption.

19. "Meatless Cities: A Workshop on How Cities Can Help Lead the Transition to a Plant-Forward Food System," Guarini Center, accessed June 28, 2023, https://guarinicenter.org/event/meatless-cities-a-workshop-on-how-cities-can-help-lead-the-transition-to-a-plant-forward-food-system.

20. Meatless Cities, "Session 3: Procurement Policies" background materials, Guarini Center, accessed June 28, 2023, https://guarinicenter.org/wp-content/uploads/2021/06/Meatless-Cities-Workshop-Session-3-Primer-on-Procurement-Policies.pdf.

21. Milan Urban Food Policy Pact, accessed September 12, 2023, www.milanurbanfoodpolicypact.org.

22. It is a complex water delivery system that includes seventeen reservoirs and three controlled lakes that together provide a storage capacity of almost 600 billion gallons. See National Academies of Sciences, Engineering and Medicine, *Review of the New York City Watershed Protection Program* (Washington, DC: National Academies of Science, Engineering and Medicine, 2020), www.nationalacademies.org/our-work/review-of-the-new-york-city-watershed-protection-program.

23. Chris Davis, "Austin Buys Carbon Credits from New Tree-Planting Program as Carbon Neutrality Goal Looms," KXAN, December 12, 2019, www.kxan.com/news/local/austin/austin-buys-carbon-credits-from-new-tree-planting-program-as-carbon-neutrality-goal-looms.

24. E.g., see Barbara Moran, "Biden Will Restore Protections to East Coast's Only Marine National Monument," WBUR, October 8, 2021, www.wbur.org/news/2021/10/07/biden-restores-protections-northeast-canyons-and-seamounts-national-monument.

25. See also Stephen M. Coan and Vikki N. Spruill, "Aquarium Chiefs: Taking a Stand for Marine Life and Our Fragile Ocean," *Boston Herald*, October 21, 2021.

26. Alex Cosmas, Linda Liu, Maurice Obeid, Jules Seeley, and Yael Taqqu, "New York: A Concrete Jungle Where Dreams Are Still Made," McKinsey and Company, December 21, 2021, www.mckinsey.com/industries/travel-logistics-and-infrastructure/our-insights/new-york-a-concrete-jungle-where-dreams-are-still-made

27. UN Environment Programme and Food and Agriculture Organization of the UN, *Becoming #GenerationRestoration: Ecosystem Restoration for People, Nature and Climate* (Nairobi, Kenya: UNEP, 2021), www.unep.org/resources/ecosystem-restoration-people-nature-climate.

28. See Timothy Beatley and J. D. Brown, "The Half-Earth City," *Environmental Law and Policy Review* 45 (Spring 2021): 775–819.

29. E. O. Wilson, *Half-Earth: Our Planet's Fight for Life* (New York: Liveright, 2017), 209.

30. See City of Vancouver, *Greenest City 2020 Action Plan Part Two: 2015– 2020*, 2015, https://vancouver.ca/files/cov/greenest-city-2020-action-plan-2015-2020.pdf.

31. See Kate Raworth, *Doughnut Economics: 7 Ways to Think Like a 21st Century Economist* (White River Junction, VT: Chelsea Green, 2017).

32. Jay Owen, "Sixty Minutes with Kate Raworth and Hazel Henderson (Replay)," Ethical Markets, June 30, 2021, https://www.ethicalmarkets.com/title-sixty-minutes-with-kate-raworth-and-hazel-henderson-recorded/.

33. Patrick Greenfield, "Investing 0.1% of Global GDP Could Avoid Breakdown of Ecosystems, Says UN Report," *Guardian*, May 27, 2021.

34. Sean Ross, "New York's Economy: The 6 Industries Driving GDP Growth," *Investopedia*, September 21, 2021, www.investopedia.com/articles/investing/011516/new-yorks-economy-6-industries-driving-gdp-growth.

Chapter 14

1. Dorany Pineda, "How L.A.'s Bird Population Is Shaped by Historic Redlining and Racist Loan Practices," *Los Angeles Times*, October 11, 2023, https://www.latimes.com/environment/story/2023-10-11/historic-redlining-bird-biodiversity.

2. Michael Laris, "A City Looks to Its Moral Compass in Lean Times," *Washington Post*, December 14, 2008.

3. Gabrielle Fonrouge, "Mayor's Highly Touted Office of Animal Welfare Barely Functioning," *New York Post*, December 2, 2020.

4. E. O. Wilson, *The Creation: An Appeal to Save Life on Earth* (New York: W. W. Norton, 2017).

5. Julia Menasce Horowitz, Ruth Igielnik, and Rakesh Kochhar, *Most Americans Say There Is Too Much Economic Inequality in the U.S., but Fewer Than Half Call It a Priority*, (Washington, DC: Pew Research Center, 2020), www.pewresearch.org/social-trends/wp-content/uploads/sites/3/2020/01/PSDT_01.09.20_economic-inequailty_FULL.pdf.

Index

Abernathy, Penelope Muse, 42
ableism, 53–55
acceptable risk, 153–54
accessibility, 48, 54, 65–66, 68–69
active design guidelines, 162–63
ADA (Americans with Disabilities Act), 53, 67
Addams, Jane, 32
aging, 54
Agyeman, Julian, 51
Albuquerque, NM, 93; Albuquerque Community Safety Department, 93
Alexandria, VA, vii–ix, 41, 150, 202–3
Alice's Garden, Milwaukee, 163
altruism, 24
American Institute of Architects, 206
Americans with Disabilities Act (ADA), 53, 67
Amsterdam, 62
Anacostia River, 15
Animal Liberation (Singer), 178
animals: basic interest of, 176–77; birds, 168, 171; coexistence with, 16, 172–75; cruelty toward, 175–77, 178–79; duties of care for, 168, 175–76; zoos and aquaria, 177–78. *See also* biophilic cities; environment; nature
Appleyard, Bruce, 68
Arieff, Allison, 55–56
artificial intelligence (AI), 106–7, 134
Asheville, NC, 60
Atlanta, GA, 59
Austin, TX, 192
autonomy, 25
awe, 170–72

Bailey, Kim Moore, 52
bans: of assault rifles, 160–61; of contributions from developers, 126; of fur, 177; of gas-powered leaf blowers, 165; of horse-drawn carriages, 176; of foie gras, 178; of smoking, 158; of trans fat, 158
"ban the box," 98
Barcelona, 57, 132–33, 176
BASE jumping, 76–77
basic income, 60, 71
Bat Conservation International, 118
beauty, 170
Bentham, Jeremy, 19, 21–22, 101–3
Bentway Park, Toronto, 137
Bethlehem, PA, 4
biocentrism, 170
biophilic cities, 168–81, 200; and ethics of coexistence, 172–75; metrics of, 171; moral vision of, 169–70
bioregions, 191
Bjornerud, Marcia, 110
Black Lives Matter, 144
Black Lives Matter Plaza, 146
Bloomer, Kent, 164
blue urbanism, 192
Bologna, Italy, 127–28, 132
Boston, MA, 50, 52, 149, 192
Bowser, Muriel, 146
Bracken Cave, San Antonio, 118
Bria, Francesca, 133
Brisbane, Australia, 173
Bristol, UK, 131
Bromwich, David, 26
Brower, Ann, 155
Browne, Jackson, 182
Bullard, Robert, 49
budgeting, participatory, 128–30
Bunch, Eric, 67
Burj Khalifa tower, Dubai, 147

Cagle, Matt, 106
calorie labeling, 158–59
Cambridge, MA, 166
Camden, NJ, 88
Carbon Neutral Cities Alliance, 184–85

carbon offsets, 192
Case, Mary Anne, 58
cathedral thinking, 116–18
Caton, James, 118–19
Champlain Towers, Surfside, FL, 155
Charlottesville, VA, ix, 103–4, 124, 148; Downtown Mall, 103–4
ChatGPT, 134
Cheh, Mary, 165
Chicago, IL, 50, 130, 165, 204
child-friendly cities, 55
Christchurch, New Zealand, 155–56
Churchill, Winston, 199
circular economy, 187
cities: ableism in, 53–55; and awe, 170–72; and beauty 170; biophilic, 168–81, 200; blue urbanism, 192; Carbon Neutral Cities Alliance, 184; and children and teens, 55; and democracy, 122, 124–26; ethical, definition of, 1–2; gentle, 24–25; governance of, 127–32; and Half-Earth Project, 193–95; "happy cities," 171; and long-term planning, 114–16; and meat consumption, 190–91; and mental health, 165–66; metrics for, 200–202; "open city," 122, 135–36; Resilient Cities Network, 184; and surveillance, 101–8; tactical urbanism, 127–28; and technology, 132–34, 201–2, 204; and virtues, 39–42; and women, 5, 55–59
citizenship, 36–39, 41, 42. *See also* cities: and democracy; voting
City Forest Credits, 192
Cleveland, OH, 94–96; pursuit policy of, 95–96
Climate Mayors, 184
Code of Conduct for Apparel Manufacturers, 187
Colau, Ada, 132
Collective Afterlife, 109
Collins, Richard, 137–38
Columbus, OH, 94
Community Commission for Public Safety and Accountability, Chicago, 204

compassion, 26–27
Compassion Charter, 27
Compton, CA, 61; Compton Pledge, 61
Confederate statues, 148
conflicts of interest, 123
Connelly, James, 142
contact hypothesis, 14, 138
Copenhagen, 40, 189
co-planning, 127–28
Coral Gables, FL, 6, 96
Creation, The (Wilson), 205
Credit Valley Hospital, Toronto, 162
Cully Park, Portland, OR, 52

Daily, Gretchen, 201
de Blasio, Bill, 42, 158, 176
de-escalation, 88–89
Democracy Voucher System, Seattle, 125
Denver, CO, 126, 160
deontological ethics, 20, 22–23, 64
Detroit, MI, 70
Dewey, Caitlin, 61
difference principle, 46
dignity, 25
disclosure of risks and hazards, 157
Doucet, Gregory, 190
Doughnut Economics, 62, 195
Downton, Paul, 194
Drayton, William, 141
driverless cars, 202. *See also* electric vehicles; technology
drones, 107. *See also* cities: and surveillance; technology
Dubai, UAE, 147
Dubal, Veena, 106
Durkin, Jenny, 153
duties beyond borders, 29–30, 182–96

Eastern Wildway, 192
Edmonton, Canada, 173
electric vehicles, 189. *See also* driverless cars; technology
empathy, 26–27
enfranchised cities, 124–25

environment, 29, 37, 78–80; climate change, 184–85; conservation, 188–93; ecological debt, 15–16; ecological footprints, 185–88; ecosystem protecion, 179–81, 191–93; environmental justice movement, 51; environmental racism, 49–51; environmental rights, 71–72; lawns, 78–80; meat consumption, 190; trees, 51, 78–80. *See also* animals; biophilic cities; nature
equality, 22, 44; of opportunity, 45, 61; of treatment, 45
ethical city: defined, 2–3; metrics for, 200–202; and physical structure, 5, 13–14; and policies, 4–5; roles of people, 3–4
ethical cues, 202
Ethical Land Use (Beatley), vii, 209
ethicists, role of, 202–3
ethics training, 203
Etzioni, Amitai, 21, 35–36
Eugene, OR, 93
Evanston, IL, 60
Everard, Sarah, 39, 56–57

facial recognition, 106–7
Feminist City (Kern), 5, 57
Finn, Pat, 147
fireworks, 173–74
First Amendment, 104, 144
Fischer, Greg, 26
Fisher, Dana, 142
fishing, 179
Fishkin, James, 131
Flint, MI, 31; water crisis in, 31–32
flourishing, 70, 152–53
Floyd, George, 48, 87
Fourteenth Amendment, 180
Frank, Mary Anne, 144
freedom, 76
Fremantle, Australia, 164
Friedman, Milton, 82
future design movement, 120
future generations, 73, 118–19; future generations commissioner, 120, 202
Future Library, Oslo, 119

Gagliano, Monica, 170
Gallego, Kate, 90
Garvin, Alexander, 139; *What Makes a Great City?*, 139
Gaudi, Antoni, 116
Genoa, Italy, 114
gentle cities, 24
gifts and gift giving, 115; from a city to the future, 114–16
Good Ancestor, The (Krznaric), 111
good life, 20–21
Graham, Hannah, 104
Grand Rapids MI, 130
Gratton, Lynda, 55
green benefit district, 128
Grossman, Katrin, 25
guaranteed income, 60, 71
guns, 143–45, 159–161; ban of assault rifles, 160–61; buybacks, 161; public health risks of, 159–61; in public spaces, 143–45; storage of, 160–61

Hadid, Zaha, 56
Hadidian, John, 174
Half-Earth Project, 194
happy cities, 171
Happy City (Montgomery), 21
harm-reduction techniques, 156–57
Hartford, CT, 130
Harvey, David, 69
health and safety, 166–67; and buildings, 161–63; and limits on freedoms, 76, 85; and noise, 165; promotion of, 152–53, 158–61; protections for, 10. *See also* mental health; policing; risks
High Line, New York, 137
Hike the Heights, New York, 143
Houston, TX, 91
Howe, Sophie, 120
Humane Society of the United States, 174
Hyde Park, London, 139

inequality, 46–47
intergenerational justice, 114–15
Intersection Repair, Portland, OR, 127
In Our Backyard, 128

Jacobs, Jane, 56, 68, 140
Johnson, Chelsea, 31
Justice Outside, 52

Kansas, MO, 67
Keckley, Elizabeth, 150
keeping options open, 113
Kellert, Stephen, 171
Kern, Leslie, 5, 57; *Feminist City*, 5, 57
Keyes, Corey, 152
Kids in the Canyon, San Diego, CA, 40
kindness, 23–25
Kit Carson Park, Taos, 148–49
Klinenberg, Eric, 163
Konijnendijk, Cecil, 169
Koretz, Paul, 177
Krznaric, Roman, 111, 114–16, 119; *Good Ancestor*, 111

Lake Erie Bill of Rights, 180
Last Child in the Woods (Louv), 16, 162
Las Vegas, NV, 79
lawns, 78–80
Lefebvre, Henri, 69
LGBTQ+ protections, 11, 59, 146–147
Lightfoot, Lori (Mayor), 50
light pollution, 165
lights out programs, 165
limits to rights, 74
Lincoln Theatre (Miami Beach), 164
Lister, Nina Marie, 78
Littleton, CO, 161
London, UK (ecological footprint of), 190
loneliness, 140
Los Angeles, CA, 49, 79, 97, 99, 126, 177
Louisville, KY, 26–27, 94
Louv, Richard, 16, 162; *Last Child in the Woods*, 162
luck, 47
Lyon, France, 190

Magpie River, Quebec, Canada, 180
Mancuso, Stefano, 170
Marris, Emma, 177
McComb, Joe, 155

McDonough, William, 187
McMahon, Rita, 168
meat, consumption of, 190
mental health, 165–66
Mexico City, Mexico, 175
Meyer, Dan, 99
Miami, FL, 95
Miami Beach, FL, 164
Miami-Dade County, FL, 189
micromobility, 58
Mill, John Stuart, 19, 21, 81–83; *On Liberty*, 81–83
Minneapolis, MN, 68
Mississauga of the Credit First Nation, 145
Montgomery, Charles, 21; *Happy City*, 21
Montreal, Canada, 176
moral debt, 15
moral hazards, 84
moral imagination, 25–26
moral status of future inhabitants, 113
Most Good You Can Do, The (Singer), 198
Mummolo, Jonathan, 89, 92
Muteshekau-shipu Alliance, 180

National Economic and Social Rights Initiative, 65
nature, 169–72; and beauty, 170–72; civilizing effects of, 141–42. *See also* animals; biophilic cities; environment; zoos and aquaria
Nehemiah (company), 99
networks, of cities, 183–85
Newsom, Gavin, 11
New York City, 42, 125, 158–63, 186, 190–94; active design guidelines, 162; AI action plan, 107; annual budget of, 198; and bans, 158, 178; bird-safe ordinance, 168–69; calorie labeling, 158–59; Civic Engagement Commission, 129; Domain Awareness System, 103; Hike the Heights, 143; horse-drawn carriages, 175–76; Meatless Monday, 190; Metropolitan Transportation Authority, 53; MillionTreesNYC, 142; Nature Goals

2050, 72, 75; Office of Animal Welfare, 176, 204; pension fund investments, 196; safe injection sites, 156–57; stop-and-frisk policy, 89; taxing cigarettes, 158; tropical hardwoods policy, 194; Watershed Protection Program, 191; Wild Bird Fund, 168
New Zealand, 180
nightingale housing, 140
no-knock warrants, 27, 91
Norfolk, VA, 114
Northwest Canyons and Seamounts Marine National Monument, 192
Nubian Square, Boston, 149

Oakland, CA, 52, 160; Oakland Goes Outside, 52
1 percent for art standard, 163
1 Percent for the Planet, 196
On Liberty (Mill), 81–83
open city, 122, 135–36
opioids, crisis, 156
Orr, David, 36
Oslo, 119, 202

Palaces for the People (Klinenberg), 163
panopticon city, 101–8
paradiplomacy, 185
Parkinson, John, 139–40
Parkland, FL, shooting in, 6
parks, 14, 15; access to, 51–52, 72–73, 169; and inclusivity, 51–52, 143, 145–46; parklets, 141–42; as social infrastructure, 137, 139, 163; use of pesticides in, 7, 154. *See also* biophilic cities; *and names of individual parks*
participatory budgeting, 128–30
patriotism, 37
Pauley, Daniel, 112
pay-to-play, 41, 126–27
Peduto, Bill, 11, 188
Pennsylvania Environmental Rights Amendment, 71
Perez, Caroline Criado, 58
Perth, Australia, 172

pest control, 177
Peterson, Kevin, 149
Philadelphia, PA, 99, 164
Phoenix, AZ, 90, 115–16
Piano, Renzo, 114
Pickett, Kate, 46–47
Pittsburgh, PA, 51, 62, 188, 205; "cracker plants" in, 188; Phipps Conservatory, 205; Pittsburgh Equity Indicators, 62; UN Sustainable Development Goals, 188
plant blindness, 28
policing: de-escalation policy, 88–89; ethical, 87–100; no-knock warrants, 27, 91; pursuit-of-vehicle policies, 93–96; stop-and-frisk policy, 89; use of deadly force in, 89–93
Portland, OR, 9, 52, 61–62, 127, 187
Porto Alegre, Brazil, 129
Port Phillip, Australia, 166
"potty parity," 57–58
precautionary principle, 154
preemption laws, 206
priming, 147–48
privacy, 101–8; benefits and limitations of, 102–3; defined, 102; key elements of, 102; zones of, 107
procurement, sustainable, 186–87
public good, 18, 20
Pugh, Catherine, 148

Quito, Anne, 39

Rana Plaza, 186–87
Rawls, John, 26, 44–45, 48, 115; *Theory of Justice*, 44, 115
Raworth, Kate, 62, 195
red-light cameras, 105–6
Rees, William, 185
reflective equilibrium, 26
Regulation on Public Collaboration for Urban Commons, Bologna, 127–28
reparations, 60–61
Resilient Cities Network, 184
restoration tourism, 193

Richmond, VA, 52
rights: to the city, 69–70; to a clean and healthy environment, 71–72; to contact with nature, 73; to health care, 70–71; to housing, 65–67; Lake Erie Bill of Rights, 180; limits on, 74; to mobility, 67–68; National Economic and Social Rights Initiative, 65; of nature, 179–81; Pennsylvania Environmental Rights Amendment, 71
Riggs, William, 68
Rikers Island jail complex, New York, 97
Ring doorbell cameras, 105
risks: acceptable, 153–54; BASE jumping, 76–77; disclosure of, 84, 157; of dockless electric scooters, 153; of driverless cars, 202; moral hazards, 84
robotics, 202
Rose, Alexander, 113

safe injection sites, 156–57
Sagrada Familia cathedral, Barcelona, 116
San Antonio, TX, 118
San Diego, CA, 40, 178
Sandler, Ronald, 34
San Francisco, CA, 7, 143, 146, 154; ban of facial recognition technology, 106–7; environmental policies of, 7, 117, 128, 154; Crosstown Trail, 142–43; and LGBTQ+, 11, 146–47; and health insurance, 7, 10, 70; parklets in, 141; policies toward animals, 176–77, 191; reproductive rights policy of, 2; South Bay Salt Pond Restoration Project, 117; Street Parks Program, 141
San Jose, CA, 78
Scheffler, Samuel, 109
Schneier, Bruce, 102
schools, 205–6; school-to-prison pipeline, 97–98
scooters, electric, 153
Scott, Andrew, 55
Seattle, WA, 98, 125
Second Amendment, 74, 144, 159
Second Chance Business Coalition, 99

second-chance cities, 97–100
Sennett, Richard, 122, 135–36
Seoul, 185
seventh-generation principle, 113
shifting baseline syndrome, 112
"Should Trees Have Standing?" (Stone), 180
Sidgwick, Henry, 19, 21
Simard, Suzanne, 170
Simmons, Robin Rue, 60
Sinek, Simon, 6
Singal, Jesse, 138
Singapore, 174; Bishan-Ang Mo Kio Park, 174
Singer, Peter, 172, 178–79, 182–83, 198–99, 201; Animal Liberation, 178; Most Good You Can Do, 198
smart cities, 202
social infrastructure, 163
Society for the Prevention of Cruelty to Animals (SPCA), 9, 205
South Bay Salt Pond Restoration Project, 117
South Mountain Park, Phoenix, AZ, 116
Stand Up against Street Harassment, 39
Stone, Christopher, 180; "Should Trees Have Standing?," 180
street harassment, 39, 56
surveillance, 101–8, 133, 140
Svendson, Erica, 142
SWAT teams, 92
Sydney, Australia, 39

tactical urbanism, 127–28
Tampa, FL, 31
Taos, NM, 148–49
Taylor, Breonna, 27, 91
technology, 132–34, 201–2, 204; digital democracy, 133–34; digital redlining, 70; digital sovereignty, 133; driverless cars, 202; drones, 107; electric vehicles, 189
Tenderloin district, San Francisco, 40
Theory of Justice, A (Rawls), 44, 115
Thompson, Scott, 87

3-30-300 rule, 169–70
time denial, 110
timefulness, 110–11
time literacy, 111
time stamps, 119
Toderian, Brent, 141
Toledo, OH, 180
tolerance, 25
Toronto, Canada, 137, 145, 165
Trillium Park, Toronto, 145
trolley dilemma, 20
Trubina, Elena, 25
Tubbs, Michael, 61

UN Sustainable Development Goals, 8, 188–89
urban actors, 199
Urban Sequoia, 190
utilitarianism, 19, 21–22, 30

Vancouver, Canada, 186, 195
Van Rossum, Maya, 72
veil of ignorance, 115
virtue ethics, 34
virtues: coexistence, 172; compassion, 26–27; Compassion Charter, 27; empathy, 26–27; kindness, 23–25; patriotism, 37; tolerance, 25; virtue ethics, 34; virtuous city, 39
virtuous city, 39

voting, 124–25. *See also* cities: and democracy; citizenship; enfranchised cities

Wackernagel, Mathis, 185
Wales Well-Being of Future Generations Act, 119–20
Walsh, Martin, 149
Washington, DC, 15, 53, 56, 99, 143, 161, 165, 177; ban of gas-powered blowers, 165; Council Office on Racial Equity, 53; 11th Street Bridge Park, 143; gun laws, 161; Washington Metro, 117; Wildlife Protection Act, 177
Wellington, New Zealand, 113
What Makes a Great City? (Garvin), 139
Whitehead, John, 104
wildlife. *See* animals; environment; nature; zoos and aquaria
Wilkinson, Richard, 46–47
Will, George, 154
Wilson, E. O., 194, 205; *Creation*, 205
Wright, Steve, 53–54

Yahaba, Japan, 120
Yellowstone to Yukon Conservation Initiative, 192

Zealandia, New Zealand, 113
Zivarts, Anna, 54
zoos and aquaria, 177–78. *See also* animals

www.ingramcontent.com/pod-product-compliance
Lightning Source LLC
Chambersburg PA
CBHW032022230426
43671CB00005B/170